BEHAVIOR MANAGEMENT STRATEGIES FOR TEACHERS

ABOUT THE AUTHORS

Dr. Joan Carol Harlan is a Professor Emeriti of Elementary Education, The University of Mississippi. This is her eleventh book that pertains to the behaviors of children and adults. She is a sought-after consultant about classroom and behavior management and has hundreds of professional publications and presentations related to the behaviors of children, teachers, and parents.

Dr. Harlan, along with her husband, Dr. Grady Edward Harlan, Professor Emeritus of Counseling and Educational Psychology, The University of Mississippi, are the proud parents of five children. This book is dedicated to her daughter, Elizabeth Ann Carson, D.O., whose development, demeanor, and character are a living testimony to the power of the strategies described herein.

Dr. Sidney Tucker Rowland is an Assistant Professor of Curriculum and Instruction at The University of Mississippi. She teaches Classroom Management, Human Development and Diversity, Effective Teaching Strategies, and other courses related to the preparation of teachers. Dr. Rowland presents professional development seminars to numerous school districts about classroom management, Attention-Deficit Hyperactivity Disorder, and Diverse Learners.

Dr. Rowland was named as Outstanding Teacher by The University of Mississippi Education Alumni Chapter for 2000-2001. This book is dedicated to her children, grandchildren, and to "Flo" for her inspiration and vision.

Second Edition

BEHAVIOR MANAGEMENT STRATEGIES FOR TEACHERS

Achieving Instructional Effectiveness, Student Success, and Student Motivation-Every Teacher and Any Student Can!

By

JOAN C. HARLAN, Ph.D.

Professor of Elementary Education
The University of Mississippi
University, Mississippi

and

SIDNEY T. ROWLAND, Ed.D.

Assistant Professor of Elementary Education
The University of Mississippi
University, Mississippi

Charles C Thomas
PUBLISHER • LTD.
SPRINGFIELD • ILLINOIS • U.S.A.

Published and Distributed Throughout the World by

CHARLES C THOMAS • PUBLISHER, LTD.
2600 South First Street
Springfield, Illinois 62704

©2002 by CHARLES C THOMAS • PUBLISHER, LTD.

ISBN 0-398-07326-0 (hard)
ISBN 0-398-07327-9 (paper)

Library of Congress Catalog Card Number: 2002018105

Printed in the United States of America
SM-R-3

Library of Congress Cataloging-in-Publication Data

Harlan, Joan C.
    Behavior management strategies for teachers : achieving instructional
effectiveness, student success, and student motivation--every teacher and any
student can! / by Joan C. Harlan and Sidney T. Rowland.--2nd ed.
        p.   cm.
    Includes bibliographical references and index.
    ISBN 0-398-07326-0 -- ISBN 0-398-07327-9 (pbk.)
    1. Behavior modification. 2. Classroom management. 3. Motivation in
education. I. Rowland, Sidney T. II. Title.

    LB1060.2 .H38 2002
    371.102'4--dc21

                                                        2002018105

Cover photograph: Elizabeth Ann Carson, D.O., Dr. Harlan's daughter.

To my parents, George and Gladys Blandon, for their continued support and love.

To my dear husband, Grady E. Harlan, for his perpetual modeling of only the most appropriate teacher, counselor, and spousal behaviors; and

To my beautiful daughter, Elizabeth Ann Carson, D.O., who is my life's pride and joy, and who is living testimony to the success of the positive procedures described herein.

J. C. H.

To students, teachers, and parents who want classrooms to be peaceful and productive;

To my grandchildren who provide "lessons" to be learned; and

To "Flo" who provides love, support, and inspiration.

S. R.

PREFACE

Two main ideas are essential to appreciating and understanding the philosophical foundation on which this text is written. First, an effective teacher is an effective behavior manager; instructional and managerial successes are inseparable. Secondly, when students are motivated and working on interesting and meaningful tasks, their learning and retention increase, and there are fewer behavior problems than if students are bored, frustrated, uninterested, or otherwise unmotivated.

Therefore, this book provides in great detail proven and tested methods for teachers to use to be successful in their behavior management and instructional efforts. It provides teachers with all the necessary strategies they need for maintaining and increasing appropriate behaviors as well as for preventing and remediating inappropriate behaviors. Teachers can select from hundreds of suggestions and approaches, all based on real classroom examples, about how to manage, motivate, and teach students of all ages, ability levels, and motivational levels.

The contents of this text reflect the authors' nearly three decades of combined experience in the field of education, as elementary and special education teachers and supervisors, teacher educators, educational consultants, researchers, and as the authors of numerous articles and eight other texts. Their experiences led to the purposeful design of this text's layout and content: namely, that teachers at all grade levels need assistance that is straightforward, easy to implement, and realistic for the variety of classroom settings and problem behaviors with which they are confronted. The text content is largely drawn from eclectic, research-based as well as common sense and practical knowledge bases, and the text is, above all, "reader-friendly" and replete with easy-to-implement, concrete, specific suggestions. Additionally, each chapter has a summary of key concepts, and references for additional reading are provided for each chapter and for the text as a whole. Each chapter also contains suggested activities and assignments that instructors can use with their students. The comprehensive index also allows readers to instantly access content and solutions as needed.

The first section of the text, Understanding Behavior and Selected Models, contains Chapters 1 through 3. Chapter 1 addresses the commonality of goals that all school personnel have for students' academic successes, appropriate behaviors, and motivation for learning. It also addresses diversity and introduces some basic concepts about behavior. Chapters 2 and 3 present numerous strategies and selected models of instruction, management, and motivation.

The second section of the text, The Basics of Behavior Management, contains Chapters 4 through 7. Chapter 4 provides critical information about antecedents, behavior, and consequences. Chapter 5 provides detailed information about using reinforcement, reinforcement menus, and various ways to schedule the delivery of reinforcement. Chapter 6 provides numerous examples of how to establish and enforce rules and procedures, with an emphasis on the importance of consistency and suggestions for the use of contingency contracting. Chapter 7 provides many examples about how to deal with students' inappropriate behaviors by using a variety of non-physical forms of punishment.

The third section of the text, The Basics of Classroom Management, contains Chapters 8 through 13. Chapter 8 describes the traits, human relations skills, dispositions, and behaviors that effective teachers cultivate, refine, and utilize as they attempt to teach and manage students. Chapter 9 includes suggestions and strategies for effective conferences, collaboration, and communication. Chapter 10 explores a variety of approaches that effective teachers use and behaviors they should model to enhance student–teacher interactions.

Chapter 11 presents numerous suggestions for creating a classroom community where diversity is respected, recognized, and responded to so that all students feel valued, accepted, and included. Chapter 12 includes information regarding legislation that pertains to students with disabilities. It describes various categories of disabilities, and it provides strategies for the accommodation, management, and motivation of students with disabilities. Chapter 13 presents parental involvement as an integral part of effective classroom management. Suggested techniques for increasing parental involvement in schools and classrooms are described.

The fourth section of the text, Legal Issues and School Violence, includes Chapters 14 and 15. Chapter 14 contains a brief analysis of some of the legal issues associated with use of corporal punishment in the public schools by school personnel. Chapter 15 provides suggestions for the creation and maintenance of a safe school environment.

Teachers, administrators, and counselors face many challenges and problems when they attempt to teach, manage, motivate, and otherwise interact with students and their parents. Successfully motivating, managing, and instructing students results in profound professional and personal satisfaction for school personnel who can then take solace in the fact that they have made a lasting and significant impact on all students.

To all readers of this book, then, we strongly encourage you to adapt and utilize this book's contents. As I indicated in one of our other (still available) books (Carson and Sykes, *Behaviors of Preschoolers and Their Teachers*, 1991: Charles C Thomas), "preschoolers are cuddly little pretzels who demand attention, sometimes defy explanation, and deserve compassion, love, and understanding" (p. 187). We add that the same is true for children and people of all ages!

And it is with great love and pride that we dedicate this book to our children, Elizabeth Ann Carson, Lynn Fleming, Leigh Fox, and our spouses, Grady Edward Harlan and Bill Rowland. They are all cuddly pretzels whose reciprocal respect, compassion, positive regard, understanding, and love make parenting, marriage, living, and teaching so unconditionally rewarding and worthwhile.

J. C. H.
S. T. R.

ACKNOWLEDGMENTS

I lovingly give special thanks to my parents for their encouragement, love, and understanding;

I sincerely express my love to my husband, Dr. Grady E. Harlan, Professor Emeritus of Counseling and Educational Psychology, The University of Mississippi;

I gratefully recognize the invaluable assistance of an outstanding secretary, Mrs. Shirley A. Messer, without whom the preparation of this and many of my previous texts would not have been possible; and

I proudly and fervently acknowledge, with evident maternal love, the overwhelming reciprocal love and devotion of my daughter, Elizabeth Ann Carson, D.O.

J. C. H.

There are a number of people that I wish to acknowledge and thank for their encouragement, understanding, and assistance.

- Special thanks to "Flo" for understanding and encouraging completion of this text.
- Special thanks to Elizabeth Anderson, my graduate assistant and friend.
- Special thanks to my husband, Bill.
- Thanks to the professionals who assisted in bringing this work to an end: Shirley Messer and colleagues at The University of Mississippi School of Education.
- Thanks to my co-author, Joan Harlan, for years of mentoring, friendship, and fun.
- Special thanks, love, and appreciation to the "twins," and to my grandchildren.

S. R.

CONTENTS

SECTION III:
THE BASICS OF CLASSROOM MANAGEMENT

SECTION IV:
LEGAL ISSUES AND SCHOOL VIOLENCE

BEHAVIOR MANAGEMENT STRATEGIES FOR TEACHERS

Section I

UNDERSTANDING BEHAVIOR AND SELECTED MODELS

Chapter 1

UNDERSTANDING BEHAVIOR

STUDENT SUCCESS/COMMON GOALS

"Elizabeth Anne is doing great in school," brags her proud mamma. "Grady is sensational in statistics," boasts a pleased Dad. You hear parents and teachers talk about "Bill, the super speller," "Diane, the wonderful writer," "Michael, the gifted geometry student," "Amanda, the accomplished artist," "Lynn, the prolific poet," and "Leigh, the magical musician." What do these boastful statements have in common? They reflect parents' and teachers' pride in students' achievements and successes.

Everyone has a need to succeed and to be recognized for success. Student success is typically conceptualized as mastering our society's educational goals and commonly accepted requisite skills and concepts. Students themselves want to succeed in school. Some students succeed in arithmetic while others succeed in art. There are students who succeed in Latin while others students succeed in linguistics. Some students succeed in social studies while other students succeed in the sciences. There are students who succeed academically and other students who succeed athletically. Some students succeed in both athletics and academics. There are students who succeed in the creative arts while other students succeed in computer applications.

Then, too, there are students who are neither athletically nor academically successful. Such students are likely to be successful at *mis*behaving or behaving inappropriately because of the attention and recognition that such misbehaviors often, albeit unfortunately, yield from peers as well as from frustrated school personnel. Since everyone–students and others–desires success, attention, and recognition, students who are not succeeding at academic or athletic tasks are likely to be successful at *mis*behaving or behaving inappropriately.

*Mis*behaving or inappropriately behaving students are typically inattentive, often disruptive, and they are a very realistic fact of life in virtually all of our public and private schools. It is critical that students, school personnel, and parents work together to help students to succeed and to behave appropriately. Students' successes and appropriate behaviors should then be acknowledged with positive attention, praise, or some other form of reinforcement.

Teachers, assistant teachers, counselors, administrators, and other school personnel want students to succeed in school for various reasons. Student success, in and of itself, is the very purpose of education and is essential to society's well-being and improvement. Student success, further, is often considered an indicator of how well students, school personnel, and parents are performing. School personnel are trained and paid to perform their professional roles in such a way as to make a significant and positive difference in students' lives. School personnel consider themselves successful if they facilitate students' school successes. Students' school successes are reflected when students become happy, healthy, competent, confident, self-sufficient, problem solving, lifelong learners capable of functioning at their maximum potential and prepared to assume a productive role in society, and *any student can!*

Parents want their children to succeed in school as a preparation for success in life. Parents are a child's first, and therefore, most important teachers. Parents can continue as such if they actively encourage and support their child and work cooperatively with school personnel. Like parents, everyone has a vested interest in students' school successes. Students who succeed in school contribute to both their own and to society's well-being. When students become capable of assuming independent and productive lifestyles, student success has positive, significant, and far-ranging personal, interpersonal, economic, social, psychological, and societal ramifications.

Though parents, teachers, principals, and students may articulate different educational goals and commonly accepted requisite skills and concepts expected of students, there are more commonalities than differences. There are personal and social goals related to self-esteem, self-understanding, self-direction, communication, compassion, and caring. There are goals related to physical fitness as well as to psychological wellness.

There are skills that may be manual, psychomotor, technical, vocational, recreational, or social in nature. The concepts that students are expected to master range from simple to complex, and they are in many different academic subject areas. The skills and concepts together equip students for success in the various roles they inevitably will assume as adults: workers, spouses, parents, community participants, and family members. As any teacher will admit, however, the educational goals will not be met if students are misbehaving, inattentive, unmotivated, and distracting other appropriately behaving students.

Students, school personnel, and parents want students to behave in ways that are consistent with achieving instructional effectiveness, and instructional effectiveness is the consummate common goal. Getting students to behave in ways that are consistent with instructional effectiveness is related to a number of student, teacher, assistant teacher, counselor, administrator, and parent behaviors; is all parties' responsibility; and is a cooperative endeavor among students, school personnel, and parents. There are motivational and management techniques that significantly impact how and/or if students succeed and behave appropriately. There are communication, counseling, and classroom management techniques that significantly impact how and/or if students succeed and behave appropriately. There are instructional, interpersonal, and intervention techniques that significantly impact how and/or if students succeed and behave appropriately. The primary focus of this text, therefore, is on the behaviors, attitudes, roles, and responsibilities that school personnel must assume if students are to succeed and behave appropriately, and *any student can*!

THE REALITY OF DIVERSITY

Long gone are the "good old days," when, by and large, school personnel had to deal with behavior problems no more worrisome than students talking out of turn, making noise, chewing gum, running in the halls, getting out of turn in line, or not putting paper in the wastebasket. While these behavior problems still exist, they are frequently overshadowed by far more serious misbehaviors which often are of a violent or life-threatening nature. Today, school personnel, students, and parents, in urban and rural communities nationwide, have to deal on a daily basis with the problems and ramifications of violence, concealed weapons, drug abuse, alcohol abuse, AIDS, pregnancy, suicide, rape, robbery, assault, gangs, vandalism, and abuse.

Each student's individual background and environment makes that student uniquely challenging for a teacher to educate and manage. There are students from single parent families, divorced families, blended families, and intact families. In terms of birth order, there are students who are the oldest or the older child within a family, and others who are younger or who are middle children. There are the only children, the twins, and in fewer cases, the triplets, quintuplets, etc. There are students from economically impoverished backgrounds and students from more economically privileged backgrounds. There are emotionally abused, sexually abused, and physically abused students as well as emotionally and physically neglected students. There are students who abuse drugs and/or alcohol, and students who have family members and/or friends in jail for a variety of offenses.

Students are from various cultural, racial, ethnic, religious, socioeconomic, educational, parental education, and linguistic backgrounds. There are students at all ability, achievement, and motivational levels. Though we decry the use of labels, there are students who are referred to as "gifted," "artistic," "talented," "creative," and "athletically inclined" students as well as "dyslexic," "dyscalculic," "learning disabled," "hyperactive," and "attention-deficit." There are "latchkey" students who, without supervision, fend for themselves after school before a working parent arrives home, as well as students who are victims of both benign and more purposeful neglect.

There are students who are avid readers and students who are television and video game junkies. There are computer literate and functionally illiterate students. There are some students who learn best by seeing and others who learn best by hearing or by tactile and kinesthetic manipulation. There are outgoing, people-oriented, gregarious students and students who are not so energized by group activities and social contact. There are physically, psychologically, and emotionally healthy students and physically, psychologically, and emotionally challenged—"differently abled" students. There are students with vastly different personalities and needs. There are anorexic and bulimic students, troubled teens, and teens who are themselves parents. There are students who prefer to work alone and students who prefer to work with others. There are students with different intelligences (Gardner identifies eight), different personality types, various learning styles and modality strengths, and different environmental preferences (all of which can enhance or detract from their learning and behavior). The Myers-Briggs Type Indicator is a scale that identifies 16 personality types and preferences on four scales: how attention is focused (Extroverted or Introverted), how information is received (Sensing or Intuition), how decisions are made (Thinking or Feeling), and how one deals with the outer world (Judging or Perceiving). Then too, there are students who learn best by seeing, hearing, and/or kinesthetic involvement, and students who are concrete, abstract, sequential, or random in their learning styles. Effective teachers assess their students' intelligences, personality types, learning styles, modality strengths, and environmental preferences, and they select and refine their instructional and management strategies accordingly.

Yet, amid the realities of today's schools and the diversity of students, all students have in common the need and the desire to succeed. *Any student can succeed and behave appropriately.* Students who remain on task—and therefore learn—do so because they are challenged by and engaged in a motivational, meaningful, and interesting task. Students so instructionally involved are also far less likely to misbehave, be inattentive, distract others, or otherwise behave inappropriately.

Consider the nursery school child who listens, spellbound, to the teacher reading a story. Think about those youngsters who cannot wait to tell their own tales, share their stories, or display their drawings. Think about the elementary school student who looks wide-eyed through a hand-held magnifier at the specimen beneath it. Observe the child who sits enraptured by the computer tutorial. Consider the team of high school students who are engrossed by a challenging geometry problem or a group of students working with microscopes who marvel at their findings.

These students, because they are engaged in learning and succeeding at their tasks, are not likely to be behavior problems precisely because they are interested in and succeeding at motivational, challenging, and interesting tasks. Another major focus of this text, therefore, is on various ways school personnel can achieve motivational and instructional effectiveness; both are required if students are to succeed and behave appropriately.

Just as the students in our schools reflect the diversity of our multicultural, multifaceted, and complex society, so too do all school personnel. It follows, then, that it is foolish, if not impossible, to expect a diverse group of parents, teachers, assistant teachers, counselors, and administrators to teach, manage, or otherwise interact with a similarly diverse group of students with only one set of philosophical assumptions about motivation or needs, and with only one instructional or management strategy. Rather, an eclectic approach that utilizes (1) various instructional techniques, (2) a wide variety of pedagogical and motivational approaches, and (3) a variety of behavior and classroom management strategies is necessary if school personnel are to succeed at having all students learn and behave appropriately.

BEHAVIOR

"Now boys and girls, be good!" says the nursery school teacher: a vague statement although probably made with good intentions. "Children, remember that you need to behave," urges the elementary school teacher: also a vague statement which lacks instructional clarity. "Students, let's not forget the rules," states the high school teacher: an appropriate statement only if the rules have been periodically reviewed with the students. "Ladies and gentlemen, please remember that the honor code is in effect at this university," coaches the college professor: an appropriate statement only if institutional policies ensure students' familiarity with the code and effective only if there are procedures in place to enforce students' compliance or address their non-compliance.

At the beginning of each new school year, parents encourage their children, "Be good boys and girls in school": again, a vague but well-intended statement. During staff development sessions prior to the opening of school, administrators stress to teachers the importance of having their students behave appropriately. At in-service sessions for school personnel, consultants elaborate on how to effectively manage students' behaviors. As each new school year begins, there are numerous articles in the professional journals about effective behavior management. At any point in time, there are countless newspaper editorials, magazine articles, and pulpit sermons about students' behaviors. Students themselves are interested in their own behaviors and in the behaviors, appropriate or otherwise, of other students.

Although the terms *behavior, conduct,* and *deportment* are sometimes used interchangeably, they are not synonymous. A quick reference to a dictionary indicates that all three of these terms refer to a manner of behaving or acting. *Behavior*, though, specifically refers to one's actions; e.g., "her behavior during the test was inappropriate." *Conduct* refers to actions as measured by an ideal standard, such as a profession's code of ethics. Deportment is behavior related to a code or to an arbitrary standard, like the rules of etiquette.

The word *behavior* refers to a response or an action. It is what people do and the way that people respond. Any action is a behavior, and when you do something you are behaving. If a teacher tells a parent "Your child is behaving" that is essentially the same as saying, "Your child is acting," or "Your child is doing." All three statements are vague and likely to prompt the parent to counter-question with, "Acting how?" or, "Doing what?" Rather, an effective teacher specifically tells a parent that "Your child is well-behaved because he follows our classroom rules," or "Your child is behaving inappropriately because he talks out of turn."

The term *behaving* does not necessarily imply appropriate behavior or "being good," even though it is often casually used to convey that the behavior under scrutiny is appropriate. Nor does the term *behaving* imply misbehavior or "being bad." Rather, modifiers such as "well-behaved" or "poorly behaved" should be used with the word *behavior* to accurately convey whether the behavior is appropriate or inappropriate.

As teachers communicate with each other and with parents, they need to label a behavior and not label the student who performed the behavior. It is preferable to identify what a student does or does not do rather than to talk in terms of the student as a "good boy" or "bad boy." Effective teachers identify and specifically describe appropriate and inappropriate behaviors, and they refrain from labeling students since no student is always "good" or "bad." The "good boy" label can be unduly stressful and anxiety-producing because it is an unrealistic expectation that the child will be unable to continually fulfill. The "bad boy" label is a fatalistic expectation that may, in fact, encourage the child to continue to *mis*behave. As Chaim Ginott (1972) says, "Focus on the deed, not the doer; on the behavior, not the student" (p. 71).

Furthermore, personal and religious convictions notwithstanding, no behavior is good, bad, right, or wrong. Rather, behaviors have to be judged in relation to the context in which they occur. Eating is appropriate in the kitchen but may not be appropriate in the bathroom. Swimming attire is appropriate at the beach but not in the boardroom. The use of clichés may be appropriate when talking informally, but not in formal writing.

Skipping, jumping, hopping, and running are appropriate during break time but not during breakfast time. A number of students talking at once is appropriate in the cafeteria but not in the classroom. Conferring with another student is appropriate at the science table but not during a science test. Shouting and cheering are appropriate during recess but not during silent reading. Coloring, doodling, and drawing are appropriate during art but not during spelling. Daydreaming and other divergent and contemplative thinking behaviors may be appropriate during creative writing but not during geography.

Even our values and judicial systems recognize the situational nature of behavior. The "little white lie" told to spare someone's feelings is far different from a deliberate misrepresentation of facts for personal gain. In a courtroom when the "extenuating circumstances" concept is invoked, shooting someone in self-defense is viewed differently than shooting someone during a premeditated robbery. Speeding for joy-riding purposes will be viewed differently than speeding a pregnant friend to the hospital for an impending delivery.

At any point in time, a student simultaneously performs a number of behaviors or actions. Think about the student working on a seatwork assignment in third grade arithmetic. The student is reading, writing, thinking, breathing, and perhaps counting out loud. The student may also be twirling her hair, tapping her feet, fidgeting in her seat, and playing with her pencil. Behaviors that are readily observable, such as writing, counting out loud, twirling, tapping, fidgeting, and playing are called overt behaviors. *Overt behaviors* are those behaviors that can be seen, counted, and measured.

Covert behaviors, by contrast, are behaviors that are not readily observable. Covert behaviors have to be inferred from overt behaviors. Values, attitudes, and feelings are examples of covert behaviors. If the student moans and groans about the assignment or the student's facial gestures and body language indicate frustration with the assignment, then we may infer that the student has a negative attitude about the assignment. But we may only infer.

Reflect on the seemingly infinite number of behaviors you are performing right now as you are reading this text. You appear to be reading, but you could be looking at the page and daydreaming. Perhaps you are also underlining or highlighting as you read, taking notes, listening to background music, talking with someone else, or snacking. You may be daydreaming on occasion, re-positioning yourself in your chair, or moving around periodically. The overt behaviors that you are engaged in are underlining, taking notes, talking, and snacking. If, as you read, you comment about the relevancy of the material or you nod in agreement at some of the text's examples, then it may be inferred that you are thinking about what you have read, and that you have a positive attitude about what you have read. But, again, we may only infer.

All of the overt behaviors just mentioned, except for breathing, are under your conscious control; that is, you chose to read, think, talk, listen, or snack. Physiological behaviors that keep you alive and functioning, such as breathing, are called autonomic behaviors. *Autonomic behaviors* are involuntary, automatic, internal responses over which, fortunately for our survival and well-being, we have no conscious control.

Our educational system, by and large, stresses and evaluates overt, measurable behaviors far more than it focuses on attitudes, values, and affect. There is more emphasis on how many books a student has read than there is emphasis on whether the student enjoys reading and, in fact, reads for pleasure. There is more attention focused on a student's level of proficiency in division than there is emphasis on whether the student enjoys and understands arithmetic and, therefore, can utilize problem solving to arrive at the correct answer. There is more encouragement and reward for writing a composition according to conventional rules of grammar than there is emphasis on creative expression and writing for enjoyment. Overemphasis on the number of facts memorized and rotely repeated trivializes the educational process. The imbalance in favor of overt cognitive behaviors over covert affective behaviors needs to be corrected because the covert behaviors of values, attitudes, and feelings integrally affect performance.

Combs (1979) recognized the interdependence of emotions and cognitions and labeled the "myth of the affective domain" as one of the beliefs that hinders progress in education. He states:

> The argument about whether education should be affective is a waste of time. The fact is, unless education is affective there will be no learning at all! How students feel about subject matter, teachers, fellow students, school, and the world in general cannot be ignored. Emotion is part of the process of learning and is an indication of the degree to which real learning is occurring. (p. 162)

Gentile (1990) rephrases Combs argument this way: ". . . facts and principles that engender no personal excitement in the learner are likely to be considered unimportant and peripheral to that person's life. In that sense, the learning that occurs will be felt to be unreal, and treated appropriately" (p. 11).

THERE ARE CHOICES TO BE MADE: APPROPRIATE AND INAPPROPRIATE BEHAVIORS

Just as students have the choice to be self-motivated and to read, think, talk, listen, or snack, so too students have the choice not to be self-motivated or to read, think, or talk. In other words, students, like the adults around them, choose their own behavior. No one and no situation can make anyone behave in a certain way. As Albert (1989) puts it:

> Though people and events and conditioning may invite a particular behavior, the invitation can be accepted or rejected. The choice exists. Once we understand that behavior is based on choice, we can begin to influence a student's decision about how to behave. The change starts with us: we need to learn how to interact with students so they will want to choose appropriate behavior and comply with the rules. (p. 8)

Before students can choose to behave appropriately or inappropriately, they need to know what constitutes appropriate or inappropriate behavior, and they need to know the natural, related, and often logical consequences of those chosen behaviors. Specific, well-articulated rules, as described in Chapter 6, assist students in making such choices. The clarity of the rules, the communications between teachers and students about the rules, and the consistency with which the rules are enforced, (also described in Chapter 6) further assist students in making behavioral choices. Identification of pairs of situation-specific appropriate and inappropriate behaviors also allows students to choose appropriate behavior and thus be in compliance with the rules, or to choose inappropriate behavior and thus not be in compliance with the rules. In either case, the student has a choice to make about how to behave and to then accept the natural, related, and often logical consequences of those behaviors.

During math class, for example, Darryl may choose either to pay attention or not to pay attention, to take notes or not to take notes, and to ask questions for clarification or not to ask questions. During a spelling assignment, Tamika may choose either to work on task or not to work on task, to talk to others or to remain quiet, and to persist and complete the task or to give up and not finish. During an examination, Rosita may choose either to follow the teacher's instructions or to ignore them, to work independently or to cheat, and to proceed in the face of difficult questions and finish the exam or to resignedly quit. During recess time, Michele may choose to abide by the playground rules or to violate them, to play fairly or to cheat, and to act aggressively or to act non-aggressively with others. In each pair of behaviors, there was one appropriate behavior and one inappropriate behavior. Effective teachers make students aware of the consequences for each type of behavior so that students can choose how they want to behave and experience the natural, related, and often logical consequences of those behaviors.

The natural, related, and often logical consequence of paying attention, taking notes, and asking questions for clarification will likely be a better understanding of the material being presented than the consequences of not paying attention, not taking notes, and not asking questions for clarification. (The word *likely* is used here because, as the content elsewhere in this text indicates, not all students need to take notes or to ask clarifying questions to effectively learn.) The natural, related, and logical consequences of working on task, persisting on task, and following task instructions will likely be better task performance than the consequences of not working on task, resignedly or prematurely quitting, or ignoring task instructions.

Once students are clearly aware of behaviors they may or may not engage in and the natural, related, and often logical consequences for each of the behaviors selected, they are in a better position to decide how they will behave. Furthermore, behaviors often have more than one consequence, and behaviors often have both positive and negative consequences.

These basic premises about behavioral choice and about awareness of the chosen behavior's natural, related, and often logical consequence or consequences, applies to student and adult behaviors alike. The driver of a car who chooses to exceed the speed limit, drive under the influence of alcohol, or knowingly operate an automobile whose brakes are faulty is likely eventually to experience serious, significant, and possibly fatal consequences of the behaviors selected. The person who chooses to be anorexic/bulimic or a substance abuser will, in all likelihood, experience different consequences than one who elects less self-injurious behaviors. The husband or wife who is emotionally, psychologically, or physically abusive to their spouse is likely to experience different consequences and responses from the spouse than one who is not abusive.

The teacher who is energetic and enthusiastic will elicit different responses from students than one who is lackluster and listless. The teacher who successfully addresses each student's needs will have greater instructional effectiveness than one who does not. The teacher who successfully motivates students to think and question will have greater success than one who merely encourages rote and often meaningless memorization. Therefore, strategies and selected models of classroom management, motivation, and instruction are presented in the next two chapters.

SUMMARY OF KEY CONCEPTS IN CHAPTER 1

1. Everyone needs to succeed and to be recognized for success.
2. Students, school personnel, and parents want students to succeed in school and collectively have a legitimate and significant interest in students' school success.
3. School success is the mastering of our society's educational goals and commonly accepted requisite skills and concepts.
4. Everyone wants students to become adults who are happy, healthy, competent, confident, self-sufficient, problem solving, lifelong learners capable of functioning at their maximum potential and prepared to assume a productive role in society.
5. Students will excel in academics, athletics, or *mis*behaving because they want to succeed and be recognized for succeeding at something.
6. Our schools' goals will not be met if students are misbehaving.
7. Misbehaving students are, by definition, inattentive and often disruptive.
8. Getting students to behave in ways that are consistent with achieving instructional effectiveness must be a cooperative endeavor among students, school personnel, and parents.
9. There is great diversity among students, school personnel, and parents.
10. Motivational, challenging, and interesting tasks are essential for learning and successfully managing students' behavior.
11. Student motivation and instructional effectiveness are required for effective behavior management.
12. Various motivational and instructional strategies are needed by a diverse group of school personnel and teachers to successfully teach and manage a diverse group of students.
13. Parents need to be integrally involved in helping their children succeed in school.
14. An eclectic approach to management, motivation, and instruction is clearly indicated if we are to expect student success and behavioral compliance.
15. *Behavior* refers to a response or an action.
16. The term *behaving*, when used without a modifier, does not signify the appropriateness or inappropriateness of the action.

17. Appropriate and inappropriate behaviors need to be pinpointed and specifically described.
18. Behaviors should be characterized; students should not be labeled.
19. No behavior is good or bad.
20. Behaviors have to be judged in relation to the context in which they occur.
21. *Overt behaviors* are those behaviors than can be seen, counted, and measured.
22. *Covert behaviors* are those behaviors that are not readily observable and, therefore, have to be inferred from overt behaviors.
23. Values, attitudes, and feelings are examples of covert behaviors.
24. *Autonomic behaviors* are those involuntary, automatic, internal responses that keep us alive and functioning and over which we have no conscious control.
25. Our educational system stresses overt, measurable behaviors more than the covert behaviors of attitudes, values, and feelings. This imbalance trivializes the educational process. School personnel need to focus on both overt and covert behaviors.
26. Covert behaviors significantly affect performance.
27. People choose their own behavior.
28. Students need to know what constitutes appropriate or inappropriate behavior, and they need to know the natural, related, and often logical consequences of those chosen behaviors.

REFERENCES

Albert, L. (1989). *A teacher's guide to cooperative discipline.* Circle Pines, MN: American Guidance Service.

Combs, A. (1979). *Myths in Education.* Boston: Allyn & Bacon.

Gentile, J. R. (1990). *Educational Psychology.* Dubuque, IA: Kendall Hunt.

Ginott, C. G. (1972). *Teacher and child: A book for parents and teachers.* New York: Avon.

SUGGESTED ACTIVITIES/ASSIGNMENTS

1. Invite a teacher to discuss classroom behaviors and classroom management.
2. Create a graph representing the diversity in a school among teachers, students, administration, and staff.

3. Visit an elementary school classroom, a middle school classroom, and a high school classroom. Observe the teacher and student behaviors that occur in each setting. Make a written record of observations. Identify behaviors as either covert or overt.

4. List the factors that impede or facilitate *your* attention and behaviors in class.

5. Research Chaim Ginott's (1972) congruent communication skills. Discuss the information with your classmates.

6. Perform this role-playing exercise: have both an overt behavior and a covert behavior demonstrated, and have a person role-play the part of a teacher addressing each of the behaviors.

7. Design a questionnaire that reveals student attitudes (covert behaviors) about a particular topic or assignment.

8. Assess your personality type using the Myers-Briggs Type Indicator. Discuss what type of instruction is best for your personality type.

9. Research Howard Gardners's forms of intelligence, the Dunn, Dunn, and Price preference surveys, or Anthony Gregoric's learning style theory to identify your preferences and learning styles.

10. Critique journal articles related to classroom behaviors, learning styles, and/or multiple intelligences.

Chapter 2

STRATEGIES AND SELECTED MODELS OF INSTRUCTION, MANAGEMENT, AND MOTIVATION–I

The models, theories, and summaries of research presented in Chapters 2 and 3 illustrate a variety of techniques for effective teaching, management, and motivation. The research on effective instruction and classroom management shows that when teachers minimize classroom behavior problems, students' achievement and learning increase. Effective teachers plan for the prevention of misbehavior. While no single model or strategy can work successfully for all teachers, with all students, at all times, virtually all the models, theories, strategies, and suggestions presented here can assist teachers in planning and implementing effective classroom management and effective classroom instruction. It is suggested that teachers study, evaluate, select, implement, and refine the strategies, models, and suggestions that suit them best so that any student can behave appropriately and learn.

EFFECTIVE INSTRUCTION

Hamachek (1990, p. 393), in an extensive review of related research on effective teaching, cites the following characteristics and predispositions teachers use for effective instruction. Effective teachers

- are **enthusiastic**;
- are not perfect, in the sense of doing and saying the right thing all of the time; they are, however, **fair**;
- are more **proactive** than reactive;
- know their subject area and are able to **communicate** what is known;

- are not only well-grounded in their subject area, they have **broad interests** that enable them to relate other areas to their teaching;
- are **thoroughly prepared;**
- **value academic achievement;**
- **assume responsibility** for students' learning;
- **consider students' needs and abilities when planning instructional strategies;**
- are as concerned about **increasing** their **students' self-esteem** as they are about increasing their students' knowledge;
- are **sincerely and personally interested** in their students;
- make sure that students have **ample time** (allocated time and engaged time) to accomplish their learning objectives; and
- are **flexible**.

Educational psychologists use a number of different concepts of time, which are defined below, when discussing teacher effectiveness. While the research indicates that there is considerable variation from teacher to teacher in the amount of time devoted to different subject areas, some of the variation was a factor of teachers' classroom management skills and was specific to the types of students found in the different classrooms. It is important that the different concepts of time be clearly understood as the related literature is reviewed (Arends, 1994, pp. 74-76):

Planned time–When teachers fill in plan books, they set aside a certain amount of time for the different subjects and activities. This is called *planned time.*

Allocated time–The amount of time the teacher actually spends on a particular subject, task, or activity in the classroom is called *allocated time.* This is also called *opportunity to learn,* and it is measured in terms of the amount of time teachers have their students spend on a given academic task.

Engaged time–The amount of time students actually spend on an activity or task is called *engaged time.* Engaged time is also called *time on task.* This type of time is measured in terms of students' on-task and off-task behaviors. If a teacher has allocated time to seatwork on math problems, and the student is working on these problems, the student is on task. Conversely, if the student is doodling or talking about football with another student, the student is off task.

Academic learning time–The amount of time a student spends engaged on a task at which he or she is successful is called *academic learning time.* This concept is most closely related to student achievement.

Time needed–The time an individual student actually needs to master a task is called *time needed.* This feature of time is usually determined on the basis of a student's ability and aptitude.

Common to numerous theories is the idea that effective teachers have specific classroom behaviors that facilitate instruction and behavior management efforts. Though different theorists and researchers may categorize or explain essential teacher behaviors somewhat differently, the following list is a synthesis of the current literature. Each essential teacher behavior is given with relevant behavioral indicators:

Clarity–*Clarity* refers to the methods used to explain content concepts, principles, skills, and ideas. It includes but is not limited to the following. Effective teachers

- provide several clearly articulated examples of each concept;
- use concrete, everyday examples students can identify with;
- carefully define new, unfamiliar, or complex terms;
- repeat difficult ideas several times with various explanations;
- write and explain key terms or ideas on the board, on an overhead, or with a handout;
- stress important points through voice changes and modulation, inflection, pausing, and other attempts at emphasis;
- speak clearly, at an appropriate volume, and without mumbling or slurring words;
- use graphs, diagrams, charts, pictures, photos, recordings, computer assisted instruction, and any other media that facilitates students' understanding of a concept;
- point out practical applications of concepts;
- utilize peer instruction, webbing, mapping, and other techniques;
- answer students' questions thoroughly; and
- encourage student problem solving and questioning.

Enthusiasm–*Enthusiasm* refers to the use of nonverbal behavior to solicit student attention and interest. Enthusiasm includes, but is not limited to, the following. Effective teachers

- present material in a dramatic, engaging, or otherwise expressive way;
- use gestures as appropriate and not as distractions;
- move around the room and up and down the aisles between students when they are speaking;
- refrain from distracting body language, other mannerisms, or dress that compete for students' attention to the lecture;
- make eye contact with students;
- punctuate content with appropriate jokes or humorous anecdotes; and
- actively engage students in class discussion.

Interaction–*Interaction* refers to the use of techniques to foster students' participation in class. Interaction includes, but is not limited to, the following. Effective teachers

- encourage students to comment or question during class;
- sincerely and generously praise students for participation;
- minimally criticize students' errors;
- call on individual students and acknowledge every student's response;
- present challenging and thought-provoking ideas;
- use a variety of instructional methods and materials/media;
- ask rhetorical questions;
- keep up to date and relevant on the material presented; and
- have a sense of humor.

Organization–*Organization* as used here refers to how subject matter is organized and structured. (In a broader context, it refers to the placement of furniture and the location of instructional materials, as discussed elsewhere in this text.) Instructional organization relates to pacing and presentational behaviors and includes, but is not limited to, the following. Effective teachers

- organize presentation/lectures with headings, subheadings, outlines, italics, emphases, and summaries;
- explain the relevancy and applicability of content;
- periodically summarize points made;
- review topics previously covered;
- stimulate student thinking and problem solving;
- use clear transitions between topics;
- avoid meaningless busywork and excessive and unnecessary homework;
- clearly state objectives and assignments;
- refrain from dwelling excessively or over-explaining obvious points; and
- avoid rambling and meaningless digressions from major themes without sacrificing incidental learning opportunities.

Rapport–*Rapport* refers to the nature of the interpersonal relations between teacher and students. Rapport is achieved when teachers are positive and more reinforcing than they are punitive, and when they convey to each and every student that they are important and cared about. Effective teachers achieve rapport with students when they address students by their names. Effective teachers are sincere when they help students with their problems, and they are tolerant of others' points of view.

Behavior management and discipline experts acknowledge that effective teachers are competent in each of the following **eight essential effective teacher behaviors.**

- They are consistent in the use of disciplinary techniques and in the enforcement of rules and policies;

- They establish **c**ontingencies (conditions) where appropriate behaviors can be rewarded and inappropriate behaviors extinguished;
- They **c**ommunicate clearly with other teachers, students, administrators, parents, counselors, and other school personnel;
- They are adept at **c**onferencing with students, parents, and fellow professionals;
- They **c**are about each and every student, and their demeanor and classroom atmosphere reflect this;
- They are **c**ompassionate in their relationships with students, and they understand the myriad of backgrounds, values, skills, and attitudes that characterize different students;
- They **c**ollaborate and cooperate with fellow faculty, staff, administrators, and other professionals to make the school experience a successful and meaningful one for all students; and
- They can successfully convey to students that it is their **c**hoice how to behave and to thus experience the resultant consequences.

Throughout this chapter, these eight essential effective teacher behaviors will be identified as they appear in the selected models, theories, and summaries of research presented. Models of discipline by Raywid (1976) and Kindsvatter (1988) indicate that a teacher's approach to discipline should be planned and conducted in three separate but successive phases: prevention, control, and behavior adjustment.

The **prevention phase** attempts to create optimum classroom conditions. In this phase, teachers are required to:
1. establish fair and reasonable expectations;
2. communicate clearly reasonable expectations;
3. create a positive classroom climate and consider students' perceptions, attitudes, and expectations; and
4. involve students in developing the expectations.

The **control phase** presents measures to abate problems, and to reestablish order following the occurrence of inappropriate behaviors. In this phase, teachers need to:
1. use reminders, restraint, and reproval;
2. be compassionate but firm;
3. be firm, fair, and considerate, avoiding anger and retaliation; and
4. analyze the group dynamics and conduct a class meeting to address group problems.

The **behavior adjustment phase** involves deciding what means are appropriate to deal with the behaviors, and to provide for long range improvement. In this phase, teachers need to:
1. enforce reasonable consequences (as described in Chapter 4);
2. use reinforcement and extinction techniques and possibly referral;

3. assess the appropriateness of teaching methods and adjust instruction and management approaches; and,

4. guide the class toward ownership of its internal problems.

The research on effective instruction and classroom climate shows that minimizing classroom behavior problems maximizes students' engaged time and achievement. Teachers who effectively manage classroom behavior problems devote time to planning the prevention of students' inappropriate behaviors.

THE KOUNIN MODEL

Kounin (1970), after several years of trying to understand discipline in the classroom, discovered that the key was not so much the way teachers controlled and disciplined individual students but, rather, the way they managed groups. He conceptualized eight different variables for describing how effective teachers manage groups:

1. **With-itness:** the ability to accurately spot deviant behavior, almost before it starts;

2. **Overlappingness:** the ability to spot and deal with deviant behavior while going right on with the lesson;

3. **Smoothness:** the absence of behaviors that interrupt the flow of activities;

4. **Momentum:** the absence of behaviors that slow down lesson pacing;

5. **Group alerting:** the techniques used by teachers to keep non-involved students attending and forewarned of forthcoming events;

6. **Accountability:** the techniques used by teachers to keep students accountable for their performance;

7. **Challenge arousal:** the techniques used by teachers to keep students involved and enthusiastic; and

8. **Variety:** the degree to which various aspects of lessons differed.

For example, monitoring "with-itness" and "overlappingness" helps teachers keep students on task and minimizes the frequency of occurrence of inappropriate student behaviors. Monitoring allows teachers a clear view of the entire classroom. When a teacher frequently scans the room observing students' behaviors, that teacher is practicing "with-itness," that is the teacher is constantly aware of what is happening in the classroom and is ready to detect and handle discipline problems. With the overlappingness strategy, teachers can manage more than one problem at a time. For example, while a teacher is helping students work independently, the teacher also monitors the rest of the class to prevent the occurrence of inappropriate behaviors.

The research on effective instruction and classroom climate, as summarized below by Kindsvatter (1988, p. 39) and with parenthetical notes by the authors, indicates that in classrooms characterized by few discipline problems, effective teachers do the following. Effective teachers:

- prevent problems by teaching and demonstrating rules and procedures at the beginning of the year and allow time for students to practice them (communication and consistency);
- maintain lesson momentum by using a brisk but appropriate pace so students stay attentive and interested (communication, collaboration, compassionate, and caring);
- establish classroom traffic patterns that avoid bottlenecks, obstacles, and long lines (caring and compassionate);
- avoid long periods of delay and confusion by establishing smooth, brief transitions between lessons and activities (compassionate and caring);
- monitor the classroom continuously and stay aware of what is occurring in all parts of the room (consistency and contingency management);
- teach students academic survival skills, such as how to pay attention, follow directions, and ask for help (caring, compassionate, conferencing, and communication);
- teach by design, with well-planned lessons and advance preparation of materials; (caring, compassionate, and collaboration);
- avoid labeling or judging students as "bad." Instead, they describe the effects of student behavior as "disruptive," "unacceptable," etc. (communication, compassionate, and caring);
- provide appropriate instruction, reteaching, remedial work, and enrichment for all students (caring, communication, compassionate, and collaboration);
- give positive feedback that specifically describes the student's accomplishment—improved handwriting, for example—rather than simply writing "good" or "A" at the top of an assignment or merely giving rewards without feedback (caring, communication, conferencing, and compassionate);
- have emergency plans for rainy days, substitutes, assemblies, and schedule changes (consistency, contingency management, and collaboration);
- teach students personal and social skills, such as conversing, listening, helping, and sharing (caring, compassionate, communication, and conferencing); and

- adopt classroom rules that are consistent with the school rules (consistency, communication, collaboration, and choice).

Not surprisingly, research on developing student responsibility in the classroom similarly reflects many of the eight essentials of effective teacher behaviors. This research, summarized by Kindsvatter (1988, p. 40) and again with parenthetical notes by the authors, indicates that in developing student responsibility in classrooms teachers need to do the following. Effective teachers

- set and enforce the limits of acceptable behaviors and hold students accountable for knowing what behaviors are acceptable (consistency, contingency management, choice, and communication);
- confront students when they do not stop their disruptive behavior following a simple warning (communication, consistency, and caring);
- do not let students exceed the acceptable limits of behaviors (caring, consistency, and communication);
- inform students that it is their choice to continue misbehaving or to stop misbehaving and make sure students understand that their decision to continue misbehaving will result in a specific consequence (communication, consistency, choice, contingency management, and conferencing);
- make sure the consequences are realistic, reasonable, and appropriate for the misbehavior, such as cleaning up the mess instead of writing an essay on not making a mess (consistency, contingency management, and communication);
- concentrate on the students' current behaviors rather than on their past mistakes (caring and compassionate);
- accept no excuses for misbehaviors (consistency); and
- have students make a commitment to change behaviors, such as a handshake, verbal agreement, or signed contract (communication, consistency, conferencing, and choice).

THE "WITH-IT" TEACHER

Kounin's (1970) concepts of with-itness and overlappingness underscore the importance of teachers being able to accurately read classroom situations and perform several different teaching behaviors simultaneously. His research also points out the need to respond quickly to "desist incidences." A *desist incident* is an incident serious enough that, if not dealt with, will lead to further and widening management problems.

Kounin (1970) identified clarity, firmness, and roughness as some types of desist behaviors. *Clarity* is the degree to which a teacher specifies what is wrong. Merely saying, "stop that!" is an unclear desist; a preferable statement would be, "Do not sharpen your pencil while I am talking." *Firmness* is the degree to which the teacher communicates, "I mean it." Simply saying, "Please don't do that" is an unfirm desist; a firm desist statement, by contrast, would be, "I will not tolerate that from you." *Roughness* is the degree to which the teacher expresses anger. Indicating, "You shouldn't do that anymore" is an unrough desist, while, "When you do that I get angry, and I intend to punish you" is a rough desist.

Extending the research of Kounin and drawing on their own work, Evertson and Emmer (1982, 1984) provide these suggestions for dealing with desist behaviors. When inappropriate behavior occurs, effective teachers do the following:

1. When a student is off task and not working on an assignment, effective teachers redirect the student's attention to the task by saying, for example, "Susie, you should be writing now." An effective teacher would check Susie's progress shortly thereafter to make sure that she is continuing on task. If Susie displays other inappropriate behaviors, she should be told to stop them. An effective teacher would maintain contact with Susie until she returns to the expected task.

2. Make eye contact with the inappropriately behaving student, and then move closer to the student until appropriate behavior occurs. Effective teachers use a signal, such as a finger to the lips or a head shake to prompt the appropriate behavior, and they monitor the student until the student complies.

3. If a student is not following a procedure correctly, simply reminding the student of the correct procedure may be effective. Effective teachers can either restate the procedure, remind the students of the correct rule or procedure, or ask the students if they remember it.

4. Ask or tell the student to stop the inappropriate behavior. Effective teachers monitor the behavior until it stops and the student begins behaving appropriately. Effective teachers ask the student to identify the appropriate behavior, and they provide feedback to the student.

5. Impose the consequence or penalty of the rule or procedure violation. Usually the consequence for violating a procedure is simply to perform the procedure until it is correctly done. When the student understands the procedure and is not complying in order to receive attention or for other inappropriate reasons, effective teachers use a mild penalty, such as withholding a privilege.

6. Change the activity. Frequently, off-task behavior occurs when students are engaged too long with repetitive and boring tasks or recita-

tions. When off-task behaviors spread throughout a class, effective teachers inject variety into the required seatwork, refocus the discussion, or change the activity to one requiring another type of student response.

7. Ignore inappropriate behavior if it is of short duration, not likely to continue, or a minor deviation, or if reacting to it would interrupt the lesson and bring attention to the behavior.

Jones and Jones (1995) offer some additional suggestions for responding thoughtfully and with a purpose **to de-escalate defiant behavior**. When a student refuses to talk, looks angry, upset, anxious, depressed, distracted, disengages from the group, or makes statements like "This stuff is boring" and "Who wants to learn this anyway?" they suggest these options (p. 292):

1. Expand on *active listening* and *identify the feelings* the student may be experiencing. An effective teacher would say: "It sounds like you're frustrated with how easy the work is," or "I would be angry too if I thought I was asked to do something I didn't think had been explained very well."

2. *Send an I-message* to let the student know the behavior is creating discomfort. An effective teacher might say "I expect all students to make only positive comments to their classmates."

3. *Offer assistance.* An effective teacher would say "Would you like me to explain it again?"

4. *Provide options.* An effective teacher would suggest a different learning strategy, a helpful resource, or would seat a student somewhere else.

5. *State the expectation in a positive manner.* For example, effective teachers remind students, "We agreed that during class discussions students will talk only when called on so it is easier for everyone to understand each other."

6. *Review available options and consequences and give the student space and time to make a choice.* An effective teacher might say, "Jeremy, remember our procedure for sharing ideas. I will call on you soon when your hand is raised, but if you talk out, we'll need to do some practice during recess."

7. Sometimes it is best to just *walk away* and give the student space. Although this is usually not desirable in cases where a major confrontation has taken place, effective teachers use this occasionally when a student seems agitated and it appears that the student will settle down if given some space.

8. Ultimately, effective teachers *clarify to students that they must make a choice about their behavior.*

THE COOPERATIVE DISCIPLINE PROGRAM

The Cooperative Discipline Program developed by Albert (1989) is predicated on the idea that students misbehave to achieve one of four immediate goals: attention, power, revenge, or avoidance of failure. Attention is a powerful reinforcer and some students misbehave for the attention and the audience that such behavior provides. Some students misbehave because they want to be the boss or at least show others that they cannot be pushed around. Vengeful students lash out and try to "get even" for real or imagined hurts. Yet other students withdraw in an attempt to avoid repeated failure.

When a student misbehaves for attention, Albert (1989) suggests the following intervention techniques. Parenthetical comments, where appropriate, are by the authors. Effective teachers

- ignore the inappropriate behavior or refuse to react to the inappropriate behavior. (Minor misbehaviors should be ignored. No single teacher can respond to each and every insignificant behavioral infraction. Teachers should **not** ignore any behavior that is a major disruption or a behavior that threatens the safety or well-being of the students or the teacher.)
- look at the student without saying anything. (The intent here is to let the student in question know that you are aware of what is going on. The intent is not to glare, stare, or otherwise scare or intimidate the student.)
- move close to or stand by the student. (Proximity of the teacher is often sufficient for the inappropriate behavior to stop. In well-run classrooms, effective teachers typically move around a good deal, and they use proximity to prevent problems.)
- cue or signal the student. For example, a written note could be placed on a student's desk that indicates "Please stop what you are doing right now!" and no conversation is needed. (This allows the teacher to continue instruction without interruption and to stop the inappropriate behavior with a minimal amount of time and effort.)
- give an "I-message" that contains an objective description of the disruptive behavior, that conveys the teacher's feelings, tells the effect of the misbehavior on the teacher or class, and requests cessation. The effective teacher might say, "Sue, when you talk during class, I get upset because I cannot concentrate. Please stop." (Be cautious that the student does not continue the misbehavior because the attention is reinforcing and/or because they enjoy upsetting the teacher.)
- legitimize the behavior and take the fun out of it. This can be done in various ways: (1) A teacher could make a lesson out of the behavior,

such as requiring the student to complete an etymology report when inappropriate language is used. (Such a report could also be mailed home to parents if this is a repeat offense.) (2) If the entire class becomes involved in paper wad throwing, have the class plot trajectories, do time and distance studies, and keep notes on their experiments so that by the time the unit is finished, the students wants nothing more to do with throwing paper. (3) If a student calls the teacher a name, such as "blimp," the student could be required either to write a three page essay on blimps that is due within one day or to go to in-school suspension until the assignment is completed. (4) A teacher could place all student notes confiscated during the week in a box on her desk. Then, on one day, a note is selected at random and read aloud to the class, omitting incriminating names or words. Notes could also be sent to the principal, sent home, or put on a bulletin board with spelling and writing corrected. (5) When a student uses obscene words, the student could be required to write the word a number of times. If this was a repeat offense, the paper with the words could be signed, dated, and mailed to a "significant other;" an interested parent, a grandparent, a Scoutmaster, or someone else who is likely to have an impact on the student if they receive such correspondence.

- use an approach sometimes referred to as the "satiation strategy," or "flooding;" namely, to extend the behavior to its most extreme form. A student has to throw paper wads for an entire period after school. A similar strategy is to have the whole class join in the misbehavior so the misbehaving child loses the special attention payoff. For example, have everyone tap their pencils on their desks if this behavior is occurring in a classroom. (A few cautions should be used with these strategies: effective teachers should inform their administrator of the tactic, provide their own paper so that they are not accused of wasting or frivolously using school supplies, and cease the strategy if the misbehavior is continuing or increasing rather than being eliminated.)

- perform an unexpected behavior which conveys that the attention-seeking behaviors will not be rewarded. Effective teachers can shut off the lights and wait a few minutes (but still observe students for safety reasons), lower their voices and/or change their tone of voice, or cease teaching temporarily and say, "Let me know when you're ready to resume the lesson." (Insist that students do absolutely nothing or else this might function as a reinforcer.)

- distract misbehaving students and focus their attention elsewhere. Effective teachers can do this by asking the students a direct question, changing the activity, or relocating students to different seats.

- reward appropriate behavior. (Effective teachers describe behavior clearly, and they only reinforce appropriate–not inappropriate–behavior. All too often, teachers ignore appropriately behaving students and are thus responsible for students' inappropriate behaviors.)

When students throw temper tantrums, are disrespectful, or are passive–aggressive ("I forgot," or "I have a mental block"), they are exhibiting power behaviors. When students are purposefully rebellious or physically and/or verbally aggressive, they are exhibiting revenge behaviors. The following suggestions are made by Albert (1989) for intervening when students "test" who is in control/*power behaviors*, or when they engage in *revengeful behaviors*. The suggestions, with parenthetical comments by the authors, require teacher restraint, control, and leadership. Effective teachers

- focus on the behavior and not the student. Effective teachers are firm and friendly, and they deal only with what is happening at the moment. (They refrain from labeling students.)
- think clearly, act logically and do not act out of anger. (Teachers must put the safety of their students and themselves first. If fights, weapons, or physical aggression are the problems, teachers need to get additional trained help immediately. They should not try to be a hero or risk anyone's safety.)
- avoid escalating the situation by yelling, sarcasm, preaching, or domination because these behaviors reduce students' self-esteem. (Hostility begets hostility, and it is a totally inappropriate behavior for teachers to model.)
- discuss the misbehavior at a later, calmer time and model self-control and nonaggressive behaviors. (Such responses require patience and practice.)
- often find it productive to hold a parent–teacher conference and consult with other personnel such as counselors, administrators, supervisors, psychologists.
- ignore minor misbehaviors (such as "muttering") as this allows students to "save face." (Effective teachers remember to deliver reinforcement for appropriate behavior while they ignore or otherwise deny reinforcement for inappropriate behaviors.)
- remove the audience and/or "table" or postpone discussion of a matter. (The issue should ultimately be revisited and not allowed to go unresolved.)
- elicit cooperation, not confrontation, and acknowledge that no one in the class is superior or inferior. (Effective teachers ensure that all students are treated fairly and equitably.)
- use time-out for a few uncomfortable moments and only after giving

students (especially confrontational students) a choice: "You may work quietly or go to time-out. You decide." (Time-out must be to a totally nonreinforcing area, and it functions best when it is coupled with an additional loss of privileges.)

When a **student misbehaves to avoid failure**, the interventions and strategies recommended by Albert (1989) focus on enhanced procedures for instructional effectiveness and student self-esteem enhancement measures. The general strategies Albert presents with parenthetical comments by the authors appear below.

- Effective teachers modify instructional methods. (Effective teachers accommodate all learning styles; they use concrete materials, manipulatives, computer-assisted instruction, and peer tutoring. They teach and reinforce one step at a time.)
- Effective teachers provide tutoring. (Effective teachers utilize fellow teachers, teacher aides, student teachers, peers, parents, and adult volunteers such as grandparents and retirees.)
- Effective teachers teach positive self-talk and build confidence. (Effective teachers minimize the effect of making mistakes. They praise students for accomplishments, and they focus on improvement by using encouragement and other reinforcers.)
- Effective teachers emphasize students' strengths rather than their weaknesses, and they acknowledge the difficulty of a complex task by breaking it down into smaller more manageable subparts.
- Effective teachers focus, analyze, and attempt to repeat past success. (Effective teachers help students to capitalize on their strengths and minimize or overcome their weaknesses.)
- Effective teachers recognize achievement. (Effective teachers realize the necessity of using both task-embedded and task-external reinforcers.)

KAGAN'S COOPERATIVE LEARNING MODEL

Albert's Cooperative Discipline program, described above, and Kagan's Cooperative Learning model, described below, use the eight essential effective teacher behaviors, but with slightly different terminology. It is clear, however, that both approaches recognize how critical it is for teachers to be consistent, to manage contingencies, to communicate, to conference, to care, to be compassionate, to collaborate, and to convey to students that it is their choice how to behave. Both programs interpret misbehavior as a message that a basic need is not being met. Both Cooperative Discipline and

Cooperative Learning emphasize structure so that all students are motivated to be actively involved in the learning process.

The four basic principles of Cooperative Learning are PIES (Kagan, 1994, p. 7):

- **P** stands for *positive interdependence*, wherein teachers create situations in which a gain for one is a gain for another, essentially a win–win approach;
- **I** stands for *individual accountability*, holding students individually and personally accountable for their learning if achievement gains are to be expected;
- **E** stands for *equal participation*; and
- **S** stands for *simultaneous interaction*

Effective teachers also foster students' positive self-concepts, and they hold high expectations for students' academic successes. They use encouragement and praise more than reprimands and criticism. They refrain from sarcasm, ridicule, verbal abuse, and other such comments that would only serve to damage students' self-esteem and reinforce any low opinions students have of themselves. The research, as summarized by the Mid-continent Regional Education Laboratory, (p. 38) and, again, with parenthetical notes by the authors, indicates that effective teachers utilize the eight essential effective teacher behaviors when they implement disciplinary techniques that focus on improving students' self-images and responsibility by

- avoiding win–lose conflicts using problem-solving activities rather than resorting to blame or ridicule (**c**aring, **c**ompassionate, **c**hoice, **c**onferencing, and **c**ommunication);
- remaining calm and courteous in the face of hostility or conflict (**c**ommunication and **c**aring);
- earning students' respect by showing that they **c**are about the students and their problems (**c**aring and **c**ompassionate);
- being **c**onsistent with all students in what they say and do (**c**onsistency and **c**ommunication);
- following through on their commitments (**c**onsistency and **c**ontingency management);
- exercising self-control and avoiding nagging, sarcasm, and bias (**c**ompassionate, **c**aring, and **c**ommunication);
- establishing rapport with students (**c**ommunication and **c**onferencing);
- treating students with respect and politeness (**c**aring and **c**ompassionate);
- keeping **c**ommunication open by being attentive listeners and clarifying students' comments (**c**ommunication and **c**onferencing); and
- using "I" messages to discuss problem behavior by stating how it makes the teacher feel (**c**ommunication and **c**onferencing).

Marshall (1989, pp 45–46) provides these specific suggestions for helping students feel that they are of value, they are competent, and they have some control:

Help students feel they are of value:

- Listen attentively to what students say. Ask for their suggestions.
- Help students identify their own positive and prosocial behavior.
- Highlight the value of different ethnic groups.

Help students feel they are competent:

- Provide experiences for students where they can succeed.
- Provide new challenges and comment on positive attempts.
- Teach strategies to accomplish tasks.
- Allow students to carry out and complete tasks by themselves.

Help students feel they have some control:

- Provide opportunities for choice, initiative, and autonomy.
- Avoid comparison between students. Avoid competition.
- Help students learn to evaluate their own accomplishments.

Marshall also stresses that effective teachers

- help students learn the skills that are necessary for interacting with others;
- let students know they have confidence in the students' ability to learn new skills;
- reappraise their expectations frequently; and
- are aware of whether their expectations differ for girls and boys and use activities in all subjects with all students.

CURWIN AND MENDLER'S
DISCIPLINE WITH DIGNITY APPROACH

The win–win theme, meeting students' needs, and a message of mutual respect comprise the vital, positive focus on multiculturalism that is at the heart of the Curwin & Mendler *Discipline with Dignity* approach (1993). They indicate that, "As a practical consideration, teachers today have no choice but to accommodate the burgeoning diversity of the students in today's classrooms. The alternative is frustration and eventual burnout. The key to success is to understand and meet the basic needs of every student," (p. 26). Curwin and Mendler's approach identifies four key principles for helping students to learn and exhibit responsible behavior. These four principles may remembered using the mnemonic device **ARMM**.

Always treat students with dignity and avoid the use of sarcasm as a means of controlling student behavior.

Responsibility is more important than obedience.

Model and teach the behaviors expected. If teachers expect students to use good manners and to respect others, then they must model those behaviors.

Make sure discipline strategies are practical. Students are quick to sense and point out "unfair" discipline strategies in classrooms. Thus, effective teachers establish the rules for behavior, and they find practical solutions to classroom problems.

Using these four principles and recognizing that students need opportunities to succeed, the effective teacher will create a classroom environment that allows and promotes success for all students.

THE ASSERTIVE DISCIPLINE MODEL

The Assertive Discipline approach to behavior management was first introduced in the mid-1970's by Lee Canter and Marlene Canter. This model suggested that teachers should approach classroom management in a firm, assertive, and positive manner, thereby creating a positive learning environment in which teachers can teach and students can learn. Since its introduction, the model has been revised to meet the ever-changing needs of students and teachers. However, the goal of the model has not changed: teach students to choose responsible behavior thus raising self-esteem and increasing academic success. The central ideas of Assertive Discipline are

- establish a classroom discipline plan that includes rules, positive recognition, and consequences;
- teach the classroom discipline plan to students, and inform administrators and parents of the plan;
- implement a system of positive recognition for appropriate behaviors;
- develop a hierarchy of consequences;
- document inappropriate behavior without taking away from instructional time; and
- enforce the classroom discipline plan in a consistent manner.

Canter identifies three types of teachers: non-assertive, hostile, and assertive. The **non-assertive teacher** fails to communicate classroom expectations to students, is inconsistent in responding to students' behaviors, and does not set and enforce firm limits. The **hostile teacher** yells, reacts emotionally, degrades, and verbally abuses students; hostile teacher behavior creates a negative classroom atmosphere which is harmful to students' motivations and self-esteem. The **assertive teacher** clearly, consistently, and firmly communicates expectations for the classroom. The assertive teacher has a discipline plan and is consistent in the use of positive recognition and consequences. The assertive teacher creates a positive learning environment in which a teacher can teach and the students can learn.

GLASSER'S REALITY THERAPY MODEL

One of the best models that uses all of the eight essentials of effective teacher behaviors is Glasser's Reality Therapy Model (1975). Glasser's 10-step discipline model is based on a teaching process about the value of reasonable rules and of how and why it is in the students' best interests to follow the rules (Mid-Continent Regional Education Laboratory, 1983, pp. 43–44). The model is presented in outline form below, with parenthetical notes from the authors about which one or more of the eight essentials effective teacher behaviors that step utilizes.

Step 1. Think about yourself and the student. Ask "What am I routinely doing with this student?" (**Caring.**)

Step 2. Then ask, "Are these things working?" If the answer is "No," make a commitment to stop what you have been doing. (**Compassionate.**)

Step 3. Make a plan to do something every day with this student that is personal, friendly, and conveys the message, "I care about you." Be persistent even though a long time passes before your student responds favorably. Stay calm and courteous no matter how your student behaves. (**Consistency.**)

Step 4. When a disruption occurs, issue a simple corrective or directive, such as, "Please stop it" or, "Please be here on time,"–nothing more. Continue with Step 3. (**Communication.**)

Step 5. If Step 4 does not work, ask the student to evaluate his or her behavior: "What are you doing?" and, "Is what you are doing against the rules?" If he or she denies doing anything, tell him or her what you see him or her doing and state the rule he or she is breaking. Put the responsibility where it belongs: on the student. Don't say anything more: just wait. (If you have trouble getting the student to admit he or she is breaking the rules, keep a tape recorder running in the classroom. Play it back to the student, or to his or her parents, to document the problem. Simply running the tape recorder will help to silence some students.) If you have been using Steps 1, 2, and 3, the questions in Step 5 are very effective in stopping the misbehavior. (Choice.)

Step 6. If the student does not stop misbehaving, then tell him or her firmly and courteously, "We've got to get together and work it out." Take time to encourage the student to come up with the plan and help if necessary. The plan should be short-term, specific, possible, and involve some form of positive action more than, "I'll stop." Get a commitment from the student to follow the plan: shake hands on it, verbalize it, or put it in writing and sign it. It is important in this step to impress upon the student that the problem is going to be worked out. If the plan is not working and the student disrupts again, accept no excuses. Ask the student, "When are you going to do what you agreed to do in your plan?" Find out what went wrong. If necessary renegotiate the plan and get a commitment from the student to follow it. (Contingency, communication, conferencing, consistency, and choice.)

Step 7. If disruption continues, repeat Step 6 once or twice. If this does not solve the problem, isolate the student at a time-out location in the room or, if necessary, in the office. (Be careful, the office can be a very interesting place to be sent for some students!) Say to the student "I want you to sit here until you have a plan that will help you follow the rules or when you are ready to work out a plan with me."

Step 8. Step 8 is in-school suspension. If the student acts up during time-out, then he or she is referred immediately to the principal: "We want you to be in class, but we expect you to follow the rules. As soon as you have a plan that will help you follow the rules, you may return to class. If you need help with your plan, I'll help you." If help with the plan is requested, the principal asks the student, "What did you do?" Then the principal asks, "What plan can you make that will help you do better?" Be prepared for lots of excuses. (Be sure the time-out room is as boring as possible—no pictures, windows, etc.) (Collaboration, communication, consistency, and choice.)

Step 9. If a student continues to misbehave, he or she is declared out of control, and parents must be notified and asked to take the student home. However, the principal tells the parents and the student, "Tomorrow is a new day. We would like your child to be with us tomorrow so long as reasonable behavior is maintained. If his or her behavior does not remain reasonable we will call you to take him or her home again." When the student returns to school the following day, if he or she misbehaves, go back to Step 8—in-school suspension— until the student makes a plan to follow the rules. (Conferencing, communication, and choice.)

Step 10. If consistent use of Steps 1 through 9 does not work, then the student must stay home permanently or receive special help provided either by the school district or community agencies. (Collaboration and conferencing.)

Glasser also contends that education, the school, the classroom, and the teaching–learning process should be organized and conducted so that students, while working at lessons, can satisfy their needs. They will thus learn, behave well, and take an interest in education. More specifically, he indicates that cooperative learning groups successfully accomplish this because learning teams give students a sense of belonging and because, he believes, teamwork is inherently motivating (Charles & Senter, 1995). Such teams, along with teachers functioning as "lead managers" rather than boss–managers, transform the classroom environment into what he calls the "friendly workplace." In the friendly workplace, students can find belonging, power, freedom, and fun: the very things that Glasser says all of us seek in life.

Relative to the manager roles that teachers have to assume, Glasser advocates that the effective teacher adopt the "lead" rather than the "boss" style. He distinguishes the "lead manager" style from the "boss" manager as follows (Charles & Senter, 1995, p. 84):

- A boss drives. A leader leads.
- A boss relies on authority. A leader relies on cooperation.
- A boss says "I." A leader says "we."
- A boss knows how. A leader shows how.
- A boss creates resentment. A leader breeds enthusiasm.
- A boss fixes blame. A leader fixes mistakes.
- A boss makes work drudgery. A leader makes work interesting.

The lead manager style aims at needs satisfaction and, "when teaching and learning produce needs satisfaction, motivation to work and behave properly follows naturally" (Charles & Senter, p. 84).

Teachers have a duty to provide a positive, productive, and safe learning environment. Every student and teacher deserves to be respected and treated with dignity. The models, theories, and approaches presented in this chapter provide effective strategies for teachers to build a classroom environment that maintains each students' dignity and treats each student with respect. Effective teachers must identify the strategies that meet the needs of their individual classrooms. They implement those strategies, and they review and refine them as necessary.

SUMMARY OF KEY CONCEPTS IN CHAPTER 2

1. Extensive research on effective teaching indicates characteristic behaviors and predispositions of effective teachers.
2. Effective teachers are enthusiastic, fair, proactive, and thoroughly prepared.
3. Effective teachers have broad interests, value academic achievement, and communicate well.
4. Effective teachers assume responsibility for student learning and consider students' needs and abilities when planning instructional strategies.
5. Effective teachers know their students well and are as concerned about increasing their students' self-esteem as they are about increasing their students' knowledge.
6. Effective teachers make sure students have ample time to accomplish their learning objectives.
7. "Flexibility" is the most frequently used adjective to describe the behavior of good teachers.
8. Effective teachers understand the different concepts of time (planned time, allocated time, engaged time, academic learning time, and time needed) and how they affect motivation, instruction, and management.
9. Research by Raywid, Kindsvatter, Kounin, and others indicates that minimizing classroom behavior problems leads to maximizing student engaged time and achievement.
10. Effective teachers devote time to planning for the prevention of misbehavior and take a proactive approach to classroom management.
11. Kounin identifies eight different variables for describing the group-management behavior of teachers: with-itness, overlappingness, smoothness, momentum, group alerting, accountability, challenge arousal, and variety.
12. Though different researchers use different models and different terminology, the eight essentials (consistency, contingencies, communication, conferencing, caring, compassion, collaboration, and choice) are common to virtually all of the selected approaches and strategies.
13. Effective teachers foster students' positive self-concepts and hold high expectations for their students' academic success.
14. Students need to feel that they are of value, that they are competent, and that they have choice, initiative, and autonomy.
15. Four principles (ARMM) are important in creating a positive classroom environment and in building student self-esteem. These principles come from the Curwin and Mendler *Discipline with Dignity*

approach (1993).

16. William Glasser's 10-step discipline model is a teaching process about the value of reasonable rules, and how and why it benefits the student to follow the rules. The steps in Glasser's model clearly reflect the eight essentials of effective classroom management.

18. Glasser stresses the importance of structuring the school as the "friendly workplace," which allows students to find belonging, power, freedom, fun, and success.

19. The lead manager style is preferable to the boss style.

20. Above all, teachers must treat all students with respect and dignity.

REFERENCES

Brophy, J. E., & Putnam, J. G. (1978). *Classroom management in the elementary grades.* East Lansing, MI: Michigan State University Institute for Research on Teaching Research, Series No. 32.

Canter, L., & Canter, M. (1976). *Assertive discipline—A take charge approach for today's educator.* Los Angeles, CA: Lee Canter and Associates.

Charles, C. M., & Senter, G. W. (1995). *Elementary classroom management.* White Plains, NY: Longman.

Curwin, R. (1992). *Rediscovering hope: Our greatest teaching strategy.* Bloomington, IN: National Education Service.

Curwin, R., & Mendler, A. (1980). *The discipline book.* Reston, VA: Association for Supervision and Curriculum Development.

Hamachek, D. (1990). *Psychology in teaching, learning, and growth.* Boston: Allyn & Bacon.

Kagan, S. (1994). The cooperative learning connection. *The Cooperative Discipline Connection, 2*(2), 1–8.

Kindsvatter, R. (1988). The dilemmas of discipline. In P. Wolfe's *Catch them being good: Reinforcement in the classroom* (pp. 32–36). Alexandria, VA: Association for Supervision and Curriculum Development.

Kounin, J. S. (1970). *Discipline and group management in classrooms.* New York: Holt, Rinehart & Winston.

Marshall, H. H. (1989). The development of self-concept. *Young Children, 44*(5), 44–51.

Mid-continent Regional Education Laboratory. (1983). Discipline. In P. Wolfe's *Catch them being good: Reinforcement in the classroom* (pp. 37–46). Alexandria, VA: Association for Supervision and Curriculum Development.

Raywid, M. A. (1976, February). The democratic classroom: Mistake or misnomer. *Theory into Practice, 27.*

SUGGESTED ACTIVITIES/ASSIGNMENTS

1. Visit the following internet sites for ideas and suggestions concerning classroom management and discipline. Share an "excellent idea."
   www.disciplinehelp.com
   www.dbeducation-world.com/perl/browse
   www.pacificnet.net
   www.track0.com/canteach/elementary/classmanl/html
   www.iloveteaching.com
2. Prepare a review of the (research) on one of the following: J. S. Kounin, L. Albert, L. Canter, E. T. Emmer & C. T. Evertson, W. Glasser, R. Curwin, or A. Mendler. Describe the principal concepts, strengths, and weaknesses in the model you choose. Your instructor may suggest other models.
3. Invite a panel of teachers to discuss how they manage their classrooms. Include a teacher from K–3, 4–8, and 9–12.
4. Role play Glasser's 10-step discipline model.
5. Role play the three types of teachers presented in this chapter.
6. Read and critique articles written by J. S. Kounin, L. Albert, L. Canter, E. T. Emmer, C. T. Evertson, W. Glasser, R. Curwin, A. Mendler, and H. Wong.

Chapter 3

STRATEGIES AND SELECTED MODELS
OF INSTRUCTION, MANAGEMENT,
AND MOTIVATION–II

In staff development training and in-service sessions, school personnel search for improved instructional, motivational, and behavior management techniques. During parent–teacher conferences, school personnel and parents wrestle with issues like (a) how to motivate students so that they want to learn and stay on task, (b) how to get students to realize the importance of what they are learning, (c) how to be an effective teacher, (d) how parents can help their children learn, (e) how to get students to read more, and (f) how to help students feel more confident about themselves. At professional meetings and conferences, there are numerous sessions that focus on effective instructional, motivational, and behavior management techniques.

There are community-wide forums for parents and teachers on various topics related to improving students' learning and behavior. There are a variety of incentive and reward programs for good grades that are sponsored by local and national businesses and industries and that reflect communities', businesses', and laypersons' interest in enhancing students' learning and improving their behavior. There are countless newspaper articles, editorials, and advice columns about teaching and parenting skills. There are numerous publications targeted for parents and teachers that contain articles about motivation, instructional effectiveness, and behavior management techniques. There are frequent magazine pieces and radio and television programs that focus on instructional and parenting practices. There are government-funded publications targeted for parents and teachers that contain articles about best parental and teacher practices.

There are undergraduate and graduate level teacher preparation programs that attempt to empower graduates with the necessary skills, concepts, teaching methodologies, motivational strategies, and behavior management techniques that can improve students' learning and behavior. Teacher educators and those involved in the preparation of school counselors and administrators research and relay, discuss and debate, and explain and emphasize effective instructional, management, and motivational strategies.

Clearly, everyone wants students to be motivated, to learn, and to behave appropriately. Students' school success must (a) be a cooperative endeavor among students, school personnel, and parents; and (b) utilize various motivational and instructional strategies by a diverse group of school personnel and teachers for successfully teaching and managing a diverse group of students. Accordingly, this chapter focuses on selected theories–of motivation, needs, choices, self-concept, and self-esteem–and on the theories' implications for successful instruction, management, and motivation.

BASIC MOTIVATIONAL AND INSTRUCTIONAL MANAGEMENT STRATEGIES

Brophy (1987) synthesized the research on strategies for motivating students to learn (p. 45). He identified the following five categories and 33 principles of motivation:

Essential Preconditions
1. Supportive environment.
2. Appropriate level of challenge difficulty.
3. Meaningful learning objectives.
4. Moderation/optimal use.

Motivating by Maintaining Success Expectations
5. Program for success.
6. Teach goal setting, performance appraisal, and self-reinforcement.
7. Help students to recognize links between effort and outcome.
8. Provide remedial socialization.

Motivating by Supplying Extrinsic Incentives
9. Offer rewards for good (or improved) performance.
10. Structure appropriate competition.
11. Call attention to the instructional value of academic activities.

Motivating by Capitalizing on Students' Extrinsic Motivation
12. Adapt tasks to students' interest.
13. Induce novelty/variety elements.
14. Allow opportunities to make choices or use autonomous organizers.
15. Provide opportunities for students to respond actively.
16. Provide immediate feedback to student responses.

17. Allow students to create finished products.
18. Include fantasy or simulation elements.
19. Incorporate game-like features.
20. Include higher-level objectives and divergent questions.
21. Provide opportunities to interact with peers.

Stimulating Student Motivation to Learn

22. Model interest in learning and motivation to learn.
23. Communicate desirable expectations and attributions about student's motivation to learn.
24. Minimize students' performance anxiety during learning activities.
25. Project intensity.
26. Project enthusiasm.
27. Induce task interest or appreciation.
28. Induce curiosity or suspense.
29. Induce dissonance or cognitive conflict.
30. Make abstract content more personal, concrete, or familiar.
31. Induce students to generate students' motivation to learn.
32. State learning objectives and provide advance decisions.
33. Model task-related thinking and problem solving.

Charles and Senter (1995) identify **charisma, caring, and enthusiasm** as three personality traits frequently seen in teachers who effectively motivate students. They describe *charisma* as hard to define and harder to acquire and characterize it as that "ephemeral quality of personality that attracts and inspires" (p. 77). Charisma includes, but is not limited to these qualities:

- an attractive appearance;
- a sparkling personality;
- the ability to envision what could be;
- steadfastness of purpose;
- faith in students' potentials;
- enlightenment;
- experience;
- wisdom; and
- the determination to persist.

Caring and *enthusiasm* also motivate students. *Caring* implies considerably more than concern. Charles and Senter (1995) describe caring as including these and other qualities:

- has a willingness to work on behalf of students;
- keeps trying when little progress is evident;
- persists even when students show no appreciation for efforts expended on them;
- encourages, cajoles, supports, or demands;

- is warm; and
- always communicates that as a teacher, he or she is not willing to let any student drop by the wayside.

Similarly, enthusiasm motivates,and it is contagious. A lack of enthusiasm is counterproductive for motivating students and is also contagious.

Charles and Senter (1995) concede that the above-mentioned personality traits may be somewhat nebulous. They offer some specific skill tasks that teachers can and should learn, practice, and perfect, as well as some things that good classroom motivators assiduously try *not* to do (pp. 78–80).

Good motivators try to:

1. use novelty, mystery, puzzlement, and excitement to energize their lessons;
2. use color, sound, movement, and student activity to attract and hold students' attention (songs, rhymes, rhythms, skits, plays, etc.);
3. assign individual and group projects;
4. state clear, reasonable expectations and requirements to avoid confusion and enlist student cooperation;
5. provide continual support, help, feedback, and encouragement;
6. listen to students' concerns and remain flexible enough to change when it is warranted;
7. provide numerous opportunities for students to display their accomplishments to both the class and to larger audiences;
8. emphasize student accountability concerning behavior, work habits, and production of quality work; and
9. work to build an "esprit de corps" and challenge students to surpass expectations and to be their best.

Good motivators do not:

1. bore students;
2. confuse students;
3. vacillate;
4. frustrate students;
5. intimidate students; or
6. punish students for failure or other shortcomings.

One additional comment relative to **student accountability** is relevant to both motivational and instructional effectiveness. Richardson (1994) reviews the six areas Evertson and Emmer identified in 1982 that teachers should attend to for developing student accountability for their academic work and their classroom behavior (parenthetical notes are by the authors):

1. Clarity of work assignments–(includes a specific set of expectations for student performance, details about form of work, and other items);
2. Communicating assignments–(includes clarity, a routine for posting

assignments or having students copy them, and conveying exactly what is required);

3. Monitoring student work–(teacher is aware of student progress, systematically checks student work, and circulates throughout the room);

4. Checking work–(students can check assignments with specific answers if procedures for checking are established; and procedures are established for collecting and returning assignments of present and absent students);

5. Giving feedback to students–(review and correct student papers, and use a grading system consistent with instructional goals and situational specifics); and

6. Clarity of instructions–(requires planning, precision, clarity, modeling, rehearsing, and periodic reviews).

An increasing body of research points to the importance of **a positive school and classroom climate** to increase achievement and students' appropriate behaviors. Goodlad (1984) used the adjectives *healthy, satisfying,* and *renewing* to describe schools that were successful in creating an academic ambience. Teachers, counselors, paraprofessionals, student teachers, teacher educators, administrators, staff, students, parents, community members, volunteers, and others can and should work together to establish a positive school and classroom climate that positively influences students' achievement, behaviors, motivation, and attitudes. There are a limitless number of ways to establish such a climate. Here are a few suggestions:

1. Recognize student progress and mastery frequently and periodically. The recognition is conveyed in a way that is meaningful to the individual student, and it is periodically conveyed to parents.

2. Encourage school clean up, spruce up, "We take pride in our environment" enhancement-type activities which involve students, faculty, and staff. Such activities and involvement allow students an opportunity to improve and personalize their work areas and the larger school environment.

3. Provide a bulletin board or other space where both students and teachers can write positive statements about each other. Teachers use the classic "suggestion box" to give faculty, staff, and students an anonymous and confidential opportunity to quietly commend, honestly criticize, or otherwise make suggestions for improvement.

4. Set aside time each day for students to read, study quietly, contemplate, or write in their personal journals. The reading, studying, or writing can be of an academic or nonacademic nature, and it should be personalized to the interests of the students and to the specifics of a particular class or situation.

5. Hold assemblies each marking period to recognize positive student accomplishments. Accomplishments may be of a behavioral, academic, creative, athletic, or other nature, and all students should receive sincere recognition for their accomplishments.

6. Have every student write or comment at the end of each day on a positive experience they had. As appropriate, these comments may or may not be shared with others, and they may or may not be made anonymously.

7. Have ongoing fund-raising, charity, community-service or other projects for worthy causes. Chose projects that involve all students and are of interest to them.

8. Create an atmosphere where parents feel comfortable visiting the school and participating in activities that contribute to its mission. So as not to compromise school security, convey ahead of time to parents the procedures for such visits.

9. Make a positive contact, by phone, letter, or e-mail with each student's parent(s) or guardian(s) weekly. This facilitates any subsequent school–home contact necessitated by a problem, and it reminds parents of a teacher's interest in their child.

10. Creatively involve resource people to address students about their special areas of expertise, hobbies, unique interests, careers, and experiences. Fellow teachers, students' parents, other volunteers, and retirees add depth and breadth to a teacher's instructional activities; they can serve as role models, and their involvement often serves to increase students' motivation.

The **momentum** of instruction and other classroom activities is an aspect of atmosphere that also impacts motivation, instruction, and management. Research by Kounin (1970) points out the importance of keeping lessons going in a smooth fashion and avoiding certain behaviors that impede momentum. Sometimes student behaviors impede momentum, and sometimes teachers do things that interfere with the flow of activities (e.g., dangles and flip-flops) or they have behaviors (e.g., fragmentation and overdwelling) that slow down the momentum of lessons.

- When a teacher starts an activity and then leaves it in midair, that behavior is a **dangle**. For example, a teacher starts to tell students to hand in their papers at the end of the lesson, and then the teacher suddenly proceeds to continue lecturing.

- Lessons are also slowed down by **flip-flops**. A flip-flop is when one activity is started and then stopped while another is begun, and then the original is started again. For example, students are instructed to begin silent reading, and then the teacher interrupts their reading to explain something, and then silent reading is resumed.

- **Overdwelling** occurs when a teacher goes on and on after instructions are clear to students. When activities are broken down into unnecessarily small units, **fragmentation** of the instructions has occurred. Effective teachers know though that what may be overdwelling or fragmentation for one class may not be with another, and it is critical that all instructions are clear to all students.

OTHER STRATEGIES

Jones and Jones (1995) extensively characterize eight general instructional management skills that enhance both instructional and behavioral management effectiveness. Their characterizations and descriptions, as outlined below with additional comments and notes from the literature and from the authors, clearly show the interrelationship between and among teachers' motivational, instructional, and management skills. There are eight skills areas for an effective teacher.

1. **Giving clear instructions**–While many suggestions are given in other chapters in this text about rules, instructions, and procedures, Jones and Jones (1995) elaborate on this first skill area as follows. Effective teachers

- give precise directions and instructions which tell students **what** they will be doing, **why** they are doing it, **how** they can get help, **what** to do with completed work, and **what** to do when they finish or if they do not finish on time;
- describe the desired quality of the work to increase students' sense of accountability and to decrease their anxiety;
- use different approaches when giving directions and instructions, vary their tone of voice, and use different media to present the instructions and to motivate students;
- use attending and listening games to improve students' listening skills;
- have students paraphrase the directions they were given, state any problems or ask any questions they have, and they require students to make a commitment to either begin a new task or to continue their work;
- positively accept students' questions about directions and create a safe, supportive, and non-reprimanding atmosphere;
- place directions where they can be seen and referred to by students;
- as appropriate, have students write out instructions before beginning an activity;
- break down the tasks into smaller segments for complex tasks or when

students are having difficulty following all of the directions;
- give directions immediately prior to the activity they describe;
- model the correct behavior; and
- hand out worksheets or outlines before a special event as a field trip or a resource speaker.

2. **Beginning a lesson**–Beginning a lesson effectively requires that teachers

- select and teach a cue for getting students' attention;
- begin only when everyone is paying attention;
- remove distractions before beginning a lesson;
- clearly describe the goals, activities, and evaluation procedures associated with the lesson being presented;
- stimulate interest by relating the lesson to the students' lives or to a previous lesson;
- use a highly motivating activity in order to make the student's initial contact with the subject matter as positive as possible;
- hand out an outline, a list of definitions, or a study guide to help students organize their thoughts and focus their attention; and
- help students to minimize transition time, the time required to settle down and begin a new task.

3. **Maintaining attention**–Effective teachers stimulate students' consistent attention to the tasks required of them. Maintaining student attention, a prerequisite for motivational, instructional, and behavioral effectiveness, is related to how the room is arranged, how and when teachers call on students, and to other factors that are listed and described below. To maintain student attention, effective teachers remember these points about **seating**:

- Arrange the classroom so that students face the speaker or teacher. Arrangements may be in a row, circle, square, or U-shape. Seating arrangements should be such that students can comfortably see and hear the teacher, group discussion is facilitated, and teachers can easily monitor seatwork.
- Adjust seating arrangements and move around the room so that all students become actively involved in meaningful classroom interaction and so the same students are not always close to or far away from the teacher. Students in the front of the room typically contribute more to class discussions, are more attentive, and are more frequently on-task than students seated near the back.

Effective teachers maintain student attention by developing these skills relative to **calling on students**. Effective teachers

- randomly select every student to respond and to answer questions, rather than predictably calling on students because this predictability often leads to boredom, inattention, and misbehavior.
- ask the question, look around the room, and give students an opportunity to consider the question. This creates interest and anticipation.
- wait at least three to five seconds after calling on a student. This gives all levels of students the opportunity to hear, process, and understand the question and time to then search for the correct answer. If teachers fail to provide the necessary time, students soon learn that they can maintain their uninvolvement simply by failing to respond immediately. Furthermore, research by Rosenthal (1973), Rowe (1978), and Tobin (1987) indicate these **advantages to increasing teachers' wait time**:
  - the length of students' responses increases;
  - the number of unsolicited, but appropriate, answers increases;
  - the failure to obtain a response decreases;
  - students' confidence increases;
  - teacher-centered teaching decreases;
  - students' questions increase;
  - lower-achieving students contribute more;
  - students' proposals increase;
  - students give more evidence to support their answers; and
  - the variety of students' responses increases.
- use games that encourage attentive listening. The **yarn activity** and **paraphrasing** are two ways to do this. With the yarn activity, only the student holding a ball of yarn may speak. After that student speaks the yarn is passed on to another student who may then speak. With paraphrasing, before a student may speak, the student must restate or otherwise paraphrase what the previous speaker or student has just said. These two approaches encourage students to listen to others rather than merely waiting for their turn to speak.
- ask students to respond to their classmates' answers and include all students.
- do not consistently repeat students' answers. If teachers parrot every response to ensure that all students hear the correct answer, students learn that they need not speak up, that they do not need to listen because the teacher will repeat the answer anyway, and that the teacher is the source of all learning in the classroom.
- model listening skills by paying close attention when students speak, and they look at the speaker and use nonverbal cues to indicate their sincere interest.
- develop a personal style and respond to students with enthusiasm.

- use straightforward and sincere praise for effort and give more positive than negative feedback.
- vary instructional media and methods and use a variety of instructional approaches and strategies that enhance students' motivation and increases the likelihood of instructional effectiveness and students' appropriate behaviors.
- create anticipation and excitement about learning.
- use silence effectively to create suspense and anticipation. Silence gives students time to slow down and assimilate material; it can be used as a signal, and it can be used to emphasize an important point.
- ask students' questions that relate to their own lives and personal experiences.
- provide work of appropriate difficulty. Students' inappropriate behaviors are often a response to work that is either too easy or too difficult. Any work that is assigned must allow for high success rates, but it must not be so easy as to bore students nor so difficult as to discourage and frustrate them.
- provide interesting seatwork and involve students in cooperative learning tasks and assignments that are related to current events, sports, hobbies, and other topics of interest to their students.
- acknowledge difficult material and let students know that help from them or from other students is available.

4. **Pacing**–Students' inappropriate behaviors can often be linked directly to poorly paced lessons. Teachers need to be aware of their teaching tempo and look to their students for nonverbal cues which indicate that students are bored, frustrated, confused, or restless. Effective teachers re-configure complex and lengthy activities into smaller more manageable steps, and they do not burden students with an inordinate amount of paperwork, worksheets, or homework. Effective teachers allow students to take short breaks, because they know that disruptive behavior is often students' method of obtaining a short respite from the rigors of a long school day.

5. **Using seatwork effectively**–Seatwork should provide meaningful practice for students, and it also enables the teacher to assess the students' progress. Seatwork should not merely be busywork. Seatwork should be as interesting as possible, and it should relate directly to the material presented immediately prior to it. Effective teachers also develop procedures for grading, monitoring, and adjusting assigned seatwork.

6. **Summarizing**–Summarizing should be used to reduce student frustration, to show students the relationships between and among the concepts they are learning, to give meaning to their school experi-

ence, and to provide students with a sense of accomplishment. Students can summarize what they have learned either orally or by writing in a journal. They can create learning displays, posters or bulletin boards that feature their work and allow them to share their accomplishments. Effective teachers also successfully summarize by relating the material learned to students' lives and interests.

7. **Providing useful feedback and evaluation**–Feedback and evaluation about performance are beneficial to both the student and the teacher. Feedback and evaluation allow for appraisal of teaching methods and materials, and they provide a basis for curriculum improvement. Feedback and evaluation show student progress and, when used correctly, can motivate improvement. Effective teachers provide honest, immediate, and specific feedback, and they de-emphasize grades and focus on students' positive accomplishments.

8. **Making smooth transitions**–The goal of a smooth transition is to prepare students to get productively involved in an upcoming activity. The physical organization of a classroom (work areas, student and teacher desk placement, movement, and accessibility) affects the smoothness of a transition. Clear pathways and a physical arrangement for accessibility allow a teacher to move around the room safely and to efficiently attend to individual student needs. Effective teachers prepare their transitions, and they post a daily schedule that clarifies the assignments.

MOTIVATION, NEEDS, AND CHOICES

Have you ever asked yourself why is it that you do the things that you do? For example, why do you like to golf or sew or play the piano? Why do you enjoy cooking or shopping? Why do you prefer a romantic movie rather than an action movie? Why do you prefer reading fiction rather than non-fiction?

Conversely, have you ever asked yourself why you avoid the things that you avoid? For example, why do you "conveniently forget" the dental appointment? Why do you postpone some of those housekeeping duties like cleaning or ironing? Why do you dread balancing your checkbook? Why do you avoid confronting an unpleasant issue?

The concept of *motivation* is a complex issue. Motivation is an ongoing process, and motivation can be either toward something or away from it. We are never unmotivated because, "Each of us, no matter who we are or what we do, is motivated to maintain and, if possible, enhance feelings of self-worth" (Hamachek, 1990, p. 262).

Motivation to do something or to refrain from doing something is a choice, a willful decision that is based on needs, and it is integrally related to people's feelings of self-worth. There are numerous theories about motivation. "Indeed, a 1992 textbook actually documents 32 distinct theories of human motivation" (Schrof, 1993, p. 52). There are also voluminous writings concerning needs, choices, self-concept, and self-esteem. What follows is a brief review of selected theorists' writing about motivation, needs, choices, self-concept, and self-esteem. Note that there are more commonalities than there are differences among the selected theories of Maslow, Rogers, Glasser, Dreikurs, Marshall, Marsh and Shavelson, and others.

MASLOW'S THEORY OF SELF-ACTUALIZATION

Maslow's (1954) **theory of self-actualization** focuses on people's constant striving to realize the potential within themselves and to develop their inherent talents and capabilities. In his "Hierarchy of Needs," Maslow delineates eight levels or categories of needs. The first four needs are lower-order deficiency needs, and they must be satisfied before higher level or actualization needs can be met. As Gentile (1990) characterized it, "Maslow's hierarchy of needs can loosely be considered to be stages through which people progress, but perhaps it is better conceived as a pyramid in which satisfaction of a more basic need is necessary for a higher need to appear" (p. 53).

The first four levels are basic needs:

1. **Physiological**–needs for water, food, oxygen, physical comfort, and sexual expression;
2. **Safety**–needs for security, comfort, freedom from fear, and peace of mind;
3. **Belongingness and Love**–need to belong, to affiliate, and to love and be loved; and
4. **Esteem**–needs for approval, recognition, respect of others, and self-worth.

These first four levels are considered by Maslow as "deficiency" needs to emphasize that a deficiency in any one of them makes it difficult to move on to a higher level. For example, if our physiological needs are not met, it is unlikely that we will be concerned about whether or not we are loved or appreciated. Likewise, if our sense of belonging and love needs are not met, it is unlikely that we will be concerned about whether or not we are self-actualized.

The next four levels, labeled by Maslow as "higher level" or "actualization" needs, are

5. **Intellectual**–needs for knowledge, understanding, exploration, and achievement;
6. **Aesthetic**–needs for order, beauty, truth, justice, and goodness;
7. **Self-actualization**–needs to fulfill possibilities, to reach potential, and to have meaningful goals; and
8. **Transcendence**–spiritual needs for broader cosmic identification.

Maslow's hierarchy helps us understand many expressions of human behavior and motivation because everyone has a hierarchy of needs. His hierarchy does not imply that any behavior is motivated only from one level. Rather, most behaviors have multiple determinants, and individuals develop their own unique hierarchy of needs as they grow and change.

A child who comes to school hungry and whose needs at the physiological level are not being met is unlikely to be concerned about learning arithmetic and succeeding at the intellectual level. Similarly, a student whose father recently abandoned the family and whose safety and belongingness and love needs are not being met is unlikely to be interested during art appreciation and unlikely to be concerned with success at the aesthetic level. There are some students for whom the needs for security, safety, or love dominate while others have more dominant needs for knowledge or intellectual achievement. "The most basic human motivation according to Maslow, at least beyond the level of physical survival, is the motivation to feel worthwhile, to feel that one belongs and is approved by persons who matter" (Hamachek, 1990, p. 59).

ROGERS' FULLY FUNCTIONING MODEL

Rogers (1969) conceptualizes motivation as growing out of the need to be more **"fully functioning."** Somewhat similar to Maslow's idea of self-actualization, the thrust of Rogers' fully functioning model is in the direction of living in closer harmony with one's inner self, that is, who one really **is** as opposed to what one **ought** to be. The self is a central concept in Roger's theory, and perceptions and behaviors are integrally related to one's sense of self. For example, a student with an adequate, healthy, positive self-concept is likely to be more open and accepting of experiences, is likely to set and achieve more realistic goals, and is more likely to have, as a result, a more positive view of self and of the school experience than a student who has an inadequate, unhealthy, and negative self-concept.

Furthermore, fully functioning individuals meet their own–not others'– expectations, and they are more self-directed than they are other-directed.

Fully functioning individuals are accepting of themselves; they are in the process of "becoming," and they tend to move toward being more open in their acceptance of their own experiences and in their acceptance of others. Fully functioning people change as a result of maturation and learning, and they have learned to trust themselves enough to take risks. Rogers characterizes fully functioning people as not looking to others for approval or disapproval, for standards to live by, or for decisions and choices. Rather, fully functioning people recognize that it rests within themselves and not within others to choose their behaviors. Fully functioning people take responsibility for their behaviors.

GLASSER'S REALITY THERAPY AND SOCIAL LEARNING

Glasser (1968) conceptualized two basic human needs: **the need for love** (to love and be loved) **and the need for self-worth** (to feel worthwhile about ourselves and others). Differences between people are conceptualized not as differences in needs but rather as differences in people's abilities to fulfill those needs. Relative to schooling, Glasser suggests that the two needs are so intertwined that they are inseparable and reducible to the concept of "identity"; namely, "the belief that we are someone in distinction to others, and that the someone is important and worthwhile" (p. 14). Self-worth in school means academic success, and a student who does not achieve success in school must find it elsewhere.

In applying his ideas to classrooms, Glasser believes that the schools must help children learn successful and responsible behaviors. Past failures and poor home conditions should not be used as an excuse for a student's inappropriate behavior. Glasser also emphasizes that the only worthwhile information from the past concerns a student's successes or achievements.

Like Rogers and others, Glasser readily acknowledges that people choose their own behaviors: "Children need to understand that they are responsible for fulfilling their needs, for behaving so that they gain a successful identity. No one can do it for them" (p. 16). Central to his "Reality Therapy" approach for dealing with unsuccessful behaviors are these two ideas:

1. students are responsible for making value judgments about their inappropriate, unsuccessful behaviors and for committing to new, better behaviors; and
2. school personnel have a parallel responsibility of not holding a student's past negative behaviors against them.

DREIKURS' CHOICES AND LOGICAL CONSEQUENCES

Related to Rogers and Glasser's theory is Dreikurs' (1968) explanation of **behavioral choices**, and the necessity of having students accept the **logical, natural consequences** of their behaviors. Dreikurs emphasizes that the responsibility for one's chosen behaviors is learned by accepting and sometimes suffering the natural, related, or logical consequences of those behavioral choices. For example, the student who refuses to properly sit in his seat loses the use of his seat for awhile. As Dreikurs (1968) explains the use of choice, "Choice is inherent in the nature of every logical consequence. The adult should always give the child a choice if possible. The child should be asked to choose between behaving in the correct manner or continuing with the misbehavior; if he decides to continue it, then the consequences should immediately follow" (p. 43).

Central to Dreikurs' theory and integrally related to the concept of self-worth is the idea that the ultimate goal of student behavior is to fulfill the need to belong. Students need (a) to feel capable of completing tasks; (b) to believe they can connect successfully with teachers and peers; and (c) to know they contribute in a significant way to the group (Albert, 1989).

SELF, SELF-CONCEPT, AND SELF-ESTEEM

Common to the above-mentioned motivation and needs theories are the concepts of *self, self-worth, self-esteem,* and *self-concept.* Maslow's theory is organized around the idea of "self-actualized" people. Glasser uses the term *self-worth,* and the concept of *self* is central to Rogers' theory.

The idea of *self* refers to our sense of personal existence. *Self-concept* is our idea of our personal identity, and it refers to the perceptions, feelings, and attitudes that people have about themselves. The term *self-concept* is the cognitive dimension of self-perception, and it designates a global conception of self. This global self-concept is made up of many dimensions, one of which is self-esteem. The term *self-esteem* (or self-worth) is the affective dimension of self-perception, and it refers to the extent to which people admire or value themselves. As Marshall (1989) puts it, "Self-esteem refers specifically to our self-evaluations—that is, our judgments about our own worth—whereas self-concept refers to other aspects as well—physical characteristics, psychological traits, gender, and ethnic identity. Our self-esteem may be affected by possessing culturally valued traits, such as helpfulness and honesty. It is also influenced by seeing that others perceive us as significant and worthy or possessing culturally valued traits" (p. 46).

According to Marsh and Shavelson (1985), the self-concept is multifaceted and includes a general self-concept, an academic self-concept, and a nonacademic self-concept. The general self-concept is a person's overall integration of the various facets of self and helps to determine the person's everyday behaviors. The academic self-concept refers to how well a person performs in various academic areas. The nonacademic self-concept is based on interpersonal relationships, emotional states, and various physical qualities. Similarly, self-esteem is multifaceted and is related to people being able to perceive themselves as competent and acquiring a sense of personal control over their environment. This sense of personal control is often referred to as an "internal locus of control," in contrast to an "external locus of control," which means decisions are in the hands of others or in the hands of fate (Marshall, 1989).

Though there may be differently articulated definitions of self-concept and self-esteem and though different researchers may examine different dimensions of self-concept and self-esteem, people clearly behave in ways that are consistent with the way they see themselves. People's beliefs about whether they can or cannot do things influence how they approach new situations; in turn, people's success in new situations affects the way they see themselves. It is essentially a circular process.

Teachers' expectations both directly and indirectly influence students' self- concept and self-esteem. If adults perceive that a certain student can do more than another, they may provide more opportunities and materials for that student, thus directly influencing the student's perceptions of his or her competence. Then too, when teachers point out a student's best work or compare one child's work with another's, they are subtly conveying their expectations and influencing that student's self-esteem. "Expectations often act as a self-fulfilling prophecy for behavior. Many times people behave in a certain manner because of the expectations they and others have for their behavior. The self-fulfilling prophecy establishes an inextricable connection between expectations about behavior and the behavior itself" (Carson & Carson, 1984, p. 117).

IMPLICATIONS

There are certain commonalities central to the writings of Maslow, Glasser, Rogers, Dreikurs, Marshall, Marsh and Shakelson, and others, as described above. Regardless of which theorist one subscribes to or which model and terminology one elects, it is nonetheless clear that:

    1. people have needs that have to be fulfilled in a somewhat hierarchi-

cal order;

2. people strive to be self-actualized or fully functioning;
3. people have a need to belong;
4. people are responsible for making decisions and choices about their behaviors;
5. people's behavioral choices—and the resultant natural or logical consequences—must emanate from within, rather than be externally controlled; and
6. people behave consistently with the way that they see themselves.

It is important, then, that teachers understand and meet their own needs and their students' needs. Effective teachers provide students with numerous and varied academic and social experiences to maximize students' successes so students become self-actualized and fully-functioning individuals who genuinely internalize and believe that they are valuable, worthy, contributing, and needed individuals. And *any student can!* It is vital that parents and teachers structure the home and school environments, respectively, so that students realize that it is they, rather than others, who are responsible for choosing their own behaviors and for experiencing the consequences of those behaviors. It is necessary that parents and teachers nurture, encourage, and recognize students' successes so that they develop a positive sense of self, and they behave in ways that are consistent with a positive self-concept.

SUMMARY OF KEY CONCEPTS IN CHAPTER 3

1. Everyone wants students to be motivated to learn and to behave appropriately.
2. Motivation is an ongoing process, and motivation can be either toward something or away from it.
3. Motivation to do something or to refrain from doing something is a choice, a willful decision that is based on need and that is integrally related to our feelings of self- worth.
4. Maslow's theory of self-actualization refers to people's constant striving to realize the potential within themselves and to develop their inherent talents and capabilities.
5. Maslow's hierarchical listing of eight universal human needs helps us to understand many expressions of human behavior and motivation because everyone has a hierarchy of need priorities.
6. Rogers conceptualizes motivation as growing out of the need to be more "fully functioning"; i.e., living in closer harmony with one's

inner self, who one really is as opposed to what one "ought" to be.

7. The *self* is a central concept in Rogers' theory, and perceptions and behaviors are integrally related to one's sense of self.

8. A positive self-concept will result in a positive view of self and of the school experience, and it is preferable to a negative self-concept.

9. Fully functioning people take responsibility for their own behaviors and are inner- rather than outer-directed.

10. Glasser conceptualizes two basic human needs: to love and be loved and to feel that we are worthwhile to ourselves and others.

11. Glasser maintains that schools must help children learn successful, responsible behaviors. Students' past failures or past negative behaviors are to be ignored and do not excuse unsuccessful or irresponsible behaviors.

12. Dreikurs, Rogers, and Glasser all readily acknowledge that people choose their own behaviors.

13. Dreikurs emphasizes that taking responsibility for one's behavior is learned by accepting and sometimes suffering the natural, related, or logical consequences of those behavioral choices.

14. Dreikurs maintains that the ultimate goal of student behavior is to fulfill the need to belong.

15. *Self-concept* and *self-esteem* are multifaceted terms.

16. *Self-concept* refers to our idea of our personal identity, and it refers to the perceptions, feelings, and attitudes we have about ourselves. It is the cognitive part of self-perception.

17. *Self-esteem* refers to the extent to which we admire and value ourselves. It is the affective part of self-perception.

18. Teachers' and parents' expectations and students' self-concept and self-esteem influence behavior, as explained by the self-fulfilling prophecy.

19. Teachers and parents need to meet their own and their students' needs. They need to help students become self-actualized, fully functioning individuals who genuinely internalize and believe that they are valuable, worthy, contributing, and needed individuals.

REFERENCES

Albert, L. (1989). *A teacher's guide to cooperative discipline.* Circle Pines, MN: American Guidance Service.

Carson, J. C., & Carson, P. (1984). *Any teacher can! Practical strategies for effective classroom management.* Springfield, IL: Charles C Thomas.

Dreikurs, R. (1968). *A parents' guide to child discipline.* New York: Hawthorn.

Gentile, J. R. (1990). *Educational psychology*. Dubuque, IA: Kendall Hunt.

Glasser, W. (1968). *Schools without failure*. New York: Harper and Row.

Hamachek, D. (1990). *Psychology in teaching, learning, and growth*. Boston: Allyn and Bacon.

Marsh, M. W., & Shavelson, R. J. (1985). Self-concept: It's multifaceted, hierarchical structure. *Educational Psychologist, 20*, 107–123.

Marshall, H. H. (1989). The development of self-concept. *Young Children, 44*(5), 44–51.

Maslow, A. (1954). *Motivation and personality*. New York: Harper.

Rogers, C. (1969). *Freedom to learn*. Columbus, OH: Merrill.

Schrof, J. M. (1993, October 25). Tarnished trophies. *U.S. News and World Report*, 52–59.

Wong, H. (1998). *The first days of school*. Mountain View, CA: Harry K. Wong Publications.

SUGGESTED ACTIVITIES/ASSIGNMENTS

1. Create a graphic organizer, a "map," or a "web" that illustrates the theories of Abraham Maslow, Carl Rogers, William Glasser, and Rudolph Dreikurs.

2. Design a set of classroom posters to enhance self-esteem, self-worth, and self-concept.

3. Visit an Internet website that provides information about "motivating" students to learn. Share the information with classmates.

4. Make a list of the students in your classroom and after each student's name, write a positive statement.

5. Use the Internet or a library to locate children's books that can improve self-esteem. Develop an annotated bibliography to share with other educators.

6. Invite a resource person who reputedly is a good motivator. Have the resource person share ideas and strategies with students.

7. Interview a classroom teacher who uses effective strategies to motivate learners. List and critique the strategies that this teacher uses.

8. Critique journal articles related to motivation and self-esteem.

Section II

THE BASICS OF
BEHAVIOR MANAGEMENT

Chapter 4

ANTECEDENTS, BEHAVIOR,
AND CONSEQUENCES

A basic understanding of essential concepts about behavior and about what happens before and after behaviors is necessary as a first step to change behavior and to implement an effective classroom management system. The essence of classroom management is the conscientious and active management of classroom environmental conditions and antecedents to prevent the occurrence of behavior problems. In this chapter, therefore, we define and describe those events that occur before and after a particular behavior, namely antecedents and consequences. We also elaborate on some essential concepts about behavior as initially presented in the first chapter. We suggest a review of Chapter 1 before reading further.

ANTECEDENTS

Antecedent conditions, hereafter simply referred to as *antecedents,* are those events that occur prior to or before a behavior. Since behaviors occur simultaneously, the particular behavior one wants to impact has to be clearly identified before its antecedent(s) can be identified.

An antecedent often influences behavior, but it does not cause a behavior to occur. An antecedent can be close in time to a behavior, or it can be more remote in time. For example, the ringing of the telephone, a recent antecedent, signals an incoming call. One's choice of a particular behavior, to either answer the call, let the phone continue to ring, or let an answering machine take the call, depends both on the situation and on the individual's personal history. If the phone rang in the middle of the night and it reminded one of a similarly timed call years ago that brought bad news, one might be reluctant or nervous about answering the call. Or, if the phone rang when one was eating dinner or at a time when telephone solicitors typically call, then one might chose to ignore the call. Both recent and remote antecedents and the specifics of a situation influence one's choice of a behavior. Furthermore, *remote* and *recent* are relative terms that have to be used and defined cautiously and in conjunction with the nature, severity, and personal significance that an antecedent has for an individual.

The nature, severity, and personal significance of an antecedent must be considered in determining the extent of that antecedent's influence on behavior. If 10-year-old Carl witnessed a friend drown two years ago, that may be perceived by Carl as so significant an antecedent that, even two years later, it influences his decision to avoid the same pool where the drowning occurred. Or, if 5-year-old Gene had a minor argument with Rick two weeks ago, that may be an insignificant, even "remote" antecedent that has little (if any) influence on Gene's decision to currently interact with Rick.

As teachers attempt to manage students' behaviors, they need to focus only on those antecedents over which they have some control. Consider Julie, a third grader who is having difficulty reading. Julie comes from an economically impoverished background, and there are no educational or reading materials in her home. She lives with her mother and an older brother who does well in school. Her mother had little or no prenatal care, and she was poorly nourished during her pregnancy with Julie. Julie is now repeating *third* grade because of her poor reading skills.

Julie's reading problems are most likely a function of both recent and remote antecedents. The remote antecedents of poor prenatal care and poor nourishment during her mother's pregnancy, and the more recent and possibly poor instruction she received during her first two years of schooling are history and, by definition, history is unalterable. Another way of looking at it, cliché though it may be, is that "you can't cry over spilled milk." Even though the remote antecedents cannot be altered, they should not be used as an excuse for not teaching Julie to read or—worse yet—for resignedly accepting Julie's difficulties in reading as inevitable.

Julie's teacher can use her knowledge of the facts—that there are no educational or reading materials at home and that Julie has an older brother who is a good reader—to help Julie improve in reading. An effective teacher would send books or magazines home with Julie, and would encourage Julie to read with her brother. However, an effective teacher knows that to successfully manage students' behaviors, they must concentrate only on factors over which they have control; for teachers, those are primarily antecedents that occur at school.

Antecedents also typically provide useful information. The following example illustrates the importance of knowing about recent and remote antecedents although knowledge of the remote antecedents is of only limited usefulness. Mario is a third grader who is failing arithmetic. He experienced anoxia at birth, and the oxygen deprivation caused some brain damage. Mario is inattentive in class, and he rarely completes his seat work or his homework assignments. His parents appear to take little interest in what Mario does at school. They have refused to come to school for a parent-teacher conference, and they have made no response to notes that the teacher has mailed home.

Mario's difficulties in arithmetic are most likely a function of both recent and remote antecedents. The remote antecedent of anoxia cannot be changed, but it is important to know about the degree and nature of any resultant brain damage so that appropriate instructional and motivational strategies can be used, and so that developmentally appropriate behavioral and academic goals are set. Mario's brain damage and delayed functioning, however, should not be used as excuses for not teaching him, and because they are unalterable, they need not be dwelled upon. Effective teachers focus only on those antecedents over which they have some control.

An effective teacher would identify and then alter the recent antecedents to Mario's tendency to not complete his seatwork. An effective teacher would closely supervise and monitor Mario's seatwork and minimize or eliminate his homework assignments. An effective teacher will recognize any improvements that Mario makes in arithmetic so that Mario's performance continues to improve.

Virtually all behaviors have one or more antecedents, although one antecedent may be more influential than another. Here are two examples:

Example 1: Fran has a history of cursing her peers. She often comes to school in a bad mood confessing to getting very little sleep the night before. Last year, Fran was exposed to a lot of cursing at home when she lived with an older brother whose behavior she often imitated. Fran's teacher does not need to distinguish which antecedent condition is more influential since all the antecedents are "history." Rather, Fran's cursing behavior and its consequences (which subsequently often become antecedents for yet other behaviors) need to be the focus of attention. For example, if the cursing receives attention, because attention is a reinforcer for most people, the cursing will continue. Ironically enough, this is true whether the attention is positive, like fellow students snickering with Fran at the teacher, or if it is negative, like the teacher scolding Fran.

Example 2: Billy hits Tommy and it appears to the teacher that Billy's aggressive behavior is the only antecedent condition to whatever response Tommy chooses. Tommy can elect to: (1) immediately retaliate and hit Billy; (2) wait and hit Billy at a later date; (3) tell the teacher; (4) tell his parents about it when he gets home from school; (5) ignore it; or any other number of possible responses. If, however, Billy has repeatedly hit Tommy in the past, then those repeated antecedents might make this instance of Billy's aggressive behavior the proverbial "straw that breaks the camel's back." The cumulative impact of Billy's aggressive behaviors towards Tommy could have a very influential impact on the response that Tommy chooses, in which case the antecedents would have an additive effect.

Antecedents can also moderate or interact with each other in ways that are often not easily identifiable. If, for example, Billy and Tommy were friends who never fought, then in the first instance of Billy hitting Tommy, Tommy's response would be moderated by their history of friendship. But, if they had fought on occasion, then the most recent instance of Billy's aggressive behavior might influence Tommy to choose a totally different response. Furthermore, one would have to look at the severity of the behavior: if Billy broke Tommy's nose, Tommy's response might be different than if Billy merely pushed him aside. As indicated before, a behavior may be influenced by any number of antecedents, and it is often difficult to determine which antecedent was most influential. Rather, teachers should concentrate on assessing relevant antecedents so they can prevent the occurrence of future behavior problems. Seating Billy and Tommy far apart will prevent another fight. Similarly, two students who are good friends may enjoy the privilege of being seated near each other only if they behave appropriately; if they are talkative and disruptive, then they too need to be seated far apart from each other.

As stated at the beginning of this chapter, it is the conscientious and active management of classroom environmental conditions and antecedents to prevent the occurrence of behavior problems that is the essence of classroom management. Countless behavior problems can be prevented by the classroom management techniques described throughout this book. An understanding of antecedents and consequences is necessary for effective classroom management.

Here are some examples of what effective teachers do with antecedents to reduce the occurrence of inappropriate student behaviors:

- Cheating on tests can be prevented by having alternate forms of the same test and by seating students far from each other to remove the temptation of cheating.
- Temporarily taking a comic book or a toy away from a student during class time eliminates the possibility that the book or the toy will distract the student during class.
- Select and use a variety of teaching strategies and instructional materials to accommodate all students' learning styles, to increase instructional effectiveness, to increase the probability of students' acquiring positive self- concepts, and to minimize the many damaging instruc-

tional and behavioral by-products of failure and poor self-concepts.

- Plan lessons and activities that are meaningful, relevant, and interesting to all students. Allow students to choose from a variety of activities to maintain high interest and involvement.

BEHAVIOR

In Chapter 1, *behavior* was defined as a response or an action. In that chapter it was explained that (a) the appropriateness or inappropriateness of a behavior has to be judged in relation to the context in which it occurs; (b) people choose their behaviors; and (c) many behaviors often occur simultaneously. As described in the first section of this chapter, antecedents impact behavior. In this section, we explain the necessity of clearly communicating behavioral expectations and how teachers can assist students in identifying and then choosing between appropriate and inappropriate behaviors.

Effective teachers assist students in choosing appropriate behaviors by clearly communicating their behavioral expectations. Some teachers often make the mistake of assuming that students know what behavior is expected of them, an erroneous assumption at best. Successful managers in industry and business do not assume that their adult employees, many of whom are professionals, know what is expected of them. Rather, they establish well-defined goals, articulate specific outcomes, and construct focused mission statements. So, too, should teachers and parents clearly communicate their behavioral expectations, although they do not necessarily always have to be in writing or presented as formal statements (unless it is in the form of a behavioral contract which is discussed in another chapter). Clearly conveying the specific, expected behaviors is especially necessary (1) when working with young students, (2) for the first few times that a "new" behavior is expected of any age student, and (3) when working with students from various cultures and backgrounds.

Reflect on the phrase, "Remember your table manners." Teachers often tell students this in the school cafeteria, but what does it really mean? This seemingly innocuous phrase could refer to the one or more of the following ten behaviors, and this list is by no means exhaustive:

1. Put your napkin on your lap.
2. Eat with your utensils rather than your fingers.
3. Do not throw food.
4. Do not trade food.
5. Eat only the food on your plate.
6. Chew quietly and with your mouth closed.

7. Do not speak with food in your mouth.
8. Keep your elbows off the table.
9. Pass the salt and pepper.
10. Bring your tray and trash to the window when you have finished eating.

If the same phrase, "Remember your table manners," is used by a parent with a child at home, it could additionally mean any of the following:

1. You may begin eating after the blessing.
2. You may have seconds after you have eaten your first serving.
3. You must wait until everyone is seated before you begin to eat.

Furthermore, there are likely to be different behavioral expectations for different meals, different foods, various settings, and across various cultures. Here are some examples: (1) At breakfast, a sweet roll may be consumed early in the meal while the sweet at other mealtimes is usually reserved for the end of the meal, at dessert time. (2) It is acceptable to eat fried chicken, hot dogs, and hamburgers with our fingers, but it is not acceptable to eat mashed potatoes or creamed spinach this way. (3) Parents might allow a brother and a sister to trade or share foods at home, but this is not appropriate for two students in the school cafeteria. (4) There are different rules of etiquette for formal and for informal dining. (5) There are different expectations about table manners across various cultures.

Thus, it is critical that both teachers and parents clearly communicate what constitutes appropriate or inappropriate behavior, and they should not assume that a vague phrase like, "Remember your table manners," will be sufficient. There is one exception to this point: if a child or a student has been repeatedly taught and reinforced for selected table manners, then it is not necessary to articulate each and every expected behavior. But it is necessary to clearly convey the expected behaviors to a child or a student of any age for the first few times that those "new" behaviors are expected.

Clear communication is something all teachers and parents should strive towards, and it takes work and practice. Behavioral expectations should be reasonable, fair, equitably applied, and age-and developmentally appropriate for a particular group of students. What is expected from a third grader will be far different from what can be expected from a high school sophomore. Some behavioral expectations may originate with the teacher, or they may be pre-determined by school, district, or state policies.

Furthermore, teachers' personal value systems, religious beliefs, and unique learning and conditioning histories further impact what they expect from students. What does "respectful" or "polite" mean? In some regions of this country and in some cultures, it means use *ma'am* and sir when addressing elders, while in other areas teachers may care more about the tone than the words that a student uses when addressing them. To many teachers "respectful" or "polite" simply means treating others with the "Golden Rule," while other teachers might interpret the terms rather authoritatively to mean "Do not talk back, and do what I say." "Respectful" or "polite" behavior might also take on a different meaning unique to a private or parochial school setting.

Effective teachers do not, however, confuse the explicit communication of behavioral expectations with lecturing or nagging. Lecturing, like scolding, is typically a lengthy and often negative harangue. Lectures are often unproductive because many children typically react to them with hostility, withdrawal, passive–aggressive behavior, or avoidance behaviors like lying and concealing. Lecturing also typically fails to send a clear message about what specific behaviors need changing. Nagging, that is, repeatedly reminding students about what to do, is also often unproductive because many students simply "tune out" the person who is nagging. Furthermore, both lecturing and nagging tend to alienate students because the tone of voice and the content are often of a condescending or belittling nature.

Effective teachers also assist students in identifying and then choosing appropriate and inappropriate behaviors. This can best be accomplished by getting students to think in terms of pairs of **incompatible behaviors**; namely, "opposite" behaviors which, by their very definition, cannot occur simultaneously. Depending on the situation and the teacher's behavioral expectations for students, one of the behaviors in a pair of incompatible behaviors will be the appropriate behavior, and the other or opposite behavior will be the inappropriate behavior. Here are some examples:

1. Elena is either on task and working on the seat work assignment (appropriate behavior), or she is off task, doodling, and not working on her seat work assignment (inappropriate behavior).
2. Leroy is either in his seat (appropriate behavior), or he is out of his seat (inappropriate behavior).
3. Maria is either looking at the teacher and listening attentively (appropriate behavior), or she is talking to a friend seated nearby (inappropriate behavior).
4. José is either working on the computer tutorial (appropriate behavior), or he is playing a game on the computer (inappropriate behavior).

Effective teachers remember that what is considered an appropriate or inappropriate behavior in one setting may not be appropriate or inappropriate in another setting because behaviors have to be judged in the context in which they occur. In Example 1, if it had been free time instead of seatwork time, doodling, reading for pleasure, or perhaps even working on homework would have been considered appropriate behaviors. In Example 2, out of seat behavior would be appropriate during recess time, but not during the administration of a standardized test. In Example 3, talking with a friend would be appropriate during break time or a peer learning activity, but not when the teacher is talking. In Example 4, playing games on the computer would be appropriate only during free time.

At this point, the reader is reminded that no discussion of behavior would be complete without stressing the basic premise of any discipline program, namely, that many student misbehaviors can be avoided when student's basic needs are being met and when students are treated with respect and responsibility commensurate to their age. (The reader is encouraged to review the theories of Maslow, Rogers, and Glasser, and the tenets of discipline programs by Mendler and Curwin, Coloroso, Albert, Mazlin, and others as presented in Chapters 2 and 3.) Students need to feel and believe that they (a) are capable and successful, (b) are listened to and cared about by others, and (c) belong and contribute in a significant way to the group. They need to feel empowered to be responsible for their behavior and to cooperate. An effective discipline program teaches students responsibility and respect; it does not expect blind obedience to authority.

Once students choose a behavior, effective teachers use appropriate consequences to impact future occurrences of behavior. *Appropriate consequences* refers to the use of natural, related, and logical consequences and/or reinforcement to either maintain or increase the frequency of occurrence of appropriate behavior and punishment or extinction to decrease or eliminate the frequency of occurrence of the inappropriate behavior. An elaboration on consequences appears in the following section.

CONSEQUENCES

Consequences are the conditions that follow the occurrence of a behavior. They have a powerful influence on behavior, and a change in the consequence(s) typically results in a change in that behavior. When a consequence is positive it is called a *reinforcer* or a *reward.* When a consequence is negative it is called a *punisher.* The process of providing positive consequences is called *reinforcement,* and the process of providing negative consequences is called *punishment.*

Consequences have these effects on behavior: they can maintain, increase, weaken, suppress, or eliminate a behavior. The process of reinforcement maintains or increases the frequency of occurrence of a behavior; discontinuing reinforcement (also known as extinction) weakens a behavior, and the process of punishment typically suppresses or occasionally eliminates a behavior.

Reinforcers are positive consequences that follow a behavior, and they serve to maintain or increase the frequency of occurrence of a behavior. Here are three simple examples: (1) If Tamara asks a question in class and the teacher's response is, "That's a good question," then she is likely in the future to ask a question in that teacher's class again. (2) If Ellen studies for an algebra exam and as she gets a good grade, then she is likely to study again the next time there is an algebra exam. (3) If Mario is periodically commended for turning in neat homework assignments, then he is likely to continue that behavior. Note that in these examples, the behaviors that are to be maintained might also increase in their frequency of occurrence, but it is almost always specific to a particular teacher or the academic subject. One can only hope, but one cannot assume, that the behaviors will generalize to other teachers and to other subjects.

Unfortunately, the same conditions that work to increase appropriate behaviors can also work to increase inappropriate behaviors because all consequences can impact both appropriate and inappropriate behaviors. Here are three simple examples. (1) If Linda throws a temper tantrum that receives a lot of attention from her teacher, even though it is negative attention, like scolding, she also receives the admiration of some of her miscreant peers. Thus, she is likely to tantrum again. (2) If Taylor cheats during an exam, he does not get caught, and the cheating results in a better grade than if he did not cheat, Taylor's cheating behavior has been reinforced, and it is thus likely to occur again. (3) If Hope is repeatedly sent to the principal's office because of misbehaving, and if she enjoys getting out of class, walking down the hall, and hanging out in the principal's office, Hope is likely to misbehave again.

In these three examples, the very behaviors that the teacher would like to decrease or eliminate were, in fact, inadvertently reinforced. Thus, those inappropriate behaviors will continue and/or increase in their frequency of occurrence. Effective teachers focus on the impact that their delivery of consequences has on students' behaviors. Put quite simply, if a behavior targeted for decrease or elimination is in fact increasing in its frequency of occurrence, then it is being reinforced, and it has not been punished.

There are also other considerations relative to these examples. In the first example, some readers might find it odd that Linda enjoyed the negative attention from her teacher. This is because any attention—positive or otherwise—is usually more reinforcing than receiving no attention at all. Furthermore, the supportive attention the tantrum received from her peers was probably more powerful than any negative attention or the scolding she received from her teacher. This is precisely why other inappropriate behaviors like cursing or acting out often continue; they shock or amuse the all-important peer group whose recognition is more reinforcing to the student's inappropriate behavior than the minimal discomfort experienced from a teacher's disapproval.

In the second example above, while some readers might consider cheating as always inappropriate, the cheating "pays off." Thus, Taylor's cheating behavior is likely to continue until he is caught cheating, is punished, or the cheating does not pay off.

The third example about Hope demands a bit more analysis. As the example described, there were many "positives" about being sent to the principal's office: getting out of a possibly boring, uninteresting, or frustrating class, walking down the hall, incurring the admiration of some peers, hanging out in the principal's office, killing time, and avoiding time in class. These "positives" may sufficiently reinforce and maintain the targeted behavior even if, once at the principal's office, Hope receives some aversive consequences. However, in many instances, being sent to the principal's office results in little consequence, and therefore it is often an exercise in futility. But if there are negative consequences to being sent to the principal's office, like a mandatory call home to parents or after school detention, then being sent to the principal's office may, in fact, function as a punisher and serve to decrease the frequency of the misbehavior. Being sent to the principal's office is most effective as a punisher with young students and with the usually well-behaved student who is being sent to the principal's office for an inappropriate behavior for the first time.

Effective teachers are very careful to reinforce only appropriate behavior, and they take seriously the importance of not accidentally reinforcing inappropriate behavior. A teacher's intention is irrelevant. The only way to know whether something is reinforcing for a particular student is to observe the impact of the reinforcer(s) on the targeted behavior. If the behavior is being maintained, or if it is increasing in its frequency of occurrence, then it is being reinforced.

Reinforcers can also be intrinsic or extrinsic to a task. Intrinsic reinforcers are those reinforcers inherent to a task or a behavior; namely the task or behavior is, in and of itself, appealing, interesting, or otherwise pleasurable. A good book, an enjoyable, favorite television program, and a preferred hobby are examples of tasks or behaviors that are intrinsically reinforcing. Ideally, academic tasks should be intrinsically reinforcing so that students will work on them and learn from them, but this is not always the case. Poor instructional methods, unmotivated students, boring materials and assignments, and students' perceptions that the material being presented has no utility or relevance are just some of the reasons that some academic tasks do not have sufficient intrinsic reinforcement.

Extrinsic reinforcers are those reinforcers externally supplied in the hopes of increasing the frequency of occurrence of a behavior. Extrinsic reinforcers are often necessary because the task or behavior required is boring, repetitive, unappealing, demanding, or otherwise aversive. An unchallenging task, a task with which a learner finds no relevance, and an overly difficult and frustrating task are examples of tasks which will require some additional external reinforcement if teachers want students to perform them.

Positive consequences function as reinforcers only if the person performing the behavior finds the reinforcer to be appealing, interesting, positive, pleasurable, or otherwise rewarding. Reinforcers occur in a variety of forms (praise, privileges, tangible rewards, freedom from aversive activities, and others). They also occur in a variety of strengths or amounts, and they can be delivered on various schedules. Reinforcement needs to be delivered immediately and consistently, especially if a teacher is trying to teach a new behavior or trying to increase the frequency of occurrence of a weak or infrequently occurring behavior. Once a behavior is part of a student's behavioral repertoire, only periodic reinforcement is needed. More detailed information on reinforcement types, delivery, principles, menus, and schedules is presented in Chapter 5.

Besides reinforcers, consequences can also be used to weaken, decrease, or eliminate the frequency of occurrence of a behavior. When a reinforcer is discontinued for a previously reinforced behavior in an attempt to weaken that behavior, that is the process of *extinction*. If Dana's off-task behaviors have been inadvertently reinforced with teacher or peer attention, when the reinforcer (attention) is removed, her inappropriate behaviors are likely to eventually cease. Effective teachers realize that any attention–positive or negative–may function as a reinforcer, and that a teacher's negative attention may be more than offset by the positive peer attention given to the inappropriately behaving student.

Extinction should be used with only with inappropriate behaviors. Teachers need to exert care not to accidentally extinguish an appropriate behavior. If John is consistently working on a task that has little intrinsic reinforcement and if he receives little extrinsic reinforcement, he will eventually get off task or otherwise misbehave, and then the teacher will probably respond. Thus, the teacher inadvertently extinguished an appropriate behavior. Effective teachers periodically pay attention or deliver some other reinforcer to students who are working on task to keep them on task.

Effective teachers "catch the student being good"; they do not wait for misbehavior. They acknowledge the student who is not squirming or fidgeting or making faces, and thus pre-empt other students from misbehaving simply to get teacher or peer attention.

Finally, consequences can be used to decrease or eliminate the frequency of occurrence of a behavior. *Punishment* refers to the application of an aversive consequence or to the withdrawal of a favored event or reinforcer.

If the consequences decrease the frequency of occurrence of the target behavior, punishment has occurred. There are many types of punishers: loss of privileges, correction, overcorrection, required interactions, restitution, time out, detention, suspension, expulsion, isolation, exclusion, and corporal (i.e. physical) punishment. More details on punishment are discussed in Chapters 7 and 15.

SUMMARY OF KEY CONCEPTS IN CHAPTER 4

1. Antecedents are those events that happen prior to a particular behavior.
2. Antecedents influence but do not cause behavior. Behaviors often have one or more antecedents.
3. There are remote and recent antecedents.
4. The nature, severity, and personal significance of antecedents must be considered in determining an antecedents' influence on behavior.
5. To effectively manage behavior, focus only on those antecedents over which you have control.
6. Antecedents provide good information about behavior but are not to be used as an excuse for inappropriate behavior.
7. Behaviors may have one or more antecedents.
8. Antecedents can have an additive, a moderating, or an otherwise interactive effect.
9. The essence of classroom management is to manage classroom environmental conditions and antecedents to prevent behavior problems.
10. Communication about behaviors must be specific and clearly articulated.
11. It is important to explicitly convey behavioral expectations and not to nag or lecture.
12. Teachers must convey to all students their expectations of appropriate behavior and academic success.
13. A successful discipline program will meet students' basic needs and teach responsibility and respect.
14. Consequences are the conditions that follow a behavior.
15. Reinforcers are positive, appealing consequences that maintain or increase the frequency of occurrence of a behavior.
16. Reinforce only appropriate behavior. Do not reinforce, even inadvertently, inappropriate behavior.
17. The only way to know whether something is reinforcing for a child is to observe the impact of the reinforcers on behavior. If the behav-

ior is being maintained or is increasing in frequency of occurrence, then it is being reinforced.

18. A pair of incompatible behaviors are two behaviors which, by definition, cannot occur simultaneously. Depending on the situation and the teacher's expectations, one behavior is an appropriate behavior and the other, or opposite, behavior is an inappropriate behavior.

19. Extinction involves discontinuing reinforcement for a previously reinforced behavior.

20. Extinction is a procedure that is best used when one wants to eliminate or weaken an inappropriate behavior.

21. Extinction should not be inadvertently used with appropriate behavior.

22. Appropriate consequences means reinforcement for appropriate behavior and withdrawal of reinforcement (extinction) or, if necessary, the use of punishment for inappropriate behavior.

23. Punishment is the delivery of an aversive, unpleasant consequence following an inappropriate behavior.

24. Punishment can suppress or decrease the frequency of occurrence of a targeted behavior if the individual perceives the punisher as aversive.

25. The purpose of punishment is to get an inappropriate behavior to decrease in its frequency of occurrence.

REFERENCES

Harlan, J. C. (1996). *Behavior management strategies for teachers.* Springfield, IL: Charles C Thomas.

SUGGESTED ACTIVITIES/ASSIGNMENTS

1. Role-play a disruptive student with a teacher who uses traditional disciplinary techniques such as minimal reinforcement and scolding inappropriate behaviors. Then role-play the exercise by demonstrating a teacher who uses a behavioral approach; namely, reinforcement for appropriate behavior and extinction or punishment for inappropriate behavior. Compare and contrast the differences in the effectiveness of the two approaches.

2. Invite a teacher to discuss discipline and classroom management problems.

3. Invite a teacher who successfully uses a behavioral approach to address the class.
4. Write about a frequently occurring behavior and identify the reinforcers maintaining that behavior.
5. Write about a behavior that was punished. Identify and describe both the behavior and the punisher.
6. Role play a situation which shows how teachers' pestering, nagging, and lecturing behaviors are often ineffective.
7. Describe the most frequently employed reinforcers used by teachers. Discuss what impact these reinforcers have on behavior.
8. Critique journal articles concerning reinforcement and rewards for students' appropriate behaviors.
9. Critique journal articles concerning the use of punishment for students' inappropriate behaviors.

Chapter 5

REINFORCEMENT: PRINCIPLES, TYPES, MENUS, AND SCHEDULES

There are some basic principles that effective teachers use to successfully manage students' behaviors, and this chapter explains those principles. In later chapters, some of these same principles will be explained relative to using negative consequences, or punishment, to weaken or decrease the frequency of occurrence of inappropriate behaviors. This chapter also explores the different types of reinforcers that should be selected relative to a student's unique conditioning history, the demands of the expected task or behavior, reinforcement menus, and reinforcement schedules (how to time and deliver reinforcement).

PRINCIPLES

There are some essential principles of reinforcement. These principles are interrelated, and they impact each other uniquely with respect to the individual student, the expected task, the type and amount of the reinforcement selected, and the timing and delivery of reinforcement. Thus, though we present the concepts below as separate principles, the reader must remember that they are almost always interrelated.

Principle 1–Appropriate Behaviors Should be Immediately Reinforced

Appropriate behavior should be reinforced immediately because that reinforcement will be more effective in influencing the behavior the closer in time it occurs to the behavior. A special privilege, such as free time, that is delivered immediately following a task will be more influential on the targeted behavior than it will be if it is promised to occur in a week. Teachers must be careful not to promise the delivery of reinforcement too distantly into the future because, as the length of time between the promise and the delivery occurs, the reinforcing effects decrease.

Regardless of when reinforcement is delivered, effective teachers follow through with their promise of reinforcement, and they deliver it as promised. If something makes delivery impossible, then at the next available opportunity reinforcement should be delivered as promised. For example, a teacher promises extra outdoor recess time on Friday, but weather conditions prohibit any outdoor recess on that day. At the next recess period, then, the effective teacher follows through as promised.

Principle 2–Appropriate Behaviors Should be Frequently Reinforced, with Frequency Defined by the Specifics of the Situation

Effective teachers test out the effectiveness of the frequency with which they deliver reinforcement until the definitive effects of reinforcement are evident, that is, until the targeted behavior is being maintained or it is increasing in its frequency of occurrence.

The principles of both immediacy and frequency are especially crucial if the appropriate behaviors are either (a) rarely exhibited by a particular student, such as attempting new material or trying new skills, or (b) demanding, frustrating, or boring. An effective teacher comments on something done correctly when Aaron is first learning penmanship. An effective teacher reinforces students for encouraging each other: "Pronouncing new words can be difficult. Let's help each other by eliminating all giggles when Sherry is attempting to sound out a new word." An effective teacher knows that if Kathy is rarely on task, then more frequent reinforcement will be needed for her than for Ken, a student who typically works on task.

Effective teachers use the principles of frequency and immediacy, along with cues, to help students develop and increase the frequency of their appropriate behaviors and to strengthen students' infrequently occurring behaviors. For example, effective teachers post on the board a list of the materials that students should have with them when they come to class, and they frequently refer to that list. Effective teachers have their classroom rules in writing, and they are posted and clearly visible to all students. Effective teachers give students handouts that clearly define the rubrics of an assignment, and they thoroughly explain the rubrics and provide students with a sample of what constitutes appropriate work.

Effective teachers also try to ensure that the work that they assign to students is developmentally, age, ability, and grade-level appropriate so that they maximize the chances of students' successes and minimize the chances of students' failures and frustration. Effective teachers realize that they must make special preparations for students who are experiencing difficulty with the assigned work. Effective teachers use reading assignments that are at an appropriate difficulty level and are not too frustrating for their students. Effective teachers realize that students who are poor readers need more immediate and more frequent reinforcement to get them to read than do students who read well and enjoy reading.

Effective teachers select, design, and/or modify all of the academic tasks they assign to be sure the tasks have some inherent interest value and are relevant, useful, or otherwise meaningful. When authentic or inherently interesting assignments are used, students will be less likely to complain, "Why do I have to learn this? I'll never use it for anything." When teachers assign tasks that have inherent interest value, they maximize the possibility of students working on task, learning, and behaving appropriately. If there is little or no interest value and/or if the behavior expected is not an authentic task, then reinforcement external to the task will be required. External reinforcement can be of any of the forms described later in this chapter.

The age and maturity level of a student impacts the principles of immediacy and frequency. For example, five-year-old Tom will need reinforcement presented closer in time to the expected behavior than will his older sister Cheryl. This is because, typically, older students can understand and better anticipate the delivery of reinforcement later in time than can younger students. Older students generally are better able to delay immediate gratification, but this does vary widely among students, depending on their maturity level and on the magnitude and type of reinforcement selected.

Here are a few additional examples that demonstrate the interrelationship of all of the factors mentioned above: (1) Praise may motivate a kindergartner and a third grader to work on task, but it may be insufficient for a high school students for whom peers are more reinforcing than the teacher. (2) A mild amount of any type of reinforcement may be sufficient to motivate any age student if the task is inherently reinforcing or interesting, but it may be insufficient with a demanding task, a new task, or a task that the student finds inherently boring. (3) A student with a history of behavioral noncompliance and the often concomitant academic failure will, in all likelihood, require more frequent doses of powerful reinforcement than will a student who typically behaves, does well academically, and is also able to delay gratification. (4) One student may quit working on a task if reinforcement is infrequent, while another student can work on the same task for longer periods of time with less reinforcement. (5) One student may enjoy the challenge and logic of deriving a geometry proof, while another student may find it frustrating or perhaps irrelevant.

Principle 3–There is No One Universal Reinforcer that Appeals Equally to All Students

Different students, like different people, have different reinforcer preferences. There are some reinforcers, like praise, positive recognition, attention, and freedom from aversive tasks that appear to be reinforcing for all students. However, it is best to test the effect of any reinforcer with the individual student by observing whether the appropriate behavior is continuing or increasing in its frequency of occurrence. Similarly, with adults in the workplace, salary increases, empowerment, relaxed dress codes, and offices with windows are considered reinforcers or "perks" for many employees but not for all. One employee may be indifferent to the office as a reinforcer and will only consider improved wages or other more tangible benefits, while another employee might consider a status-conferring office a more powerful reinforcer.

Most young students perceive praise, an award, or some other form of positive recognition from either their peers or their teacher as reinforcing. A younger student might consider a compliment or a commendation from a teacher as reinforcing, but an older student may not. Ironically, many junior high and high school students perceive being labeled the "trouble-maker" or "class clown" as reinforcing, even though it may seem perverse that students would value negative attention. In all likelihood this is because older students want to avoid being viewed as the "teacher's pet" or as a "nerd," and the attention they receive from their peers is more important than the attention they receive from their teacher. Furthermore, negative attention is a form of attention, and attention is an almost universal reinforcer.

Students who are motivated by getting good grades would be reinforced by an extra credit assignment that, if successfully completed, will add points to their scores. In contrast, such an optional assignment would not be considered reinforcement for students who are more indifferent to the grades that they receive.

Principle 4–Provide Students with the Opportunity to Chose from a Wide Variety of Reinforcers

By allowing reinforcement choices, the process of satiation can be averted, and an effective teacher increases the likelihood of reinforcer effectiveness. Satiation occurs when the same reinforcer is so over-used that it loses its effectiveness. Satiation typically occurs with mild or marginally appealing reinforcers and/or if the task's demands exceed the appeal of the reinforcer.

Teachers should allow students to suggest their own reinforcers, but the effective teacher makes the final decision about which reinforcers will be used. On occasion, a teacher may have to exert "veto power" with a reinforcer chosen by students that is inappropriate, harmful, or impractical to deliver. Students could be allowed to choose a reinforcer from a weekly list. Other teachers and students' parents also can provide helpful suggestions about appropriate reinforcers. Effective teachers observe students carefully to determine what they find reinforcing. Effective teachers notice which students like to work or play together as these privilege-type activities often function as effective reinforcers. More information on selecting reinforcers and using reinforcement menus appears later in this chapter.

Principle 5–Reinforcement Should be Delivered Consistently and Frequently with Complex Tasks and with New Tasks

Complex behaviors and/or new tasks need to be initially restructured into smaller components with reinforcement delivered at frequent intervals. This principle is essentially the idea of "shaping"; namely, reinforcing in small steps successively closer and closer approximations of the final target or goal behavior. Shaping is a good management tool and a good instructional tool. It is good management because it provides for the delivery of frequent, periodic reinforcement, especially when progress towards the final outcome is lengthy or slow. It is good instruction because it allows for learning smaller, and thus more manageable, amounts of (typically) new material.

For example, when preschoolers are taught the alphabet, they are not expected to learn all 26 A through Z characters at once. Rather, they learn the first "chunk" of material as "A, B, C, D, E, F, G," and then they are reinforced. Then they learn the next "chunk" of material "H, I, J, K, L, M, N, O, P," and then they are reinforced for adding that to the first set of letters. Finally, they are taught to add the remaining sequence–"Q, R, S, T, U, V, W, X, Y, and Z"–to the first two lists, and then they are reinforced. Similarly, when counting is first taught, the first 100 numbers are taught in this usual sequence: first, mastery of recognizing and understanding the single digit numbers and numerals is reinforced; then understanding about place value is reinforced, then mastery of recognizing and understanding the double digits is reinforced, and so forth.

Good management, consistent and frequent reinforcement, and improved instructional effectiveness are inseparable. Effective teachers know that they must break down multi-step and complex behaviors into small, manageable, and easily reinforcible component parts. For example, complex geometry proofs need to be preceded by more elementary geometric concepts, and students best learn good penmanship one letter at a time.

Consistently and frequently reinforcing appropriate behavior is the best way teachers can prevent classroom behavior and learning problems. Effective teachers do not wait for problems to occur, but rather they prevent their occurrence by using a positive and proactive approach to management. Individual student compliance with the rules as well as a group's compliance can and should be periodically reinforced.

When a teacher reinforces the entire class for desirable behavior, this is known as a "group contingency." Reinforcement is dispensed contingent upon the collective behavior of the entire group. Using a group contingency is an effective management approach because it allows a teacher to influence the entire group's behavior by dispensing a single reinforcer. One difficulty with the use of a group contingency, however, is the selection of a consequence that is reinforcing for everyone in the group. These reinforcers tend to be successful for group use: a pizza party, a field trip, free time, freedom from homework, and extra recess time. An extensive discussion of all the types of reinforcers is in the next section.

Effective teachers use these principles of reinforcement to periodically acknowledge the student who is working on task, and they compliment the student who is behaving appropriately. Effective teachers periodically recognize all students when they are industrious and persistent with difficult assignments. Effective teachers do not ignore students' appropriate behaviors; if they do, they run the risk that the ignored student (i.e., the appropriately behaving student who is unacknowledged) will eventually behave inappropriately because it will yield some attention, even if it is negative attention. This is the traditional discipline paradigm that is to be avoided and replaced with periodic and positive attention for appropriate behavior. Effective teachers use these principles of reinforcement, and they make sure that all students, those who consistently behave appropriately and those who behave inappropriately but are now behaving appropriately, are periodically reinforced.

TYPES OF REINFORCEMENT

There are two types of reinforcement: positive reinforcement and negative reinforcement. *Positive reinforcement* involves the appearance or addition of a new stimulus that maintains or strengthens a behavior. *Negative reinforcement* involves the disappearance or removal of a stimulus.

The reinforcers discussed so far and hereafter are pleasurable, desirable, positive consequences. Teachers should try to make schools and classrooms pleasant and positive environments; therefore, we encourage a greater use of positive reinforcement and a lesser use of negative reinforcement. However, because the concept of negative reinforcement is often misunderstood, we include brief information on it for clarification.

Negative Reinforcement

Negative reinforcement is a type of reinforcement. Negative reinforcement is not punishment. Negative reinforcers are unpleasant, aversive consequences that maintain and/or increase the frequency of occurrence of a behavior. Negative reinforcers have reinforcing value because they cause an unpleasant or aversive situation to cease to exist. With negative reinforcement, a person controls the removal of an aversive condition by performing a certain behavior, and it is this removal which is reinforcing.

Here are some examples of behaviors that are negatively reinforced. The ring of an alarm clock is unpleasant or annoying. The behavior, shutting off the alarm to stop the noise, is negatively reinforced. An irritating buzz or beep sound occurs when a key is left in an automobile ignition when the transmission is put into park. The behavior, removing the key from the ignition to stop the sound, is negatively reinforced. In these examples, the noise or sounds also function as cues or prompts for the expected behaviors of getting up and shutting off the alarm and removing the ignition key, respectively.

Here are two more examples. A baby cries, and crying is aversive to the parent or the caretaker. The behavior, picking up the crying baby, often stops the crying so it is negatively reinforced. Consider the student who feigns a toothache to get out of class right before an exam. Because the behavior allows the student to escape the aversive situation of the test, that behavior is negatively reinforced. Though negative reinforcement is reinforcement, we strongly encourage teachers to use only positive reinforcement.

Positive Reinforcement

Positive reinforcement can take many forms. It is important for teachers to be knowledgeable about the different types of reinforcers (sometimes called rewards) that are available so they can successfully impact behavior.

At this point, the reader is reminded of reinforcement Principle 3, presented previously: there is no one universal reinforcer that appeals equally to all students. Just as there are differences among students, there are differences in students' preferred reinforcers. Praise, positive recognition, attention, and freedom from aversive tasks appear to be reinforcing for most students, but effective teachers test the effect of any reinforcer with the individual student by observing whether the appropriate behavior is continuing or increasing in its frequency of occurrence. The effective teacher never assumes that one reinforcer will be effective for everyone.

One group of reinforcers includes acknowledgments that recognize and certify students' accomplishments or successes, praise, and positive attention. These reinforcers are powerful and effective for most students, and they are simple to use.

Acknowledgments that Recognize and Certify Students' Accomplishments or Successes. Examples of acknowledgments that certify students' accomplishments or successes are awards, citations, ribbons, badges, posters, personalized certificates, trophies, plaques, letters of commendation, a special designation such as "student of the week," a special appointment such as class representative, positive publicity about student behavior, and positive communications to parents about a student's behavior.

The tangible forms listed above, such as awards, letters, posters, and certificates, can be teacher-made or purchased. Teacher-made items are less costly, but they require teacher time and effort. Teacher-made items may also appear to be more personal and less commercial. Younger students tend to be more easily satisfied with teacher-made items than are older students. With all students, though, effective teachers accompany the delivery of a tangible reinforcer with an appropriate positive comment, praise, and perhaps some other form of positive attention.

Praise and positive attention. Praise is easy to deliver, it does not cost anything, and it is relatively non-controversial. When praise is delivered according to the guidelines presented below, few parents should object. If you are uncomfortable or if praising seems somewhat unnatural to you, practice praising until it becomes natural and sincere. Practice will help you to eliminate any feelings of artificiality or self- consciousness. Similarly, if a student appears to be self-conscious or is embarrassed by the praise, then effective teachers recognize that they need to express their approval privately with such a students and not publicly in front of the class. Effective teachers also realize that videotaping their interactions with students helps them critique and thus improve how they and their students communicate and interrelate.

Adults who did not receive much praise when they were children may be hesitant to use praise. Adults who received more negative feedback than positive feedback when they were children may be more likely to criticize than to commend. Furthermore, positive feedback is usually less specific ("Good girl!") than is negative feedback ("Stop pulling Jessica's hair!"). Thus, people typically receive specific criticism about their weaknesses, and they receive only general information about their strengths. If any of these apply to you and your personality, then you need to practice thinking and being positive. Be sure that any praise you use sounds and is natural and sincere. Some teachers find it necessary and effective to put up a sign or some other reminder to be positive and to praise.

For praise and positive attention to be effective, teachers must remember to praise according to the following guidelines. Effective teachers

- Use behaviorally descriptive praise and target it to a specific behavior. "That's good Nick" is vague because many behaviors occur simultaneously. "Nick, I am pleased you are working on the spelling assignment" is much more targeted and clear.
- Use a variety of words and phrases when praising. Avoid the repetitive use of trite words or phrases. *Good* and *great*, for example, are so overused that their use is often only mildly effective or may, in fact, be ineffective.
- Are genuinely enthusiastic about a student's achievement or behavior.
- Deliver the praise energetically, with a smile and make eye contact with the student.
- Personalize the praise they deliver with the student's name.
- Praise sincerely and genuinely.
- Deliver praise in a manner that reflects warmth and appreciation about the student's behavioral improvement or academic achievement.
- Are in close proximity to the student when they praise.
- Make a concerted effort to praise every student as often as possible.

The actual construction of praise and its delivery will vary with the individual teacher. Even small increments of growth, improvement, or achievement are to be encouraged, nurtured, and otherwise reinforced. Effective teachers know that if they are positive with students, their classroom becomes a pleasant environment for learning and for students' appropriate behaviors.

There are these two final and important comments about praise. Because many behaviors occur simultaneously, teachers have to be careful to avoid "mixed messages." A *mixed message* refers to a statement or two which have a positive component and a negative component. With mixed messages, the negative component often cancels out the reinforcing value of the positive component. Effective teachers also avoid making any comments that are sarcastic or demeaning to students. Effective teachers make a positive, specific comment according to the guidelines suggested, and then they stop talking. Should constructive criticism or a reprimand be necessary, effective teachers do so by utilizing the "sandwich technique" as described in Chapter 10.

Tangible or material reinforcers. Tangible or material items are another group of popular reinforcers. They can take many forms: toys, prizes, supplies, trinkets, books, t-shirts, posters, and other gifts. Tangible reinforcers can be inexpensive or costly, cost is one of their drawbacks, and they should be used sparingly.

Tangible reinforcers are also controversial. There are some parents who mistakenly perceive the contingent dispensing of tangible reinforcers as bribery. The use of tangible reinforcers is not bribery, because bribery is an inducement to do something that is typically illegal or improper. It is not bribery when a teacher attempts to help students learn or behave appropriately.

Then, too, there are some parents who erroneously perceive the use of tangible reinforcers as "paying students to do what they should do anyway." This argument incorrectly equates tangible reinforcers with payment. This perception ignores the fact that different students have different abilities and motivational levels, and that all students are often faced with assignments that lack intrinsic appeal, thus necessitating the use of rewards external to the task, and often these are tangible or material reinforcers.

Furthermore, the leaders and managers of successful businesses and industries use tangible and material reinforcers to encourage their employees' performance and productivity. Many businesses have established partnerships with schools to materially reward students for academic success because their executives recognize the efficacy of using tangible rewards to motivate and encourage students' appropriate behaviors. There are local businesses and national franchises that give students tangible rewards if they amass good grades or refrain from inappropriate behaviors. The tangible rewards take a variety of forms but are typically items such as coupons for free meals, pizza parties, arcade games, movie passes, or other material types of reinforcement.

Gold stars, points, check marks, and tokens are also earned rewards which are reinforcing because they can be exchanged for something of value. In a token economy (discussed in detail elsewhere), students can earn points, stars, or tokens for appropriate behavior. At a later and more convenient time, students exchange them for something more reinforcing.

Privileges. Privileges and the right to participate in a variety of preferred activities are another group of popular reinforcers. They are powerful reinforcers because most students find the opportunity to engage in a preferred activity or to enjoy a privilege as reinforcing. There are an unlimited number of preferred activities and privileges. As with identifying other kinds of reinforcers, effective teachers observe students, and they ask students about which activities and privileges they consider reinforcing.

Reinforcing activities and privileges can be of an academic, personal, or social nature. Reinforcing academic learning activities and privileges can take many forms. Students could be allowed to have extra time in the computer lab, learning center, or library. Students could be provided with unique or extra opportunities to participate in special activities or assignments. Because such activities and privileges are academic in nature, they are not controversial with parents, but they may be insufficiently rewarding for more difficult students or with very demanding, frustrating, or boring assignments.

Reinforcing personal and social activities are privileges that are typically non-academic in nature, and they too can take many forms. Free time to engage in behaviors that are typically not allowed or only infrequently allowed in the classroom is a powerful privilege for students of all ages. Students can use their free time to do homework in class, listen to music so long as it does not interfere with others, complete puzzles, talk quietly with their friends, write letters, or participate in special school events or functions.

An elementary school student could be given a preferred seat placement, a preferred locker space or locker partner, or be allowed to lead the class to the lunchroom. A junior high school student could be allowed to make a five-minute, non-emergency, local, social telephone call or be allowed the opportunity to engage in a preferred creative or athletic activity. A high school student could be allowed to go off-campus for lunch or be allowed to reserve a special library carrel.

Other personal and social activities involve allowing students to earn classroom or school appointments that convey status, responsibility, or importance. Students could be appointed as special tutors, helpers, monitors, or messengers. Students could be allowed to perform special jobs like feeding the classroom pet, collecting papers, watering the plants, sharpening the pencils, cleaning or reorganizing areas in the classroom, emptying the waste baskets, leading the flag salute, or reading to the class.

Effective teachers do the following when dispensing personal and social activities and privileges. Effective teachers deliver these reinforcers like they do all other types of reinforcers, contingent upon students' appropriate behaviors. Effective teachers do not label students as "special" or "privileged." They dispense activities or privileges that are perceived by their students as reinforcing, and they define the parameters of what constitutes an appropriate activity or privilege. If a student wants to engage in a dangerous or otherwise unsuitable behavior, the effective teacher exerts "veto power" and explains why. Effective teachers also explain when the privileges may be enjoyed, and they insure that their delivery does not interfere with what other students are doing.

Furthermore, effective teachers know that younger students might consider selected classroom tasks such as clean-up or emptying the waste basket appealing, while older students might consider such tasks menial in nature or otherwise be offended or, insulted and therefore not be reinforced by them. But a really effective teacher would present the same reinforcer in this context: "Who can I trust to empty the waste basket? Who can be responsible enough to take the basket all the way across campus to the dumpster and return to class in five minutes?" This same reinforcer takes on a new appeal to a student who now views it as an opportunity to get a brief break from class.

Effective teachers also allow students to select as privileges or reinforcers those very behaviors which were considered inappropriate in other settings. For example, two students who are friends tend to talk to each other frequently. Talking is not an inherently inappropriate behavior, but talking during an exam is an inappropriate behavior. Thus, the students may be allowed to talk with each other as a reinforcer, but only at acceptable times like during a cooperative learning assignment or during free time. Doing homework is another example of a behavior that is certainly not inherently inappropriate. However, doing homework during class time when students are expected to complete assigned seat work makes it an inappropriate behavior. Teachers must remember that the appropriateness of a behavior has to be judged in relation to the context in which the behavior occurs.

Generalized Rewards. Another group of reinforcers are earned reinforcers which have little or no value in and of themselves; they are reinforcing because they can be exchanged for something of value. These reinforcers are called *generalized rewards.* Generalized rewards are typically items like gold stars, points, check marks, and tokens.

Generalized rewards are effective for a number of reasons. They are rarely subject to satiation, the outcome that occurs when a weak or mild reinforcers loses its effectiveness because of its repeated use. Generalized rewards are easy to deliver; they are of little or no cost; they provide a small amount of immediate reinforcement; and they allow the delivery of more powerful reinforcement at a later, more convenient time.

In the classroom, generalized rewards like stars, points, check marks, or tokens are typically used in a token economy. A token economy is essentially an exchange system. The stars, points, check marks, or tokens are given to students immediately following the occurrence of appropriate behavior. Students accumulate these generalized rewards, and they exchange them for various forms of reinforcement. Well-structured token systems have built-in penalties for students' repeated noncompliance. There are additional details about structuring a token economy in another chapter.

Edible reinforcers. Another group of reinforcers are edible rewards. There are a limitless number and variety of edible reinforcers, and they are very powerful. However, edible reinforcers are controversial for a variety of reasons. Edibles can be costly, and a school district may not allow teachers to use their instructional supply money for them. The use of edibles also affirms the appropriateness of between-meal snacking, which may conflict with some parents' values and philosophies. (Some parents perceive between-meal snacking as having a negative influence on students' eating behaviors during mealtime.) Eating between meals may also encourage dental cavities, especially if sweet edibles are used and/or if students cannot brush their teeth after eating them.

Edible reinforcers also cause handling, sanitation, and storage problems that are not associated with other kinds of reinforcers. Furthermore, if the edible reinforcer is provided while a student is on task, it can function as a competing event because the student may become more interested in the edible than in continuing the task.

There is also some controversy about the appropriateness of teachers providing edibles for reinforcement, and for their withholding of them as punishment. Some people consider this inappropriate because it focuses on food. For example, some people believe that many adults have weight and dietary problems because their parents dispensed or withheld food.

One of the most critical objections to the use of edibles has to do with the type of food or snack used. The most popular edibles are candies, other sweets, soft drinks, sugared cereals, pretzels, and chips—most of which are high in fat, salt, sugar, and calories. The use of these kinds of edibles is contraindicated with students who are obese, diabetic, or those who have high cholesterol or blood pressure. Some parents may also object to the use of edibles in a party situation if their religious values prohibit such an activity.

Some teachers and parents also object to the use of the most popular edibles because they believe that it teaches poor nutritional habits. These problems can be overcome by the use of less objectionable and healthier items, such as dried or fresh fruit, popcorn, or vegetable sticks. While both teachers and parents might more readily approve of these healthier edibles, fruits and vegetables are costly; they pose additional handling, storage, and shelf-life problems; and, most importantly, they are typically less reinforcing than are the candies, sweets, and chips.

Students with special dietary needs also have to be considered when selecting edible reinforcers. There are students with allergies or intolerances to common foods like wheat, milk, soy, peanuts and other nuts, various nut oils, and sunflower seeds. Many edibles also typically have some of these items in them, frequently as "hidden" or not immediately recognizable ingredients. Then, too, there are students with diabetes and other health problems who should not receive many of the more popular edibles. Teachers also need to exercise care in the delivery of edibles which contain ingredients that the students seated nearby have allergies or intolerances to, and they must do so without making the allergic student ostracized. So when edible reinforcers are used in the classroom, teachers must select edibles to meet the needs of all students; they must supervise their appropriate delivery; and they must exercise care that no student is excluded or made to feel rejected because of their allergies, food intolerances, health problems, or special dietary needs.

We therefore recommend that teachers use edible reinforcers on an infrequent basis. Teachers should follow these suggestions and any additional school or district-wide policies concerning the dispensing of edible reinforcers. At the beginning of the school year, teachers should get a signed permission slip from parents about what edibles can and cannot be used with their children. Teachers should keep a copy of the permission slip and file a second copy in the principal's office. The parents' preferences and suggestions should be strictly followed. Teachers should not dispense any edibles until they receive permission from their students' parents. If a written permission slip is not received, the parents should be called, and the teacher should take notes on the conversation.

Effective teachers observe students to get ideas about their edible reinforcer preferences, and they ask students about their reinforcement preferences. Teachers should become knowledgeable about students' food needs and preferences and about the ingredients within the edibles selected. Teachers need to be sure that all the edibles dispensed are fresh, clean, untainted, and properly stored, handled, and dispensed. Teachers will also need to institute clean-up procedures following the use and delivery of edible reinforcers.

Freedom from aversive or unpleasant activities. The last category of reinforcers includes "freedom from aversive or unpleasant activities." For example, for most students, freedom from homework is very reinforcing. Many students also consider being exempted from close teacher supervision or from certain assignments as reinforcing. Some other students may perceive relocating their seat assignment away from an unpleasant location such as a window or a door. As with the other kinds of reinforcers, reinforcers in this category must be carefully selected so that the chosen amount and type are reinforcing to the individual student and to the demands of a task. Additional content on the process of aversive conditioning (something far different from these "freedom from aversive or unpleasant activities" which function as reinforcers) appears in another chapter. The material discussed in the following two sections on reinforcement menus and reinforcement schedules should assist teachers in effectively selecting and dispensing reinforcers.

REINFORCEMENT MENUS

A restaurant menu provides the food and beverage options that are available. A computer program menu indicates a number of options that the user may access. Similarly, a reinforcement menu provides a list of reinforcer options from which a student may select. The reinforcer selected is then delivered contingent upon a student's satisfactory performance of an appropriate behavior.

A reinforcement menu has many advantages. The advantages relate to student's reinforcement preferences, satiation, the demands of the task, and other situation-specific issues and practical matters that impact the selection of an appropriate reinforcer. Because a reinforcement menu provides students with a choice of reinforcers, its use helps teachers to accommodate different students' reinforcer preferences. Effective teachers remember that there is no universal reinforcer; what is reinforcing to one student may not be reinforcing for another student. For reinforcement to successfully motivate academic behaviors and behavioral improvement, it must be both meaningful and relevant to the student whose behavior a teacher is trying to impact. A reinforcement menu should contain three or more options. It should be posted on the bulletin board or printed and distributed to students.

The use of a reinforcement menu also allows teachers to prevent the occurrence of satiation. As mentioned previously, satiation occurs when the same reinforcer is so overused that it loses its effectiveness. Satiation typically occurs with the mild or marginally appealing reinforcers and/or if the task's demands exceed the appeal of the reinforcer. Therefore, teachers should periodically change the reinforcement options in the menu, especially if student compliance is decreasing, if the reinforcer is for a particularly demanding task, or if the reinforcer is being used to encourage a new, weak, or infrequently occurring behavior. Periodically revising the reinforcer options in the reinforcement menu also accommodates those reinforcers that are only available at selected times (pep rallies, class parties, and guest speakers) or for unpredictable occurrences like the field trip that is canceled because of bad weather.

The options provided in a reinforcement menu should be of approximately equal appeal and value, and all reinforcers should be available and delivered as promised. The options must be clearly and specifically described to prevent any misunderstandings that could undermine the efficacy of the system. Effective teachers make sure that their students understand the amount and type of reinforcement that they can earn and when reinforcement will be delivered if they behave appropriately. Effective teachers also make it clear to students what words like "completed" or "satisfactory" mean. For example, specification that "The assigned seatwork has to be completed with at least 80% accuracy" preempts the possibility that students will rush through an assignment without sufficient regard to accuracy and solely to receive the reinforcement.

When using a reinforcement menu, provisions also have to be made for unforeseen events. For example, a student works on task according to teacher directions and earns 10 minutes of extra time in the computer lab on Friday. But a special event is planned for Friday in the computer lab, which means that the reinforcer cannot be delivered as promised. The effective teacher explains this to the student and then follows through and remembers to deliver the reinforcer at the very next opportunity.

The reinforcer options in the reinforcement menu should be selected by the teacher and the students together. Parents could also be consulted. Effective teachers observe the students to see what they enjoy, and they ask students about their reinforcer preferences. And, as mentioned previously, some student behaviors are considered misbehaviors only because of the context in which they occur. Allowing students to talk with friends, write letters, or work on homework are reinforcing activities that can be included as options in a reinforcement menu, so long as those activities occur at an approved time.

It is also likely that there will be some discrepancies between students' reinforcer preferences and teachers' reinforcer preferences. A student might cherish free time to work on a nonacademic task, while a teacher might prefer to offer extra time to work on an academic task. To ensure that the selected reinforcer options are reinforcing to an individual student—in light of the student's preferences, the nature and difficulty of the specific task, and the specifics that make every classroom unique—teachers could use a **reinforcement preference inventory**.

A reinforcement preference inventory allows students to express their reinforcement preferences. Such inventories can use either an open-ended or a closed format. In an open-ended format, students complete statements such as: "If I had free time in class, I would like to . . ." or "The jobs I like to help the teacher with most are. . . ." In a closed format, students respond to statements that resemble items on a multiple choice test like this one: "The job I like to help the teacher with most is (a) being an office monitor; (b) collecting the paper; or (c) putting the daily assignment on the board.

Effective teachers poll students periodically throughout the school year to ensure that the reinforcement options they once preferred are still appealing. If students' preferences have changed, the options offered need to be changed accordingly.

REINFORCEMENT SCHEDULES

Reinforcement schedules specify the timing and frequency of reinforcement. For practical classroom use (as opposed to more formal use in a research setting), we recommend that teachers use these schedules informally and without data collection. For classroom use, the schedules do not need to be in writing, and teachers do not need to chart, count, or graph behaviors or use precisely timed schedules. Rather, when teachers dispense reinforcement, they need to be aware of the following information concerning the timing and frequency of the delivery of reinforcement. Also, effective teachers always assess the impact of their intentions to reinforce a behavior, namely, a behavior is reinforced only if it is being maintained or it is increasing in its frequency of occurrence.

Continuous schedule of reinforcement. If a behavior is on a continuous schedule of reinforcement, reinforcement is delivered each and every time the targeted behavior occurs. A continuous schedule is essentially a fixed ratio (FR) schedule, wherein reinforcement is delivered following each and every occurrence of a certain behavior. In the professional literature, a continuous schedule of reinforcement is described as a *fixed ratio one* (FR1) schedule.

A continuous schedule of reinforcement is required when trying to get a new or an infrequently occurring behavior underway. A continuous schedule of reinforcement provides a maximum amount of reinforcement for a behavior. Effective teachers use this schedule with new behaviors, which are typically weak and therefore occur infrequently, because it provides a generous amount of reinforcement. A student who has repeatedly been off task will need a continuous schedule of reinforcement, such as reinforcement delivered for every 10 minutes of uninterrupted work on task. A student who has a history of not finishing the arithmetic seatwork will also require a continuous schedule of reinforcement.

Once an appropriate behavior is established through the use of a continuous schedule, the behavior will require some periodic reinforcement if it is to continue. To put it another way, after a new behavior is established, teachers should provide reinforcement on an unpredictable schedule to encourage persistence. Effective teachers make a gradual transition from dispensing reinforcement on a continuous schedule to dispensing reinforcement based on one of the partial schedules of reinforcement described below. This transition is sometimes referred to as *leaning out* or *thinning out* the schedule.

Effective teachers also make sure that appropriately behaving students receive some reinforcement occasionally. Effective teachers do not take students' appropriate behaviors for granted. If periodic reinforcement is not provided for a behavior that has been continuously reinforced, it is very likely that the appropriate behavior will diminish in its frequency of occurrence, or it may cease altogether.

Partial schedules of reinforcement. Schedules of reinforcement which are not continuous schedules are partial schedules of reinforcement. With a partial schedule of reinforcement, reinforcement is provided following only some occurrences of the appropriate behavior. A student who is usually off-task only occasionally would be a good candidate for a partial schedule of reinforcement. Such occasionally delivered reinforcement serves to maintain or increase the frequency of occurrence of the appropriate behavior. When reinforcement is delivered on a partial schedule, the unpredictability of when reinforcement will next occur serves to encourage student persistence and maintains or increases the frequency of occurrence of the appropriate behavior.

The delivery of reinforcement on a partial schedule can be based primarily on either students' behaviors (their performance of an appropriate behavior or their refraining from performing an inappropriate misbehavior) or on the passage of time. Partial schedules that use behavior as the primary determinant for the delivery of reinforcement are called ratio schedules. Partial schedules that use time as the primary determinant for the delivery of reinforcement are called interval schedules.

In practice, ratio and interval schedules overlap. Ratio and interval schedules are not mutually exclusive because in both schedules reinforcement is typically delivered based on a behavior that is expected to occur within some time frame. Effective teachers need to generally understand the impact and effects of different schedules on students' behaviors, and then they need to time and deliver reinforcement as it is most appropriate to the specifics of their classroom.

Ratio schedules. There are two types of ratio schedules: the fixed ratio schedules and the variable ratio schedule. With ratio schedules, reinforcement is delivered primarily on students' performance of appropriate behaviors or their refraining from performing inappropriate behaviors.

With the *fixed ratio* (FR) schedule of reinforcement, a reinforcer is delivered after the specific fixed number of behaviors have occurred–for example, after every five correct geometric proofs or after every three short stories read and summarized. This same specific, fixed component of the fixed ratio schedule makes anticipation of the next reinforcer predictable. Students might stall before starting the next set of five correct geometric proofs, because they know that reinforcement will not occur until after the completion of another five correct proofs. Students might be slow to start reading and summarizing the next set of three short stories, because they know that reinforcement will not occur until after the completion of reading and summarizing three more short stories.

Thus, when a fixed ratio schedule is used, teachers can expect some students to display a decrease in the frequency of occurrence of the appropriate behavior for a time immediately following receipt of a reinforcer. This decrease in response rate is known as a *post-reinforcement pause*: students pause or wait before starting the next round of behaviors after completion of which they will earn reinforcement. The post-reinforcement pause is most likely to occur either when a large number of behaviors are required for receipt of a reinforcer, or if a weak or only marginally powerful reinforcer is used.

The second type of ratio schedule is called a *variable ratio* (VR) schedule. In a variable ratio schedule, reinforcement is delivered after a varying, often unspecified, but rather average number of appropriate behaviors have occurred. The actual number of behaviors required for receipt of reinforcement varies, and reinforcement is typically delivered for an average number of behaviors. A variable ratio schedule is unpredictable since the student does not know when the next reinforcement will be delivered. This unpredictability typically results in a persistent and often high behavior response rate with little, if any, decrease in behavior after delivery of reinforcement.

Look at this example about using a variable ratio schedule, but remember that in practice teachers typically do not need to be encumbered by formally timing or counting of behaviors (unless they find it to be helpful). If a teacher wants a student to complete a spelling assignment of 20 words, the teacher could deliver reinforcement after the student correctly spells 3 words, then again after the students correctly spells 8 more words, then again after the student correctly spells 4 more words, and finally, after the student correctly spells the remaining 5 words. In this variable ratio schedule, reinforcement was delivered four times for 20 words $(3 + 8 + 4 + 5 = 20$ words) for an average reinforcement rate of 5 (20 words $\div$ 4 deliveries of reinforcement). When using a variable ratio schedule, effective teachers deliver reinforcement only after a varying number of performances of appropriate behavior, and the first reinforcement is attainable for a small number of appropriate behaviors. In this example, the student first had to spell three words correctly. The reinforcement was delivered thereafter on an unpredictable and therefore highly motivating schedule.

Effective teachers are also careful not to deliver reinforcement for either an increasing or a decreasing number of performances of appropriate behaviors. If reinforcement delivery is contingent on an increasing number of performances of appropriate behavior, students may "catch on" and cease to respond, because they understand that subsequent reinforcers will require increasing amounts of appropriate behavior. Conversely, reinforcement delivery should not be on a decreasing number of performances of an appropriate behavior because the initial demand of performing many behaviors before reinforcement is received often results in too "lean" a schedule, that is, an insufficiently reinforcing schedule.

Variable ratio schedules of reinforcement typically are very powerful, resulting in behaviors that become imbedded if not habitual. Adult gambling and playing other games of chance are examples of behaviors that are reinforced on a variable ratio schedule of reinforcement, and those behaviors are maintained or strengthened by the occasional and unpredictable delivery of reinforcement. Receipt of reinforcement is unpredictable, so playing the slot machines continues or possibly increases in its frequency of occurrence. A gambler hopes that it will be the next game of chance—the next hand, or the next lottery ticket—that will be the winner or "the one that hits the jackpot." Hence, gambling behaviors continue and/or increase. In a classroom, when a teacher "spot checks" homework assignments, students are more likely to complete their homework assignments with regularity, because they never know which day's work will be checked.

Interval Schedules

The other two types of partial schedules of reinforcement are based primarily on the passage of time. Schedules where time is the primary determinant for the delivery of reinforcement are called *interval schedules.* There are two types of interval schedules: *fixed interval* (FI) schedules and *variable interval* (VI) schedules. It is important to remember that interval and ratio schedules are not mutually exclusive. There is almost always a behavioral component expected when reinforcement is delivered using interval schedules, and there is almost always a time component involved when reinforcement is delivered using ratio schedules.

With the *fixed interval schedule,* a reinforcer is provided following the first appropriate behavior that occurs after a specific and fixed amount of time has elapsed since the last appropriate behavior. Because it is a fixed schedule, it is predictable. Because the receipt of reinforcement is predictable, behaviors on a fixed schedule will rapidly decrease in their frequency of occurrence if the time for reinforcement passes and no reinforcement is received.

For example, if all class exams are scheduled weekly and their occurrence is predictable, many students are likely to cram or to only study right before the exam. By contrast, if some exams are "pop quizzes" that can occur at any time, many students will study at a more consistent and frequent rate. Thus, students' cramming behaviors for weekly exams occur with a fixed interval schedule, while students' ongoing and consistent studying behaviors occur with a variable interval schedule. Furthermore, while studying and test-taking are not reinforcing behaviors per se, they are reinforced–and they therefore continue–if the studying results in increased test scores.

We digress a moment to discuss the use of scheduled exams and "pop quizzes." Scheduled exams create less stress and tension for students than do "pop quizzes." Scheduled exams are typically lengthier than are "pop quizzes." The advantages and disadvantages of both types are specific to each unique classroom, the subject matter, and the individual students in a class. Generally speaking, teachers at all grade levels should use a combination of scheduled exams and "pop quizzes." Teachers should use scheduled, predictable exams with younger students and in classes in which the material is complex or extensive. Teachers should use "pop quizzes" with older students, and to assess students' knowledge of small amounts of material.

The other form of an interval schedule is the *variable interval schedule.* Like the variable ratio schedule, this is a powerful schedule. The variability of this schedule leads to a higher response rate, that is, the appropriate behaviors being reinforced are likely to continue or to increase in their frequency of occurrence. Behaviors that are on a variable interval schedule typically occur steadily, and there is often very little pause after receipt of reinforcement. With a variable interval schedule, reinforcement is provided at varying amounts of time since the last appropriate behavior occurred and was reinforced.

Teachers should use these principles about scheduling the delivery of reinforcement informally and without encumbering data-collection paperwork. Of course, if such record keeping assists their management efforts, then they can do so. But in most cases, teachers can accomplish their management goals by merely observing the impact of the reinforcer they dispense on a behavior's frequency of occurrence. Teachers simply must remember that if a behavior is being maintained or increasing in frequency it is being reinforced, and if a behavior is decreasing in frequency it is not being sufficiently reinforced.

One final comment about reinforcement schedules. We include the following material to facilitate readers' understanding of journal articles in the professional literature that pertain to the use and timing of reinforcement. In research articles about the efficacy of different schedules of reinforcement in research, clinical, experimental, and a variety of institutional settings, researchers typically collect, record, and graph their data.

In these articles, the researchers often use graphs to display the frequency of occurrence of behaviors across four distinct phases. In Phases 1 and 3, reinforcement is dispensed using the same schedules and contingencies. Phase 1 is the baseline period, when researchers determine how often the appropriate and inappropriate behaviors occur. Then, in Phase 2, the researchers typically institute a treatment program which, if successful, results in an increase in the frequency of occurrence of the appropriate behavior and a decrease in the frequency of occurrence of the inappropriate behavior. It is at this point that we encourage teachers to continue the timing and delivery of reinforcement and to go no further. In research settings, however, researchers typically use two additional phases to assure that the efficacy of the treatment was not random or otherwise attributable to chance. In Phase 3, the consequences as they existed during the baseline period are reinstated, and the appropriate behavior typically decreases while the inappropriate behavior typically increases. The final phase, Phase 4 is a return to the delivery of reinforcement as it occurred in Phase 2, and if the appropriate behavior increases while the inappropriate behavior decreases, the researchers can be confident in their findings. We again stress that teachers can use minimal data collection and simply observe the effects of their timing and delivery of reinforcement. We also encourage teachers to read the professional literature to learn more about the selection, use, delivery, and timing of reinforcement.

SUMMARY OF KEY CONCEPTS IN CHAPTER 5

1. Appropriate behaviors should be immediately reinforced.
2. When a reinforcer is promised, it must be delivered.
3. Appropriate behaviors should be frequently reinforced, with frequency defined by the specifics of the situation.
4. The only definitive way of knowing if a behavior is reinforced is if it is being maintained or if it increases in its frequency of occurrence.
5. The principles of both immediacy and frequency are especially crucial if the appropriate behaviors are rarely occurring and/or if the tasks are perceived as too demanding, frustrating, or boring.
6. Assignments need to be developmentally, age, ability, and grade-level appropriate.
7. All learning tasks should be selected either because they have some inherent interest value or because they can be shown to be relevant, useful, or otherwise meaningful.

8. There is no universal reinforcer; however praise, positive recognition, attention, and freedom from aversive tasks appear to be reinforcing for virtually all students.

9. A reinforcement menu provides students with the opportunity to choose from a wide variety of reinforcers.

10. The use of a reinforcement menu minimizes the occurrence of satiation. Satiation occurs when the same reinforcer is overused and thus loses its effectiveness. Satiation typically occurs with mild or marginally appealing reinforcers and/or if the task's demands exceed the appeal of the reinforcer.

11. Reinforcement should be delivered consistently and frequently with complex tasks and with new tasks or behaviors. Teachers should use reinforcement continuously and immediately with new and infrequently occurring behaviors.

12. Shaping involves reinforcing in small steps successively closer and closer approximations of the final target or goal behavior.

13. The shaping technique is a good management tool and a good instructional tool.

14. The shaping technique is almost always required when teaching new material.

15. Multi-step and complex behaviors need to be broken down into smaller, more manageable and reinforceable component parts.

16. Consistently and frequently reinforcing appropriate behavior is the best way to prevent classroom behavior and learning problems.

17. Teachers should not wait for behavior problems to occur. Teachers can prevent behavior problems by using a positive and proactive approach to management.

18. Teachers should periodically reinforce all students for appropriate behavior.

19. Teachers should avoid using the traditional approach to discipline which ignores students' appropriate behaviors and focuses on their inappropriate behaviors. Instead, teachers should periodically reward appropriate behavior and ignore students' mistakes and their other non-disruptive and non-injurious inappropriate behaviors.

20. When a teacher uses a group contingency, reinforcement is dispensed contingent upon the collective behavior of a group of students.

21. Positive reinforcement involves the appearance or addition of a new stimulus that maintains or strengthens a behavior.

22. Negative reinforcement involves the disappearance or removal of a stimulus that maintains or strengthens a behavior.

23. Negative reinforcement is a form of reinforcement. Negative rein-

forcement is not punishment. Negative reinforcers have the same effect on behavior as do positive reinforcers.

24. Teachers are encouraged to use only positive, rather than negative, reinforcement in the classroom.

25. Reinforcers are also sometimes called *rewards*.

26. Praise, positive attention, and a limitless number of other forms of acknowledgments that recognize and certify accomplishments are powerful reinforcers for most students.

27. Praise should be sincere, targeted to the specific behavior being commended, and energetically delivered.

28. Teachers should avoid the use of mixed messages when praising because the negative component of the mixed message may cancel out the reinforcing value of the praise or other positive component in the mixed message.

29. The routine dispensing of tangible and edible reinforcers is to be avoided in the classroom. Teachers should use these types of reinforcers only occasionally because they are controversial.

30. There are a limitless number of academic, personal, or social activities and privileges that teachers can use as reinforcers.

31. Teachers should dispense all reinforcers contingent upon students' performance of appropriate behaviors.

32. Generalized rewards, such as gold stars, points, check marks, and tokens are earned rewards which are reinforcing because they can be exchanged for something of value.

33. In a token economy, students can earn points, stars, or tokens for appropriate behavior. At a later and more convenient time, students exchange them for something more reinforcing.

34. Freedom from aversive or unpleasant activities, such as homework, function as reinforcers for many students.

35. A reinforcement menu provides students with a choice of reinforcers. Options in the menu should be selected by the teacher and the students. A reinforcement preference inventory allows students to express their reinforcement preferences.

36. The amount or magnitude of reinforcement, the timing and delivery of reinforcement, and a task's demands are interrelated and impact the effectiveness of reinforcement.

37. If a behavior is on a continuous schedule of reinforcement, reinforcement is delivered each and every time the behavior occurs.

38. A continuous schedule of reinforcement (FR1) is required to get a new or infrequently occurring behavior underway.

39. Once a behavior is established with the use of a continuous schedule of reinforcement, it will require some periodic reinforcement for it to

continue.

40. With a partial schedule of reinforcement, reinforcement is provided following the occurrence of only some of the times that a student performs an appropriate behavior.

41. The unpredictability of partial schedules encourages student persistence and serves to maintain or increase the frequency of occurrence of appropriate behavior.

42. Partial schedules of reinforcement that use behavior as the primary determinant for the delivery of reinforcement are called ratio schedules.

43. Partial schedules of reinforcement that use time as the primary determinant for the delivery of reinforcement are called interval schedules.

44. Ratio and interval schedules overlap and are not mutually exclusive.

45. Reinforcement can be delivered on a fixed ratio schedule, after a fixed number of students' performance of appropriate behavior.

46. A post-reinforcement pause, a decrease in response rate immediately following receipt of reinforcement, occurs with the use of a fixed ratio schedule.

47. In a variable ratio schedule, reinforcement is delivered after a varying, often unspecified, but typically average number of appropriate behaviors have occurred.

48. In a fixed interval schedule, a reinforcer is provided following the first appropriate behavior that occurs after a specific fixed amount of time has elapsed since the last behavior.

49. In a variable interval schedule, reinforcement is provided at a variable amount of time since the last occurrence of an appropriate behavior occurred and was reinforced.

50. Teachers are encouraged to read the professional literature to learn more about the selection, use, delivery, and timing of reinforcement.

REFERENCES

Woolfolk, A. E. (1995). *Educational psychology.* Boston: Allyn & Bacon.

SUGGESTED ACTIVITIES/ASSIGNMENTS

1. Design a list of ten academic activity reinforcers that would be appropriate for elementary school students, junior high school students,

and high school students.

2. Design a list of ten personal or social activity reinforcers that would be appropriate for elementary school students, junior high school students, and high school students.

3. Design a list of ten tangible reinforcers that would be appropriate for elementary school students, junior high school students, and high school students.

4. Create a reinforcement preference survey for students at a particular grade level.

5. Student input into reinforcer selection assures reinforcer appropriateness. What reinforcer would you select that would motivate you to study more? What reinforcer might your friends select for the same task? Poll 10 people, compare their responses, and report the results in class.

6. Construct five citations/awards to motivate students. Specify the grade level.

7. Identify a personal behavior that is on a partial schedule of reinforcement. Describe the behavior and the reinforcers that are maintaining that behavior.

8. Think back to when you were in elementary school, junior high, or high school. What assignments did you find particularly reinforcing? What assignments did you find irrelevant, meaningless, or boring?

9. Think of 50 different ways to praise an elementary school students, a junior high school student, or a high school student.

10. Critique journal articles related to the selection, use, delivery, and timing of reinforcement.

Chapter 6

RULES AND PROCEDURES, CONSISTENCY, AND CONTINGENCY CONTRACTING

Effective teachers at all grade levels devise, use, and teach their students the required rules and procedures. Effective teachers consistently enforce their classroom rules with the appropriate consequences for students' compliance or non-compliance. Effective teachers also use written behavioral contracts with selected students when other more informal management strategies have been unsuccessful. This chapter describes the effective use of rules and procedures, consistency, and some basic principles about behavioral contracting.

RULES AND PROCEDURES

The term *rules* refers to expectations or standards for a behavior and the conditions under which the behavior may occur. Well-constructed rules give students guidance about appropriate behaviors, and they are necessary for effective instruction and teacher–student interaction. Every teacher has to decide which rules are most appropriate for his or her classroom and his or her particular group of students, although some rules about generally-accepted behaviors and some procedures for routine activities are appropriate for virtually all classrooms. Effective teachers devise and use rules according to these factors: the specific classroom, the students and their developmental levels, the teachers' instructional goals, and school and district-wide policies.

Rules are a fact of life, and they govern peoples' behavior in a variety of settings: make a full stop at the stop sign; no smoking permitted; all visitors to the school must register with the principal's office and get a visitor's pass. Living in a social setting and working in a group setting requires that some individual freedoms be regulated to accomplish the goals of the group. Because classrooms are made up of groups of students often under crowded conditions for relatively long periods of time to accomplish specific and varied purposes, students' classroom behaviors have to be regulated through the use of explicit rules and procedures. The consistent use and enforcement of classroom rules and procedures assist teachers in regulating students' behaviors so that learning occurs, personal injuries and damage to school and personal property are avoided, and the frequency of occurrence of inappropriate behaviors decreases.

The term *procedure* refers to a particular course of action or way of doing something. Effective teachers establish procedures for routine classroom behaviors such as distributing and collecting materials and papers, computer use, library use, and movement within and out of the classroom. Effective teachers use rules and procedures to achieve order, to enhance students' learning, and to facilitate students' appropriate behaviors. Effective teachers clearly explain their rules and procedures. They use signals and cues to prompt students' compliance with the rules and procedures, and they spend time explaining and rehearsing procedures with students.

Effective teachers devise rules and procedures according to the specifics of their situation and their students. There will and should be differences in how individual teachers phrase rules and describe expected procedures. There is no magic number of rules or procedures teachers should have because each classroom situation is different, and effective teachers realize that it is impossible to have a rule to cover every situation.

Effective teachers construct their rules and procedures according to the many suggestions that follow. First and foremost, effective teachers plan for the school year before the year begins, and they present the most important rules and procedures on the very first day of school. Effective teachers plan for the use of classroom space, the location and movement of students, and the location and accessibility of materials and work areas. When devising rules and procedures, teachers have to make decisions about all of the following (additional content on the use of space, seating arrangements, and furniture location appears in Chapter 8):

- where to put the teacher's desk so the teacher can see and monitor all students easily;
- where to seat students to minimize inappropriate student behaviors;
- where to locate special equipment, computers, laboratory, and other supplies;
- where to display instructional materials so that they are easily visible to all students;
- where to store frequently used materials so that they are easily accessible;

- where to locate students who need special help so that they can receive assistance from the teacher's aide, the student teacher, or the teacher, without distracting other students;
- where to seat students to minimize distractions that compete for their attention;
- how to begin and end the lessons so that instruction flows with continuity, and students are engaged on the expected academic tasks;
- how they will present, collect, and return assignments to students;
- how they will allow students to leave the room for the restroom, the principal's office, the cafeteria, the nurse's office, the counselor's office, the library, etc.; and
- how they will use, store, organize, and access their instructional materials.

The very first day of school is when the most effective teachers establish with their students their expected rules and procedures. Later on in the year, as additional or situation-specific rules are required, effective teachers introduce those. What teachers do on the first few days of school often determines their management success or failure for the remainder of the year. Effective teachers have positive expectations for students' successes, and through the effective use of rules and procedures, they provide a work-oriented, organized classroom atmosphere that facilitates students' learning and appropriate behaviors.

Effective teachers are visible, available, and in charge on the first day of class. The rules and procedures they devise require organization, preparation, and effective time-management. Effective teachers have their rules, procedures, and schedules written, posted, or otherwise displayed so they are clearly seen by all students, and they have them ready to distribute to students when they arrive to class. Effective teachers carefully plan, implement, and consistently maintain their management system throughout the school year.

On the first day of school, effective teachers provide designated places for students to sit, and they indicate where students are to store and access their belongings. Effective teachers explain to students about any special areas of the room, their purposes, and the procedures associated with their use. Effective teachers describe and demonstrate the appropriate behaviors required by their rules and procedures. Effective teachers have students practice the expected rules and procedures, and they provide feedback to the students on how well they have done. On the first day of school, effective elementary school teachers, in particular, provide students with name tags. On the first day of school, effective teachers with junior high and high school students use a sharing activity to allow students to get to know each other and to feel comfortable with each other.

Early in the school year, effective teachers inform parents about the rules for behavior and about selected procedures so that they can be supportive of the teacher's management efforts. Parents can be informed regarding rules and procedures through the school handbook or by a teacher-made handout that is sent home or distributed during a parent–teacher conference. Effective teachers put the rules in writing, something which conveys the idea that the rules are to be taken seriously. Effective teachers distribute the written rules and procedures to parents with instructions that parents read and discuss the rules and procedures with their children.

In some school districts, parents are required to "sign off" on the rules. Their signatures constitute an agreement that they understand what is expected of their child and that they have discussed the rules and procedures with their child. While the parents' signatures are not binding, such a policy makes an impression on parents and students about the importance of the expected rules and procedures.

Effective teachers carefully plan and specifically instruct students on the expected rules and procedures. Early in the school year, effective teachers clearly communicate their requirements for seat work, homework, extra-credit, and other assignments. Effective teachers clearly communicate their expectations for incomplete work, work that is completed late, and make-up work for absentees.

Effective teachers specifically convey to students the procedures they will use for (a) monitoring students' progress and completion of assignments, (b) how and when students' work will be checked and monitored, (c) how and when students can typically expect to receive feedback on their assignments, (d) how assignments are to be turned in and/or collected, and (e) how students' work will be displayed. Effective teachers specifically communicate their expectations about how assignments will be graded, their policies about extra-credit assignments, and the weight and percentage of each component used in their grading system. Effective teachers clearly convey the administrative and record-keeping functions they will use: completing course cards, taking attendance, checking rosters, and so on. Effective teachers explicitly communicate their expectations for routinely expected behaviors: what students are to do when the bell rings; what students are to do if their pencil breaks and needs sharpening; what students are to do when the fire drill bell rings; what students are to do if the bus does not show up on time; what students are to do if they have a question; what students may do if they finish an assignment early; what students are to do if they need to use the restroom, and so on.

Effective teachers use the following guidelines and suggestions when determining the rules and procedures they expect of their students.

• The expected rules and procedures enhance rather than detract from teachers' and students' ability to see each other and to see instructional materials and media. All students should be easily able to see instructional materials and media. The effective teacher has a clear and unobstructed view of all students at all times.

- The expected rules and procedures must also enhance rather than detract from teacher–student accessibility to each other. High traffic areas (the pencil sharpener or the door to the hallway) should be located separately from each other and be kept clear and accessible.

- The rules and procedures should minimize student distractions. Arrangements that compete with the teacher for students' attention, such as seating students facing the windows, playground, or face to face with each other but away from the teacher, should be avoided.

- The expected rules and procedures are clearly and explicitly stated so that students know precisely what is expected of them. Clearly and explicitly stated rules and procedures should be firmly but politely and respectfully presented to students. For example, "Please be in your seat and ready to work when the bell rings," specifies what students are to do, and it is stated politely and respectfully. However "You will be in the right place at the right time" is so vague that a teacher will inevitably have to further clarify and interpret what it means.

- The expected rules and procedures should be described briefly, and there should be separate rules for different behaviors. Constructing rules and procedures in accordance with this guideline makes the rules easier for students to understand, remember, and therefore hopefully comply with. Clearly stated rules empower students to make better decisions about their behaviors. However, the length of the rule statement or the description of the expected procedure should not comprise its clarity.

- The expected rules and procedures should specifically summarize expected student behaviors. For example, "Please raise your hand and wait until you are called on before speaking," provides students with guidance about what they are to do, but "Don't call out" lacks clarity and provides no such guidance.

- Whenever possible, the expected rules and procedures should be presented in the positive rather than the negative. For example, "Please walk in the halls," clearly articulates that walking is the only acceptable form of movement when students are in the halls. "Don't run in the halls" is too vague to be effective because it will, in all likelihood, need to be modified to include other types of unacceptable hall behaviors like skipping, jumping, and hopping. The expected rules and procedures can be stated in the negative for emphasis with injurious, offensive, or clearly forbidden student behaviors such as "No smoking allowed anywhere on campus;" "No alcoholic beverages allowed any-where on campus;" and "No firearms or weapons allowed anywhere on campus." When so stated, these statements will still require further clarification to explicitly inform students and parents about, for example, what constitutes a "weapon."

- The rules and procedures that teachers want students to comply with must be reasonable and appropriate behavioral expectations. Unreasonable or otherwise inappropriate behavioral expectations are very difficult to enforce. What constitutes "reasonable and appropri-ate" behavioral expectations will vary with the situation and with the age and developmental characteristics of a particular group of stu-dents. For example, "We speak softly when we are eating breakfast or lunch in the school cafeteria" is a rational, reasonable, and appropri-ate behavioral expectation, because mealtime should be a social time as well as a time to eat. But "No talking during lunch" is an unrea-sonable behavioral expectation because in the typical school cafeteria students sit close to many other students, many students have been properly taught that mealtime should also be a social and relaxed time, and lunch time is often perceived by students as a welcome break from academic class activities and a chance to socialize with friends.

- The rules and procedures expected should be conducive to creating a positive and nurturing classroom climate and school-wide atmos-phere. If teachers construct many rules that are negative, students may perceive the rules as arbitrary, which can lead to teacher–student conflicts that defeat the goal of establishing a positive and nurturing classroom climate and school-wide atmosphere.

- Effective teachers remember that the appropriateness or inappropri-ateness of a behavior depends on the specifics of the situation. Thus, a classroom rule, "No talking," can and should be enforced during a competitive examination, but it is an inappropriate expectation for stu-dents when they are engaged in cooperative learning activities, labo-ratory work, or at recess. Effective teachers enforce their classroom rules firmly and fairly, but they are flexible and can accommodate unforeseen or unpredictable events that inevitably will occur.

- Effective teachers give students a written copy of the expected rules and procedures. Effective teachers formally teach students the expect-ed rules and procedures, and they provide the rationales for the rules and procedures. An explanation of the rationales for the rules and procedures is almost always necessary when teachers have to enforce unpopular rules like dress codes. Effective teachers realize that while all students should be initially taught about the rules and procedures, only some students will need reminders about them.

- Effective teachers model or demonstrate the expected rules and procedures. They rehearse them with their students, and they provide feedback to the students. Effective teachers know that when students understand why the rules and procedures are required, they are more likely to comply with them.
- Effective teachers construct rules and procedures that are consistent with and not in conflict with school-wide and district-wide rules, procedures, and policies. Teachers' classroom rules, however, should not merely be duplicative of school-wide and district-wide rules, procedures, and policies.
- Effective teachers know the school-wide and district-wide rules, procedures, and policies regarding emergencies and disasters such as tornadoes, earthquakes, chemical spills, bomb threats, and guns or hostage situations, and they explain and enforce these rules with their students. Effective teachers are also aware of what student behaviors are expressly required (e.g., "Students must get a hall pass when outside the classroom.") or expressly forbidden (e.g., "No firearms or weapons allowed on campus.") by school-wide or district-wide rules, procedures, and policies.
- Effective teachers have the expected rules and procedures conspicuously posted, and they refer to them frequently. Having the rules and procedures posted and highly visible reminds students about them and serves as a cue to students about what is expected of them. When a student complies with a rule, an effective teacher points that out periodically and as frequently as possible: "I am so pleased Jay that you remembered Rule 3, to please raise your hand and wait to speak until you are called on." Conversely, when a student fails to comply with a rule, an effective teacher points that out and refers to the rules' list as a cue: "Jay, kindly remember Rule 3, to please raise your hand and wait to speak until you are called on." With older students, effective teachers describe the rules and procedures in course syllabi or other handouts.
- Effective teachers often involve students in selecting rules and procedures. Effective teachers involve students in establishing some of the rules and procedures because they know it encourages ownership, and thus helps the class to function well as a unit. The rationales for the rules and their actual construction also form the basis for empowering class discussions during which students can voice their concerns and validate their understanding. Even young students can understand that if everyone is talking at once no one will be heard; hence the necessity of the rule "Only one person talks in class at a time." Older

students are often capable of setting rules and procedures creatively and from their unique perspectives. Of course, students should not be permitted to establish rules or procedures that are contrary to school-wide or district-wide policies, or that permit illegal, discriminatory, injurious, or otherwise inappropriate behaviors. In some school districts, "codes of conduct" rather than rules are used. These codes function like rules and are typically collaboratively established by administrators, teachers, staff, students, and parents.

- Effective teachers periodically review and revise their rules and procedures. New tasks and activities implemented as the school year progresses—such as field trips, guest speakers, or prom night—often require additional task or activity-specific rules and procedures. Effective teachers introduce the additional activity-specific rules and procedures as necessary, not prematurely, and close in time to when the expected behaviors are to occur, for example, a few days before the field trip, the visit by a guest speaker, or prom night.

- Effective teachers use a minimum number of rules and procedures. Effective teachers avoid overloading students with unnecessary or trivial rules. Effective teachers also have separate, specific rules and procedures for students' behaviors in school settings other than their classroom: the cafeteria, the playground, the computer center, the library, etc.

- There are some rules about generally accepted behaviors and some procedures for routine activities that are appropriate for virtually all classrooms: "Please follow directions the first time they are given;" "Please raise your hand and wait for permission to speak;" "Please keep hands, feet, and other objects to yourself;" and "Please be in your seat when the bell rings."

- Effective teachers know that most behaviors expected of students are complex and made up of a number of smaller discrete behaviors. For example, coming into class in the morning may require that students have to perform all of these and possibly additional behaviors: remove jacket; hang up or store jacket; take out their notebook, texts, pencil, pens or other work materials; place their homework in the basket on the teacher's desk; get their work folder; sharpen their pencils; and begin working on the first assigned activity. Effective teachers demonstrate, model, and rehearse with students each step of a complex behavior or expected procedure.

Effective teachers know that after the establishment of their classroom rules and procedures, they need to make clear to students what the consequences will be if students abide by the rules or violate them. Effective teachers provide frequent, periodic, and positive consequences for students' appropriate behaviors. Effective teachers strive to actively, enthusiastically, and frequently reinforce all students for appropriate behaviors. Effective teachers use students' appropriate behaviors to impact other students' behaviors.

CONSISTENCY

Effective teachers consistently deliver reinforcement for students' appropriate behaviors, and they consistently use punishment or withhold reinforcement for students' inappropriate behaviors. Effective teachers are consistent in their use of management techniques, and they are consistent in their enforcement of the expected rules and procedures. When teachers are consistent, students learn to associate the consequences of their behaviors with their behaviors. Students can then choose how to behave, and hopefully they will behave appropriately more frequently than inappropriately.

Each student's behavioral and conditioning history, the type and amount of reinforcer or punisher used, and the demands and appeal of a particular task determine how quickly a student's behavior changes. Some students continue appropriate behavior after receiving only one or two reinforcers, or they refrain from inappropriate behavior after receiving only one or two punishments. Other students may need many doses of reinforcement to continue appropriate behavior or many doses of punishment to refrain from inappropriate behavior.

Effective teachers consistently deliver reinforcement on a continuous schedule for students' new behaviors and for their infrequently occurring behaviors. Consistency in the administration of reinforcement is of utmost importance when teachers try to teach a new behavior or if they are trying to strengthen an infrequently occurring behavior. For example, a student who is reluctant to answer questions in class should be consistently reinforced for responding each and every time that behavior occurs (i.e., reinforcement is delivered on a continuous schedule of reinforcement). Then, once the student is frequently answering questions, reinforcement should be delivered only some of the times that the behavior occurs (i.e. reinforcement is delivered on a partial schedule of reinforcement). The transition from continuous reinforcement delivery to periodic delivery is often referred to as "thinning out the reinforcement schedule" or making the reinforcement schedule "lean."

Effective teachers consistently use appropriate consequences to manage students' behaviors. *Appropriate consequences* refers to teachers' consistent use of periodic reinforcement for all students' appropriate behaviors so those behaviors continue. *Appropriate consequences* also refers to teachers' consistent withholding or denial of reinforcement for all students' inappropriate behaviors.

Effective teachers are careful not to accidentally extinguish appropriate behaviors; when behaviors that were previously reinforced continue without reinforcement, they are likely to cease. For example, sometimes teachers ignore students who are on task, performing their seatwork, working quietly, or otherwise behaving appropriately. This typically happens because those teachers find themselves spending a disproportionate amount of time and effort focusing on the inappropriately behaving student (the traditional discipline paradigm). Teachers who ignore appropriately behaving students, though, will soon find that the appropriately behaving students will misbehave because their appropriate behaviors have been extinguished. So it is imperative—in order to be effective in increasing appropriate student behaviors and decreasing inappropriate student behaviors—teachers provide all students with periodic and frequent reinforcement for appropriate behavior.

While effective teachers are consistent for all the reasons suggested, effective teachers are also flexible. Effective teachers realize that individual behavioral infractions by individual students with individual behavioral histories, and in different situations are never identical, and they flexibly adjust the delivery of appropriate consequences accordingly.

At this point, the reader is encouraged to review the material presented in Chapter 5 on schedules of reinforcement, and to pay particular attention to the effects on behavior of partial versus continuous schedules of reinforcement. Behaviors that are on a partial schedule of reinforcement become imbedded and highly resistant to extinction. Effective teachers deliver periodic and frequent reinforcement for students' appropriate behaviors because behaviors that are reinforced only some of the times that they occur become imbedded and highly resistant to extinction. Effective teachers also exercise painstaking care to be sure that inappropriate behaviors are not inconsistently punished or otherwise accidentally reinforced. Instead, effective teachers consistently punish students' inappropriate behaviors.

All teachers will be occasionally inconsistent in their use of reinforcement and punishment. There are many reasons why teachers are inconsistent in the reinforcement of students' appropriate behaviors or in their punishment of students' inappropriate behaviors. Some teachers have unreasonable rules and unworkable or unrealistic procedures that they expect students to perform. Some teachers fail to monitor students sufficiently, so some students' inappropriate behaviors go unpunished or, worse yet, those behaviors are inadvertently reinforced. Some teachers' inconsistency in the delivery of punishment for students' inappropriate behaviors is directly responsible for misbehaving students "testing the system to see what they can get away with." Some teachers require tasks that students do not perceive as meaningful, inherently interesting, or otherwise intrinsically reinforcing. With such tasks, inappropriate student behaviors–like not working on task or interfering with other students who are working on task–will increase if no appealing external reinforcers are provided.

Finally, all teachers will occasionally be inconsistent in their use of reinforcement and punishment because there are so many student behaviors to manage. Effective teachers conserve their time and effort to focus only on the most important behaviors, rules, and procedures.

CONTINGENCY CONTRACTING

The word *contingent* means conditional. When consequences are delivered on a contingent basis, that means a reinforcer is delivered only after an appropriate behavior occurs and a punisher is delivered or reinforcement is otherwise denied after an inappropriate behavior occurs. Effective teachers establish the contingencies for consequences using the same guidelines suggested for the construction and use of classroom rules and procedures. Effective teachers consistently deliver the appropriate consequences in accordance with the contingencies established.

Contingency contracts or *behavioral contracts* are formal, written agreements between a teacher and a one or more students which specify (1) the behaviors students are to engage in, and (2) the consequences that will occur if students comply with the conditions of the contract. They are essentially no more complex than formal communications between the parties about what students are to do (or not to do) and what the consequences will be. The simple process of writing down the behavior and its consequences and having all parties sign the contract emphasizes a student's commitment to behave a certain way, and thus increases the likelihood of a student's compliance with the terms of the contract. Behavioral or contingency contracts often use an "if–then" construction: "If I, . . . (student's name), do this . . . (identify the appropriate behavior), then this . . . (specification of the reinforcer) will occur." For example, "If Joan works on the spelling assignment and gets at least 90% of the words correct, then she can write in her diary for 10 minutes this afternoon after lunch."

The "when–then" construction can also be used, but it conveys to students that they have no choice, and they must perform the behavior. It's use may be required, on occasion, or it may be totally inappropriate, depending on what behavior is expected.

Effective teachers use formal behavioral contracts occasionally and only when other, less formal approaches to management have been unsuccessful. Effective teachers realize that the following items are important when using contracts:

- the contracts are simple;
- the expected behavior is clearly stated;
- the expected mastery level is clear;
- the focus of the contract is positive on the performance of an appropriate behavior rather than on the cessation of an inappropriate behavior;
- the reinforcer that will be delivered for the appropriate behavior is clearly specified;
- the reinforcer(s) used can be of any variety, including generalized rewards such as points, tokens or stars that can be exchanged at a later date for another reinforcer;
- the reinforcers are selected by the teacher, with some student input to ensure that they have reinforcing value;
- the type and amount of reinforcers selected are appropriate to the amount, difficulty, and nature of the behavior expected;
- the delivery of reinforcement is specified in the contract; and
- a reinforcement menu is used to prevent satiation.

Homme (1973) provides these ten basic rules relative to contingency contracting. The first five refer to the use of reinforcers in contracting, and the second five describe essentials of proper contracts.

1. The contract payoff (reward) should be immediate. It is important that the presentation of the reinforcer be contingent only on the adequate performance of a behavior and not merely on the passage of time.
2. Initial contracts should call for and reward small, simple-to-perform approximations of the final behavior or performance desired. Instead of, "Do all of your math work and then you may watch a video," effective teachers use; "Do the first five problems correctly and then you may watch your video for five minutes."
3. Reward frequently with small amounts. This is particularly important when the student is initially learning about contracting.
4. The contract should call for and reward accomplishment rather than obedience. A reward for accomplishment leads to independence while a reward for obedience leads to dependence.
5. Reward the performance after it occurs not in anticipation of its occurrence.
6. The contract must be fair, and the amount of the reward should be appropriately related to the amount of the performance.

7. The terms of the contract must be clear so students know what is expected of them and what they can expect as reinforcement.

8. The contract must be honest, carried out immediately, and carried out according to the terms specified in the contract.

9. The contract must be positive and should contribute to the student's experience and learning.

10. Contracting as a method must be used systematically and maintained, and care must be taken not to reward inappropriate behaviors.

When teachers establish rules and procedures according to the suggestions in this chapter, consistently enforce them, and use formal behavioral contracts appropriately, occasionally, and as necessary, they are likely to experience instructional success and appropriate student behaviors. When students' inappropriate behaviors continue to occur, they can be addressed using the strategies provided in the next chapter.

SUMMARY OF KEY CONCEPTS IN CHAPTER 6

1. Rules describe expectations or standards for a behavior and the conditions under which the behavior may occur.

2. Effective teachers devise and use rules according to, but not limited to, these factors: the specific classroom, the students and their developmental levels, the teacher's instructional goals, and school- and district-wide policies.

3. Procedures are a particular course of action or way of doing something.

4. The consistent use and enforcement of classroom rules and procedures assists teachers in regulating students' behaviors so that learning occurs, personal injuries and damage to school and personal property are avoided, and the frequency of occurrence of inappropriate behaviors decreases.

5. Effective teachers plan for the school year before the year begins, and they present the most important rules and procedures on the very first day of school.

6. Effective teachers plan for the use of classroom space, the location and movement of students, and the location and accessibility of materials and work areas.

7. Effective teachers have positive expectations for students' successes, and through the effective use of rules and procedures, they provide a work-oriented, organized classroom atmosphere that facilitates stu-

dents' learning and appropriate behaviors.

8. Effective teachers describe and demonstrate the appropriate behaviors required by their rules and procedures.

9. Early in the school year, effective teachers inform parents about the rules and procedures so that they can be supportive of the teachers' management efforts.

10. Effective teachers put their rules and procedures in writing because this conveys the idea that the rules and procedures are to be taken seriously.

11. Effective teachers are visible, available, and in charge on the first day of class.

12. The rules and procedures that effective teachers devise require organization, preparation, and effective time-management.

13. Effective teachers enforce their classroom rules firmly and fairly, but they are also flexible and can accommodate unforeseen or unusual events that inevitably occur.

14. Effective teachers use rules and procedures that enhance visibility, accessibility, and utility.

15. Whenever possible, the expected rules and procedures should be presented in the positive rather than the negative.

16. The rules and procedures that teachers want students to comply with must be reasonable and appropriate behavioral expectations.

17. The rules and procedures should be conducive to creating a positive and nurturing classroom climate and school-wide atmosphere.

18. Effective teachers remember that the appropriateness or inappropriateness of a behavior depends on the specifics of the situation.

19. Effective teachers formally teach students the expected rules and procedures, and they provide rationales for the rules and procedures.

20. Effective teachers construct rules and procedures that are consistent with and not in conflict with school-wide and district-wide rules, procedures, and policies.

21. Effective teachers know the school-wide and district-wide rules, and they explain and enforce them with their students.

22. Effective teachers have the expected rules and procedures conspicuously posted, and they refer to them frequently.

23. Effective teachers involve students in establishing some of the rules and procedures because they know that this encourages student ownership of the rules and thus helps the class to function well as a unit.

24. Effective teachers periodically review and revise their rules and procedures.

25. Effective teachers consistently deliver reinforcement for students' appropriate behaviors, and they consistently use punishment or with-

hold reinforcement for students' inappropriate behaviors.

26. Effective teachers consistently deliver reinforcement on a continuous schedule for students' new behaviors and for infrequently occurring, appropriate behaviors.

27. *Appropriate consequences* refers to teachers' consistent use of periodic reinforcement for all students' appropriate behaviors and the consistent withholding or denial of reinforcement for all students' inappropriate behaviors.

28. When consequences are delivered on a contingent basis, a reinforcer is delivered only after an appropriate behavior occurs or a punisher is delivered, or reinforcement is denied, after an inappropriate behavior occurs.

29. Contingency contracts or behavioral contracts are formal, written agreements between a teacher and one or more students which specify the behaviors students are to engage in and the consequences that will occur if students comply with the conditions of the contract.

30. Effective teachers use formal behavioral contracts occasionally and only as necessary when other, less formal approaches to management have not been successful.

REFERENCES

Albert, L. (1995). Discipline tips from the expert: Rule is a 4-letter word. *Teaching Kids Responsibility, 1*(1), 2.

Homme, L. (1973). *How to use contingency contracting in the classroom.* Champaign, IL: Research Press.

SUGGESTED ACTIVITIES/ASSIGNMENTS

1. Invite a former teacher to discuss the disciplinary problems he or she encountered.

2. Write five classroom rules that you think are appropriate for use with elementary school students, junior high school students, and high school students.

3. Describe the rules and procedures your teachers required that you remember as being reasonable and appropriate. Provide your rationale.

4. Describe the rules and procedures your teachers required that you remember as being unreasonable and inappropriate. Provide your

rationale.

5. Invite classroom teachers from different levels to address the class about the rules and procedures they use.

6. Invite an administrator to address the class about a school districts policies and procedures.

7. Have a panel discussion with parents discussing how they support the teacher and his or her procedures.

8. Design a behavioral contract for a student. Specify the expected behavior, the consequences to be used, and rationales.

9. Critique journal articles concerning the use of contingency contracting or behavior contracts with elementary age students, junior high students, and high school students.

Chapter 7

DEALING WITH INAPPROPRIATE BEHAVIOR

Previous chapters focused on understanding behavior; selected models of classroom management, motivation, and instruction; and basic principles about antecedents, behavior, consequences, reinforcement, and classroom rules and procedures. The major focus of this chapter is on non-physical punishment strategies that teachers can use with students' mildly disruptive inappropriate behaviors. Chapter 15 presents strategies for preventing school violence and for dealing with students' more troublesome and severe inappropriate behaviors.

When teachers have to manage a student's mildly disruptive inappropriate behavior, the best strategy is a combination of reinforcement of the student's appropriate behavior and extinction of the student's inappropriate behavior (via denial of reinforcement for a behavior that has been previously reinforced). This strategy is effective if it is carried out in accordance with the principles that govern the use of reinforcement and extinction. It may not be successful, though, for these reasons: the amount or type of reinforcer offered is too weak or is of the wrong type; satiation renders the reinforcer ineffective; the reinforcer offered is not commensurate with the nature or the difficulty level of the task; and/or the processes of reinforcement and extinction are not correctly implemented. Thus, all too often, frustrated teachers prematurely abandon this strategy, and they resort to punishment.

Effective teachers do otherwise. Effective teachers persist in their use of reinforcement for students' appropriate behaviors and extinction for students' inappropriate behaviors until they are successful. But with the realization that some punishment may nonetheless be necessary, the following information about punishment is presented in the hope that teachers will use punishment of any form only as a last resort.

PUNISHMENT

Punishment can involve the application of an aversive consequence, or it can involve the withdrawal of a favored event or reinforcer. In either case, the consequences must decrease the rate of the target behavior in order to be considered punishment.

Punishment should be used only when reinforcement and extinction procedures have been exhausted and have failed to produce the desired result. Punishment should be used as a last resort because the main effect of punishment is to suppress behavior in the presence of the person delivering the punishment (the punishing agent). When the punishing agent is not present, the previously punished behavior is likely to resume because nothing is done to eliminate the original reinforcing consequence. For example, Barbara learns not to cheat on an exam in Mr. Woods' class because Mr. Woods closely monitors his students' behaviors during tests. Barbara does not necessarily refrain from cheating altogether, but rather she learns not to cheat only in Mr. Wood's class, or worse yet, she learns how to cheat in Mr. Woods' class without being caught.

Teachers who manage their students primarily with the use of punishment find that students learn ingenious ways to engage in the punished behaviors without detection. The typical avoidance behaviors that result, lying, truancy, and sneaking around, are elaborated on below.

When teachers rely strictly on punishment as a management technique, they create a negative classroom atmosphere. Furthermore, using only punishment or using more punishment than reinforcement focuses on the negative—on what not to do—and it does not teach students about how to behave appropriately. Effective teachers realize that, while punishment may temporarily reduce or suppress a student's inappropriate behavior, it typically is ineffective on a long-term basis for eliminating a student's undesirable behavior.

Punishment can be physical punishment (i.e., "corporal punishment") as discussed in Chapter 14, or it can take a variety of non-physical forms: loss of privileges, the correction procedure, the over-correction procedure, time-out, isolation, exclusion, non-exclusion, required interactions, satiation, reprimands, response cost, penalties, conflict resolution, and peer mediation. Before discussing each of these types of non-physical punishment, however, it is important to understand that when teachers over-rely on punishment for inappropriate student behaviors, they are likely to encounter these undesirable outcomes (Carson & Carson, 1984):

• **Punishment works unpredictably**. Sometimes teachers' attempts at punishment actually result in an increase rather than a decrease in the frequency of occurrence of a student's inappropriate behavior. Consider the case of Anne who is repeatedly sent to the principal's office and continues to behave inappropriately. If Anne enjoys getting out of class, perceives peer approval for being the "difficult" student as appealing, and if Anne associates only a minimum amount of aversiveness with this strategy, Anne is likely to repeat her inappropriate behavior. Furthermore, because the teacher enjoys some immediate reinforcement for the time that Anne, the misbehaving student, is out of the class, the teacher is likely to continue with the use of this punishment even though it is not having the desired impact on Anne's inappropriate behavior.

• **Punishment is inefficient for teaching a new behavior.** This is true because punishment focuses on the negative, that is, on the inappropriate behavior or what *not* to do rather than focusing on the positive, that is, on the appropriate behavior, or what *to* do. Rather, effective teachers use active, periodic, and frequent reinforcement to shape students' small and successively closer approximations to a final target or goal behavior.

• **Punishment decreases a teacher's reinforcing value.** Put simply, when a teacher dispenses only occasional reinforcement but frequent punishment, that teacher is less powerful when he or she tries to dispense reinforcement.

• **Punishment promotes avoidance behaviors.** Avoidance behaviors are those that keep one from getting close to punishment or a punishing situation. Many students engage in lying, sneaking, hiding, concealing, and skipping school to avoid punishment. These typical avoidance behaviors—students' skipping school, in particular—are contrary to everyone's educational goals.

• **Punishment is often harmful to a student's self-image.** Negative, punitive, critical, or derisive statements about students' inappropriate behaviors are inappropriate for teachers to use, but they often occur as a result of teacher frustration. Such statements are damaging to student's motivation and self-esteem. Instead, effective teachers lavishly reward, praise, and otherwise encourage students' progress, achievement, and appropriate behaviors.

• **Punishment often results in students disliking school and the teacher and becoming sullen, negative, withdrawn, and antagonistic.** When school becomes aversive and totally unrewarding, many students respond antagonistically or aggressively with behaviors like vandalism or violence, or they respond more passively by withdrawing, becoming obstinate, wanting to drop out, or feigning sickness to get out of or away from school.

Two additional undesirable outcomes are specifically associated with the use of physical, or corporal, punishment:

• **Physical punishment models aggressive behavior.** Students imitate what they see others do. The use of physical punishment with students by teachers or by other adults in a child's environment functions to condone the use of aggressive physical methods with others.

 • **Physical punishment is considered by many to be inhumane, and it is also often unjustly administered.** Physical punishment is often ineffective when the punishment is mild. Increasing the severity, though, only serves to the increase both the likelihood of inhumanity and the possibility of abusiveness of the procedure. Furthermore, certain groups of students—boys, minorities, low socioeconomic groups, and young children—receive physical punishment disproportionately more frequently than do other students.

Effective teachers understand some basic principles about the delivery of punishment. Many of these principles are similar to the ones presented in Chapters 4 and 5 concerning consequences and the delivery of reinforcement. When punishment is necessary, Woolfolk (1995, p. 219) and others provide these suggestions for its use. Effective teachers:

 • are consistent in the use of punishment. Effective teachers let students know in advance what the consequences are for breaking the rules, and they provide those predetermined consequences.
 • avoid the inadvertent reinforcement of behaviors they are attempting to punish. Any confrontations between a student and a teacher are kept as private as possible to avoid making the misbehaving student a "hero" in the eyes of his or her peers for standing up to a teacher in a public showdown.
 • inform students that they will receive only one warning before punishment will be delivered for the next infraction of a rule or the next occurrence of inappropriate behavior. Effective teachers give the warning in a calm and firm tone, and then they follow through with delivery of an appropriate and related form of punishment as promised.
 • insist on an action, such as the performance of appropriate behavior, rather than accepting a student's promise to behave appropriately. Students should not be allowed to convince teachers to change the terms of an agreement concerning behaviors and their consequences.
 • deliver punishment immediately contingent upon a student's inappropriate behavior and make the punishment unavoidable.
 • deliver punishment with a focus on students' actions, not on the students' personality or on the students' personal qualities.
 • deliver reprimands and constructive criticism in a calm but firm voice.
 • avoid vindictive words, sarcasm, or a nasty tone of voice.
 • stress to students that they need to stop the inappropriate behavior. They do not express any negative feelings that they may have for the

inappropriately behaving student.

- adapt the severity and type of punishment to the infraction.
- realize that they cannot stop every student's inappropriate behavior.
- ignore students' minor inappropriate behaviors which do not disrupt the class or which are harmless to others.
- use a disapproving glance, a signal such as flashing the lights or the act of moving closer to the inappropriately behaving student to stop a student's inappropriate behavior without disturbing the flow or momentum of the lesson.
- use removal of the inappropriately behaving student from the group as a powerful punisher, especially if it appears that the student is misbehaving to gain peer acceptance and approval. Essentially, this is time-out from a reinforcing situation, and it works especially well with junior high and high school students.
- refrain from the use of extra homework or other academic activities as punishers so that students do not perceive them as negative or distasteful. (An aside from these authors: The purpose of homework is to extend students' learning time. Homework should not be assigned carelessly or frivolously. Students should be given homework that they can perform successfully and on their own. Homework should not merely involve the continuation of instruction, but rather should be a continuation of practice and/or a preparation for the next day's instruction. Parents should be informed of their expected involvement in special assignments like science fairs or other major projects. Effective teachers provide students with immediate, positive, and constructive feedback about their completed homework assignments. Effective teachers provide fair rules and procedures for homework, and they instruct students on what the consequences are for completion of homework on time, and for incomplete late homework.)
- analyze the situation if inappropriate student behaviors continue and make adjustments accordingly. Effective teachers often realize that the punishment they used is ineffective because it is too weak or because it is not perceived by the misbehaving student as punitive. Some teachers inadvertently reinforce the very misbehavior they would like to eliminate; therefore, effective teachers analyze their intents and actions, and they carefully observe students' behaviors to see if their management efforts and intentions are successful.

NON-PHYSICAL FORMS OF PUNISHMENT

There are a number of non-physical forms of punishment: loss of privileges, the correction procedure, the over-correction procedure, time-out, isolation, exclusion, non- exclusion, required interactions, satiation, reprimands, response cost, penalties, conflict resolution, and peer mediation. These are described below but not in any order of preference or suitability. Rather, effective teachers realize that they have to select the appropriate form of non-physical punishment depending upon the ages, abilities, and preferences of their students, their students' unique behavioral and conditioning histories, the particular inappropriate behaviors that they are trying to impact, and the myriad of factors that are unique to their classroom. Furthermore, effective teachers analyze the effect that their management strategies have on students' behaviors, and they continually refine or alter the strategies to be sure that they are accomplishing their objectives.

Loss of privileges. For different students, some activities function as privileges or reinforcers, and the inability to participate in those activities functions as a punishment. Loss of privileges, such as free time, play time, going on class field trips, or attending an assembly program, functions as punishment for many students. The loss or delay of the use of objects brought from home, such as sports equipment or cell phones, also functions as punishment for many students. For yet other students, the loss or delay of access to school areas such as the lunchroom, the computer lab, or the commons functions as punishment.

As with the the selection of reinforcers, teachers must carefully select the punishers they use, and they should not assume that the loss of a certain privilege will function as punishment for all students. Granted, most students enjoy recess or free time, but that is not necessarily true for all students. Rather, teachers need to assess the impact that their intended disciplinary strategy yields; if the inappropriate behavior that they are trying to punish decreases in its frequency of occurrence then it is being punished, but if it is continuing or increasing in its frequency of occurrence then it is being reinforced.

When teachers use loss of privileges with students, they make sure that the consequences are related, reasonable, and respectful. Related consequences are logically connected to the inappropriate behavior. For example, if a student continually tips back in his chair endangering himself and others, he would then lose the right to sit in the chair and have to stand for the rest of the period. Or if two students are disruptive when they are seated near each other in the cafeteria, they should be temporarily denied the right to sit and eat lunch together. Reasonable consequences are those that are equal in proportion and intensity to the inappropriate behavior. For example, if two students are rowdy during the first recess period, a reasonable consequence would be to deprive them of the next recess period. If the same two students were repeatedly rowdy during recess, it would also be reasonable to deny those students of the next three or four recess periods. Respectful consequences are those that are politely and unemotionally stated, carried out in a way that preserves a student's self-esteem and delivered without shaming or embarrassing the student.

Loss of privileges is typically a very effective form of punishment if the privilege withheld is truly reinforcing to the student. It is a easy to administer, and it is non-controversial. If loss of privileges entails taking away a student's property temporarily, then teachers must be sure that the student's property is returned at a later and more appropriate time, like after class or at the end of the school day.

The correction procedure. The correction procedure requires an inappropriately behaving student to make amends for an inappropriate behavior, to undo the effects of the behavior, or to otherwise make restitution such as return, replacement, and/or repair. The correction procedure is essentially the restoration of something back to its original state prior to the inappropriate behavior.

Here are three examples of how the correction procedure can be used. (1) Louise scribbles on the bathroom wall. The correction procedure would require that she clean the wall where she scribbled. (2) William litters on the playground. The correction procedure would require that he pick up the litter and dispose of it properly. The clean up should occur during recess or free time–not during academic or class time because then the strategy could backfire simply because William wants to get out of class. (3) Dwayne vandalizes another student's locker. The correction procedure would require that Dwayne restore the locker to its original condition and that he pay for or replace any of the items that he damaged.

The over-correction procedure. The over-correction procedure is closely related to the correction procedure just described. The over-correction procedure requires the inappropriately behaving student not only make amends or make restitution for the inappropriate behavior, but to go one step further, typically a requirement that necessitates further time, effort, service, or money. Like the correction procedure, the over-correction procedure is essentially the restoration of something back to its original state prior to vandalism or another inappropriate behavior. Here are two examples of how the correction procedure can be used: (1) Roy sprays graffiti on school property. The over-correction procedure would require not only that he clean up the graffiti but that he also clean other areas of school property. As with the correction procedure, the clean up should take place during Roy's free time or after school–not during academic activities or class periods. (2)

Marina hits another student. The over-correction procedure would require that she apologize to the student and that she write an essay on why it is inappropriate to hit. Thus, the effective use of restitution requires that the student making the restitution learn from the process about how to relate to others or how to treat property rather than simply performing restitution as an isolated event.

Both the correction and the over-correction strategies are effective punishers that are easy to use. They both teach students about being responsible for their behaviors, because they are similar to procedures used outside the classroom whereby those who damage property or are otherwise offensive to others and their property are responsible for restitution, regret, and/or repair.

Time-out. The term *time-out*, means time-out from reinforcement. It is often referred to in the professional literature as *TO* once it has been referred to as time-out. In research settings, time-out is often used in conjunction with a point, star, or token economy, and it functions as a punisher because it removes a person from the opportunity, (i.e., it "costs" a person the chance) to accumulate points, stars, or tokens which are exchangeable at a later date for a reinforcer.

Recently, though, time-out has become a popular punishment strategy for use by both teachers and parents, and it is used as a technique by itself and not necessarily in conjunction with a token economy system. Effective teachers view time-out as an extension of the idea of non-reinforcement, whereby an inappropriately behaving student is removed from the setting that is reinforcing the inappropriate behavior and temporarily placed in a different setting that is not at all reinforcing.

There are three types of time-out: isolation, exclusion, and non-exclusion. **Isolation** requires the temporary removal of the inappropriately behaving student from the classroom. It is comparable to the concept of solitary confinement, but the removal time in minutes should not exceed the child's age in years. Under no circumstances should a time-out be in excess of 30 minutes. **Exclusion** requires the inappropriately behaving student to remain in the classroom, but the student is required to sit apart from or is otherwise excluded from contact with other students. **Non-exclusion** limits the extent of the inappropriately behaving student's involvement in ongoing activities. It is comparable to the loss of privileges strategy, whereby the inappropriately behaving student has to continue working while other students, those who were behaving appropriately, have free time or another reinforcing activity.

Teachers can use time-out successfully if they follow these suggestions. Effective teachers

- count the frequency of occurrence of the inappropriate behaviors before and after the use of time-out to be sure that its use is having the intended effect.

- explain how the time-out will proceed and make sure their students understand the process by having them explain it in their own words.
- use a kitchen timer or watch alarm for the timing of time-out and to signal the end of the time-out period.
- clearly establish the procedures and time limits for students' going to and remaining in time-out.
- post a description of the offenses that will lead to time-out in a prominent and highly visible place, periodically reviewing them with their students.
- prepare alternative punishers for students who refuse to go to time-out.
- do not yell, scream, threaten, or intimidate the student who is sent to time-out. When a student returns from time-out, the punishment is over, and no further punishment for that offense should be delivered unless the inappropriate behavior re-occurs. Furthermore, as soon as the student returns from time-out and starts to behave appropriately, effective teachers reinforce that student.
- give students a choice before using time-out: "You may work quietly or you may go to time-out. You decide."
- add additional time to be served in time-out if a student behaves inappropriately while in time-out. If repeated or more serious inappropriate behaviors occur while a student is in time-out, an additional form of punishment, such as a loss of privileges, is warranted.
- make sure that the area selected for time-out has absolutely no reinforcing or appealing features. It must be an area that is devoid of all reinforcement.
- use time-out consistently and apply it as quickly as possible following the occurrence of the inappropriate behavior.
- instruct the students who are not in time-out to have no contact or interaction with the student who is in time-out.
- place only one student at a time in time-out.

In the classroom, a time-out area can be easily configured by simply screening off a safe corner of the classroom where there are no materials, no distractions, but simply a chair behind a screen for the inappropriately behaving student to sit on. If a special time-out booth, box, or a classroom area like an empty closet, cubicle, or book room is used, it must be safe, free of all distractions and reinforcers, and properly heated, cooled, and ventilated.

In some schools, teachers mistakenly think they are using time-out when they send an inappropriately behaving student to the principal's or counselor's office or they the student in the hall. While these two approaches are not inherently problematic for certain inappropriate behaviors and for certain students, they are not time-out.

Required interactions. This strategy requires inappropriately behaving students to meet with others to discuss their inappropriate behaviors. Joan could be required to meet with Carol if Joan's inappropriate behavior involved Carol. She could also be required to meet with her teacher, the administrator, the counselor, the school psychologist, the attendance officer, other school personnel, or with her parents at school. For many students, having to discuss their inappropriate behavior and meet with others is perceived as unpleasant; therefore, this strategy is often quite effective for preventing the re-occurrence of the inappropriate behavior.

Satiation. The use of satiation as a non-physical form of punishment is not to be confused with the concept of satiation presented in the context of reinforcer use, selection, and delivery. In that context, satiation refers to a reinforcer losing its effectiveness because it is repeatedly used.

Satiation is an effective strategy that teachers can use to get students to stop inappropriate behaviors. Sometimes satiation as a punishment strategy is also referred to as *flooding*. Satiation is essentially insisting that students continue the inappropriate behavior until they are tired of the repeated performance of the behavior. For example, students who write notes at inappropriate times in class or hurl paper airplanes can have their behaviors modified by being required to write many notes or fold numerous paper airplanes. The teacher or the student should provide the necessary paper or supplies. Effective teachers use satiation only with behaviors that, when repeatedly performed, are not physically or emotionally harmful or dangerous to the student or to others.

The satiation strategy should not be used at a time when repetition of the inappropriate behavior interferes with class activities. And again, effective teachers ignore students' non-interfering, harmless, mildly inappropriate behaviors until they stop.

Reprimands. Reprimands are an expression of disapproval about a student's inappropriate behavior. A reprimand is usually a verbal statement, but it is often accompanied by a disapproving gesture such as shaking a finger or nodding behaviors that indicate, "Stop it." Combining a reprimanding verbal statement with a disapproving gesture or other action is typically more effective than using a verbal statement by itself. Reprimands are easy to deliver immediately after the occurrence of an inappropriate behavior, and they require little or no preparation.

Effective teachers know that reprimanding the inappropriately behaving student quietly and privately is more effective than loud, public reprimands. Woolfolk (1995) points out, "Some students enjoy public recognition for their misbehavior. Perhaps public condemnation encourages a student to save face by having the last word" (p. 218).

Effective teachers avoid the circuitous "criticism trap" that can occur with the use of reprimands. For example, Mrs. White says, "Sit down," and Mary does. Mrs. White is immediately reinforced for having attended to Mary when she was behaving inappropriately. Repeated instances of this, coupled with Mrs. White's non-reinforcement of Mary's in-seat behavior, often will result in Mrs. White continuing to respond to Mary's out-of-seat behavior. Mrs. White is now a victim of a trap her behaviors created, a trap from which she needs to extricate herself.

Axelrod (1983) presents this similar caution about using reprimands. "Reprimands are a form of attention. If reprimands are the only form of attention a student receives, or if they are lengthy explanations and discussion, they can serve to reinforce rather than punish an undesirable behavior. To avoid this problem, reprimands should be brief and incisive and should be combined with approval for appropriate behavior" (p. 34).

Effective teachers give reprimands in a calm but firm tone of voice. The focus of the reprimand should be on the behavior. The reprimand should not label the student or attack the student personally. Effective teachers avoid the use of labels altogether. Labels can be remarkably enduring: many negatively labeled students work to honor their assigned roles ("class clown" or "troublemaker"), while positively labeled students may find their labels ("genius" or "math whiz") frustrating and stressful to repeatedly measure up to.

Response cost. Response cost entails removing a reinforcer, contingent upon the occurrence of an inappropriate behavior. It is similar to the loss of privileges strategy. Inappropriately behaving students are denied free time, working with a group, eating with their friends, going on a class trip, or some other reinforcer because of their inappropriate behavior.

Response cost can be used with individual students as well as with groups of students. It is an easily applied procedure than can produce an immediate and significant decrease in the frequency of occurrence of inappropriate behaviors. It takes little time to administer, does not disrupt ongoing activities, and typically does not require the inappropriately behaving student to leave the classroom.

Penalties. A penalty is essentially a punishment, a negative or unfavorable consequence that is delivered as a result of inappropriate behavior. Penalties can successfully deter students' repeated violations of rules and procedures. Penalties can be delivered for all types of student behaviors: aggression, noncompliance with behavioral rules, incomplete, missing, or poorly done assignments, etc. Penalties can take many forms, and this category of nonphysical punishers overlaps with other forms of non-physical punishment. Several examples of penalties—a reduction in score or grade, loss of privileges, fines, demerits, detention, referral to the principal, and confiscation—are briefly discussed below.

Effective teachers inform their students of what the penalties are and how they will be delivered. Effective teachers plan how they will use penalties. They select penalties that are appropriate for the offense, and they deliver penalties in a uniform and consistent manner. Effective teachers select penalties that are related to the inappropriate behavior and that are reasonable in their degree and amount relative to the inappropriate behavior. Effective teachers use penalties sparingly and mostly as deterrents to students' inappropriate behaviors; instead, they rely on reinforcement and encouragement to maintain students' appropriate behaviors.

When students turn in their assignments, they should get immediate feedback for their work. If a student repeatedly turns in late, incomplete, or poorly done work, two penalties teachers commonly use are reducing the score or grade for that assignment and/or keeping the student after school to complete the work. Reducing a student's score or grade can dampen a student's enthusiasm and motivation; therefore this technique should be used sparingly, mostly for repeated offenses, purposefully sloppy work, or lackadaisical effort. With ongoing or repeated inappropriate behaviors, the effective teacher contacts the student's parents. Keeping a student after school or in Saturday detention to complete the work is often very effective, but it is impractical without parental cooperation and often their transportation (e.g., for bussed students).

The penalties, loss of privileges, fines, and demerits should be used when students repeatedly violate rules and procedures, particularly if their behaviors indicate a willful refusal to comply with reasonable requests. Loss of privileges is a particularly effective penalty because of the logical relationship between the inappropriate behavior and the lost privilege. For example, a student who abuses laboratory or athletic equipment is denied access to the equipment for a period of time. If the student repeatedly abuses the equipment, two or more penalties could be used for a more powerful impact on behavior: The student loses the right to use the equipment for the first infraction; for repeated infractions, the student loses the use of the equipment and also experiences another penalty.

Fines and demerits can also be utilized for students' repeated violations of some classroom rule or procedure, like continued talk that disrupts instruction, wandering around the room, not working on task, or otherwise disturbing other students. A fine is a penalty that requires some sort of financial or non-financial "payment" or "service." In schools the "payment" has traditionally been repetitious work such as copying sentences, spelling words, multiplication tables, or other material that has low intrinsic interest so the copying work is distasteful. The repetitive work should be nonacademic in nature so that students do not associate spelling or multiplication with drudgery. Service or student labor activities serve as good fines.

The traditional demerit system uses a check mark or a demerit to record each incidence of inappropriate student behavior. The first demerit often serves as a warning to students, and the accumulation of additional demerits causes an additional penalty to be levied. Since the focus of a demerit system is on inappropriate behavior, it is recommended that it not be used alone, but in conjunction with a point, star, or token economy that recognizes and reinforces appropriate behavior. Effective teachers often report the demerits to parents.

Effective teachers limit the use of fines and demerits to easily observable behaviors that represent major infractions of rules and procedures. Effective teachers realize that fines and demerits must be used consistently, which requires that they immediately identify students' inappropriate behaviors when they occur. Effective teachers attend to significant and important behaviors. Effective teachers make every effort to periodically and frequently reinforce students' appropriate behaviors, rather than attending only to students' inappropriate behaviors with the use of punishment.

Detention requires that the inappropriately behaving student spends time before school, after school, on Saturdays, or in a designated school area such as an assembly or other room that is monitored by school personnel. During this time the student is expected to work on an academic task. Parents have to be notified of the use of detention so they can make transportation arrangements. Saturday detention should not be used with students whose religions prohibit Saturday school attendance.

Referral to the principal is similar to required interactions. It is a penalty that is best reserved for students' serious and repeated infractions of rules and procedures. Some school policies require that the inappropriately behaving student meet with the principal, school counselor or psychologist, with or without their parents present, before they are permitted to return to the classroom.

Confiscation occurs when students lose possession of items that are forbidden on school property, such as weapons, guns, knives, alcohol, tobacco, and gang or drug- related paraphernalia. The confiscation, storage, and disposal of such items has to be done in strict accordance with school and district policies, and teachers must be fully aware of what those policies require. Confiscation should also be used with students' possessions that, if retained by them, typically serve as competing events to their working on task. Items such as comic books, trading cards, and toys may have to be taken from students if they are distracting students from working on task. They should be returned to the students at the end of class or at the end of the day.

Conflict resolution and **peer mediation** are two approaches effective teachers use to help students resolve their conflicts peacefully and constructively. They are processes that allow school personnel to establish a school environment that is calm, safe, comfortable, and conducive to learning. *Conflict resolution* refers to various methods and strategies that allow people to interact with each other in positive ways to resolve their differences. *Peer mediation* refers to programs that are based on a foundation of applied conflict resolution. Both techniques empower students to share the responsibility for creating a safe and secure school environment. Trained student-mediators help their peers learn how to take responsibility for their behaviors and to solve their problems.

There are many similarities between conflict resolution and peer mediation. They are both problem-solving processes that involve a neutral third party who guides the disputants to a mutually satisfactory resolution. Initially, trust is established and the structure and definition of the problem are defined in terms of each disputant's perspective. Then these processes utilize fact-finding, isolation of the issues, and identification of options and alternatives for solution. The options are then evaluated, issues are clarified, and a written implementation plan is developed. Resolution review and processing occur next, and the last stages involve the implementation of the agreement, evaluation of the results, review and revision as necessary, and discussion of the entire experience.

The most essential component of conflict resolution and peer mediation programs is the instruction of students regarding conflict management skills. Peer mediators are trained to listen, and they act as a neutral third party to help disputants work out their disagreement. Hereford (1993) provides these suggestions concerning the active listening skills that peer mediators need. We believe they are effective management and listening strategies for teachers:

- be committed to understand what is said;
- move away from distractions (noise, music, people watching);
- maintain eye contact;
- lean slightly toward the person speaking;
- acknowledge the speaker by smiling or nodding;
- listen for the main idea;
- clarify by asking questions and to get more information about events and feelings;
- restate in your own words what the speaker says;
- summarize what you hear to assure the speaker that you understand what has been said;
- do not interrupt or give advice; and
- do not interject your own feelings or experiences.

Various model conflict resolution and peer mediation programs provide manuals that specifically and thoroughly explain the processes used for resolution or mediation. Generally speaking, students and teachers are encouraged to listen to each other carefully and to be fair, respectful, and honest in their interactions. Student mediators are instructed to lead the mediation privately and confidentially and not to place blame, take sides, or give advice. Resolution and mediation should occur during non-academic school time such as recess, lunch, or free time. Students' participation in conflict resolution and peer mediation activities is strictly voluntary; if the conflicting parties do not wish to participate in these activities, school authorities intervene with established disciplinary measures.

Generally speaking, students, faculty, counselors, and administrators who have utilized conflict resolution and peer mediation programs report decreased pressure on teachers to serve as disciplinarians and increased opportunities for students to develop and use creative solutions to disputes. Peer mediators learn and develop leadership skills and enhanced communication and problem-solving skills. Students become actively involved in the problem-solving process. They assume greater responsibility for solving their own problems, and they recognize that adult intervention in their disputes may not always be necessary. Many programs report success as measured by the decrease in number of student conflicts and the decrease in the number of conflicts referred to the principal. Furthermore, there may be carry-over to students' home situations, wherein parents and their children become more effective at resolving conflicts.

THE SCHOOL COUNSELOR

Teachers' instructional and management efforts can be enhanced if they utilize the services of other professionals. A multi-disciplinary approach typically increases the chance of teacher success because of the different perspectives and expertise each professional brings to a particular problem. Teachers often confer with fellow teachers, school administrators, and parents. They may refer students to nurses, physicians, optometrists, dentists, or psychologists. They may consult with social workers, special educators, speech therapists and others–like the school counselor.

Teachers can and should seek assistance for their management efforts from the school counselor. School counselors have expertise counseling, conferencing, referring, consulting, and in testing and interpreting standardized test scores. The school counselor is an invaluable resource to teachers and parents. A brief description of the school counselor's functions follows.

Harlan (1996) indicates that school counselors use their training and skills to help students to become better adjusted, to understand developmental issues in their lives, and to understand themselves better. The relationship between a student and a counselor is confidential, and it provides an environment in which a student feels free to discuss personal issues without censure. This confidential relationship is necessary so that a student does not feel inhibited to discuss any issue, no matter how personal or sensitive.

Younger students typically need more direct assistance with developmental issues such as how to get along with peers, how to make the transition from home to school, how to survive in a classroom with 20 or more other students, and how to contend with the normal stressors of functioning in a structured environment. Preschool and elementary age children, when placed in the school environment, typically have not had the experience of having to respond to adult authority other than their parents, and they often have problems adapting to the school environment. The school counselor has the best vantage point to serve as an advocate for children and for helping them learn to cope with and adapt to their new environment.

In order for the school counselor to be successful with students, the counselor needs to be viewed by students as a friend and a confidant whom they can seek out on demand. Children and other individuals typically do not have an adequate concept of the counselor's roles and function. Therefore, it is imperative that counselors spend the time and energy necessary to help students, teachers, administrators, parents, and others understand their roles. Teachers need to help students to understand and value school counselors and the services they can provide.

Middle school students typically present a different set of developmental problems. They are growing and developing rapidly, both physically and emotionally. Physical growth changes are accompanied by many emotional responses to growing up. Like younger children, children at this stage need assistance adjusting to the challenges and demands made by school and by their peers. Societal influences, which range from the prevalence of gangs and drugs to abusive, dysfunctional, or unsupportive family members, further add to the myriad of possible adjustment problems facing this, or for that matter any age student.

The counselor's role changes with high school students because students in this age group are in a transition from adolescent concerns to the problems of young adulthood. They are also in the process of making lifelong choices and decisions. Counseling high school students presents the counselor with the challenge of helping them learn to cope with adult problems and to navigate the challenges of peer group pressures. High school students are confronted with the pressures and stresses of the transition from the adolescent world to the adult world. High school students are attempting to establish themselves in adult roles of learning so they can begin to independently and effectively manage their lives. Since these individuals are also confronted with the developmental problem of making major, possibly irrevocable, choices, this is typically a highly stressful period for these students and for their teachers and parents.

Teachers and school counselors have the training and expertise to view and evaluate students' school behaviors. These professionals spend more time interacting with students during the school year than any other group of school personnel. Their observations of students' behaviors, and their combined skills, expertise, and abilities place them in the best position to construct, implement, and refine educational and behavior management programs.

School counselors also perform a vital role in helping parents understand the behavior of their children. Effective counselors are accessible to parents, and they are non-threatening in their interactions with them. Effective school counselors help parents understand the cognitive, emotional, and social development of their children.

In their referral role, school counselors have contacts with other treatment professionals who are trained to handle problems beyond the scope of their training. Referral sources include the following agencies and services: mental health centers, employment service counselors, learning development centers, physicians, social service agencies, legal services, and many other human service agencies.

The magnitude of problems facing students, teachers, administrators, and parents mandates the use of a multidisciplinary approach. To achieve instructional and management effectiveness and to ensure that all students grow and develop properly, effective teachers avail themselves of the skills and expertise of school counselors.

SUMMARY OF KEY CONCEPTS IN CHAPTER 7

1. An effective management strategy is a combination of reinforcement for appropriate behavior and extinction for inappropriate behavior.
2. Punishment should be used only when reinforcement and extinction procedures have been tried and have failed to produce the desired results.
3. Punishment should be used only as a last resort.
4. Punishment can involve the application of an aversive consequence, or it can involve the withdrawal of a favored event or reinforcer. In either case, the consequences must decrease the rate of the target

behavior in order to be considered punishment.

5. Punishment focuses on inappropriate behavior or what not to do. It is a negatively oriented procedure that is inefficient for teaching a new or appropriate behavior.

6. Punishment works unpredictably, and its use may actually increase rather than decrease the frequency of occurrence of an undesirable behavior.

7. Punishment decreases a teacher's reinforcing value.

8. Punishment promotes avoidance behaviors such as lying, sneaking, hiding, concealing, and skipping school.

9. Punishment is often harmful to a student's self-image.

10. The frequent use of punishment often results in students disliking school and the teacher and in the student becoming sullen, negative, withdrawn, and antagonistic.

11. Physical punishment models aggressive behavior.

12. Physical punishment is considered by many to be inhumane, and it is often unjustly administered.

13. The effective use of punishment requires that it be delivered consistently, immediately, and contingent upon a student's inappropriate behavior.

14. There are several common forms of nonphysical punishment: loss of privileges, the correction procedure, the over-correction procedure, time-out, isolation, exclusion, non-exclusion, required interactions, satiation, reprimands, response cost, penalties, conflict resolution, and peer mediation.

15. Loss of preferred activities or privileges, lost or delayed use of objects or equipment, and lost or delayed access to special school areas serve as punishers for many students.

16. When loss of privileges is the punishment strategy selected, teachers must be sure that the consequences are related, reasonable, and respectful.

17. The correction procedure requires an inappropriately behaving student to make amends for their inappropriate behavior.

18. The over-correction procedure requires inappropriately behaving students not only to make amends or make restitution for their inappropriate behaviors, but to go one step further, typically requiring further time, effort, service, or money.

19. Both the correction and the over-correction procedures essentially require that the inappropriately behaving student restore something back to its original state prior to the vandalism or other inappropriate behavior.

20. Time-out is an extension of the idea of non-reinforcement, wherein the inappropriately behaving student is removed from the setting that is reinforcing the inappropriate behavior and is placed in a different setting that is not at all reinforcing.

21. There are three types of time-out: isolation, exclusion, and non-exclusion.

22. Isolation requires the temporary removal of the inappropriately behaving student from the classroom.

23. Exclusion requires the inappropriately behaving student to remain in the classroom, but the student is required to sit apart, away, or is otherwise excluded from contact with other students.

24. Non-exclusion limits the extent of the inappropriately behaving student's involvement in ongoing activities.

25. The amount of time the inappropriately behaving student spends in any form of time-out should not exceed in minutes the student's age in years and should never exceed 30 minutes.

26. The required interactions form of non-physical punishment requires inappropriately behaving students to meet with someone—other students, the teacher, an administrator, the counselor, their parents, or possibly other school personnel—to discuss their inappropriate behavior.

27. The satiation strategy consists of having inappropriately behaving students continue the inappropriate behavior until they are tired of it.

28. Reprimands are an expression of disapproval for a student's inappropriate behavior.

29. Reprimands should be delivered in a calm but firm tone of voice, and they should be given quietly and privately to the inappropriately behaving student.

30. Penalties are negative or unfavorable consequences that result when students behave inappropriately.

31. Examples of penalties are a reduction in score or grade, loss of privileges, fines, demerit, detention, referral to the principal, and confiscation.

32. Teachers must be fully informed regarding school and district policies concerning weapons, guns, knives, alcohol, tobacco, and gang or drug-related paraphernalia.

33. Conflict resolution refers to various methods and strategies that allow people to interact with each other in positive ways to resolve their differences.

34. Peer mediation programs are based on a foundation of applied conflict resolution, and they empower students to share the responsibilities for creating a safe and secure school environment.

35. School counselors, who have expertise in counseling, conferencing, referral, and consulting, are an invaluable resource to teachers and parents.

REFERENCES

Allen, R. B. (1988). *Classroom common sense discipline.* Tyler, TX: Common Sense Publications.

Bercovitz, J. (1984). *Social conflicts and third parties.* Boulder, CO: Westview Press.

Carson, J. C., & Carson, P. (1984). *Any teacher can! Practical strategies for effective classroom management.* Springfield, IL: Charles C Thomas.

Evertson, C. M., Emmer, E. T., Clements, B. S., Sanford, J. P., & Worsham, M. E. (1984). *Classroom management for elementary teachers.* Englewood Cliffs, NJ: Prentice Hall.

Folberg, J., & Taylor, A. (1984). *Mediation: A comprehensive guide to resolving conflicts without litigation.* San Francisco: Josey-Bass.

Glass, J. (1993, August). Are you still wearing your childhood label? *Redbook,* 50–56.

Harlan, J. C. (1996). *Behavior management strategies for teachers.* Springfield, IL: Charles C Thomas.

Hereford, N. J. (1993, September). Kids helping kids. *Instructor: Middle Years,* 31–35.

Katz, N. H., & Lawyer, J. W. (1985). *Communication and conflict resolution skills.* Dubuque, IA: Kendall Hunt.

McGiboney, G. W. (1993, Spring). Developing a comprehensive school discipline program. *School Safety,* 15–17.

Miller, P. (1994). *The relative effectiveness of peer mediation: Children helping each other to solve conflicts.* Unpublished Dissertation, University of Mississippi.

Stomfay-Stitz, A. M. (1994). Conflict resolution and peer mediation: Pathways to safer schools. *Childhood Education, 70*(5), 279–282.

Stulberg, J. B. (1987). *Taking charge/managing conflict.* Lexington, MA: Heath and Company.

Walton, R. E. (1987). *Managing conflict.* Reading, MA: Addison-Wesley.

Woolfolk, A. (1995). *Educational Psychology.* Boston: Allyn and Bacon.

SUGGESTED ACTIVITIES/ASSIGNMENTS

1. Write recollections of teachers who appropriately utilized reinforcement for students' appropriate behaviors and extinction for students' inappropriate behaviors.
2. Write recollections of teachers who over-utilized punishment for stu-

dents' inappropriate behaviors and under-utilized reinforcement for students appropriate behaviors.

3. Model the appropriate use of reprimands.
4. Demonstrate how teachers can inadvertently fall victim to, "the criticism trap."
5. Poll elementary, junior high, and high school students about what school privileges they enjoy and would rather not lose as punishment.
6. Explain which punishment techniques their teachers used with them and whether they were effective or ineffective and why.
7. Design a model time-out program.
8. Give an in-school example of the effective use of the correction procedure or the over-correction procedure.
9. Research referral options to other professionals in the community.
10. Role-play a conflict resolution or peer mediation approach with emphasis on the necessary skills for effective and active listening.
11. Interview principals about what they do when inappropriately behaving students are referred to their office.
12. Read and critique journal articles about the use of time-out.
13. Read and report on articles in popular publications, magazines, and newspapers that relate to the use of time-out.
14. Read and critique journal articles related to different approaches to conflict resolution and peer mediation.
15. Interview a counselor to learn more about how counselors can help teachers in their instructional and management efforts.

Section III

THE BASICS OF
CLASSROOM MANAGEMENT

Chapter 8

THE EFFECTIVE TEACHER

There are numerous traits, human relations skills, dispositions, and behaviors that effective teachers cultivate, refine, and utilize as they attempt to instruct students, effectively manage their students' behaviors, and establish a motivating, positive, friendly, nurturing, success-oriented classroom atmosphere. There are also numerous traits and behaviors that effective teachers refrain from. This chapter describes those traits and behaviors that teachers should adopt and those they should avoid; thus, it also provides suggestions for establishing a classroom atmosphere that facilitates students' learning and appropriate behaviors. The traits and behaviors are not presented in any order of importance or priority because their value will vary with the specifics of a classroom, the teacher, the students, and their behaviors.

THE TRAITS AND BEHAVIORS OF EFFECTIVE TEACHERS

Self efficacy. Self-efficacy is an expectancy construct initially discussed by Bandura (1986) and then more recently investigated by Gibson and Dembo (1984) and Emmer and Hickman (1991). Bandura (1986) defined *self-efficacy* as "A judgement of one's capability to accomplish a certain level of performance " (p. 391). It is important to consider the construct of self-efficacy relative to classroom management because as Page (1994) indicated, "These expectations influence thoughts and feelings, choices of instructional activities, amounts of effort expended, and the extent of persistence in the face of obstacles" (p. 47).

A brief digression concerning the use of expectations: We generally, perhaps somewhat idealistically, discourage teachers from having preconceived notions or expectations about their behaviors or about their students' behaviors. But, in reality, teachers and students will all have some preconceived notions or expectations. That being the case, we strongly encourage teachers and students to have only positive rather than negative expectations for their own behaviors and for the behaviors of others. We remind the reader of the importance of positive expectations with respect to the construct of self-efficacy, and later on in this chapter relative to establishing a motivating, positive, friendly, nurturing, success-oriented classroom atmosphere.

The following 36 teacher efficacy items are from Emmer and Hickman's (1991) instrument, *The Scale for Measuring Teacher Efficacy in Classroom Management and Discipline*. Each of the 36 items relates to one of three efficacy factors that the scale covers: (1) classroom management and discipline efficacy items; (2) external influences efficacy items; and (3) personal teaching efficacy items. Each item is important; the different items have different correlational strengths related to management effectiveness, and the items are inter-related.

Effective teachers analyze the expectations they have for themselves and for their students. They objectively assess themselves and their behaviors for self- improvement. We suggest, therefore, that teachers assess themselves on the Emmer and Hickman instrument, presented below. The assessment can best be done by using the five-point response format ranging from very unlikely to very likely, as utilized in the original Emmer and Hickman research. Once teachers complete the assessment, they gain insight into what they expect their effectiveness to be as they attempt to manage and teach students.

1. When a student does better than usual, many times it is because I exerted a little extra effort.
2. If a student in my class becomes disruptive and noisy, I feel assured that I know some techniques to redirect him quickly.
3. The hours in my class have little influence on students compared to the influence of their home environment.
4. I find it easy to make my expectations clear to students.
5. I know what routines are needed to keep activities running efficiently.
6. There are some students who won't behave, no matter what I do.
7. I can communicate to students that I am serious about getting appropriate behavior.
8. If one of my students couldn't do an assignment, I would be able to accurately assess whether it was at the correct level of difficulty.
9. I know what kinds of rewards to use to keep students involved.
10. If students aren't disciplined at home, they aren't likely to accept it at school.
11. There are very few students that I don't know how to handle.
12. If a student doesn't feel like behaving, there's not a lot teachers can

do about it.

13. When a student is having trouble with an assignment, I am usually able to adjust it to his or her level.

14. Student misbehavior that persists over a long time is partly a result of what the teacher does or doesn't do.

15. Student behavior in classrooms is more influenced by peers than by the teacher.

16. When a student gets a better grade than usual, it is probably because I found better ways of teaching that student.

17. I don't always know how to keep track of several activities at once.

18. When I really try, I can get through to most difficult students.

19. I am unsure how to respond to defiant students.

20. A teacher is very limited in what can be achieved because a student's home environment is a large influence on achievement.

21. I find some students impossible to discipline effectively.

22. When the grades of my students improve, it is usually because I found more effective teaching approaches.

23. Sometimes I am not sure what rules are appropriate for my students.

24. If a student masters a new concept quickly, this might be because I knew the necessary steps in teaching the concept.

25. The amount that a student can learn is primarily related to family background.

26. I can keep a few problem students from ruining an entire class.

27. If parents would do more with their children at home, I could do more with them in the classroom.

28. If students stop working in class, I can usually find a way to get them back on track.

29. If a student did not remember information I gave in a previous lesson, I would know how to increase his or her retention in the next lesson.

30. Home and peer influences are mainly responsible for student behavior in school.

31. Teachers have little effect on stopping misbehavior when parents don't cooperate.

32. The influences of a student's home experiences can be overcome by good teaching.

33. Even a teacher with good teaching abilities may not reach many students.

34. Compared to other influences on student behavior, teachers' effects are very small.

35. I am confident of my ability to begin the year so that students will learn to behave well.

36. I have very effective classroom management skills.

Here are two examples of how to analyze responses to this scale. Example 1: Ms. Tucker gives consistent responses of "very likely" or "likely" to Items 3, 6,10, 12, 29, 21, 25, 27, 30, 31, and 34. The response pattern indicates a resigned, defeatist, negative attitude about her expectations; therefore, there is a lesser likelihood that she will successfully teach and manage certain students. By contrast, if Ms. Tucker gives consistent responses of "very unlikely" or "unlikely" to these same items, the response pattern indicates a proactive, take-charge, positive attitude about her expectations; therefore, there is a greater likelihood that she will successfully teach and manage certain students. Example 2: Mr. Saunders gives consistent responses of "very likely" or "likely" to Items 2, 4, 7, 9, 11, 26, 35, and 36. The response pattern indicates his confidence in his ability to convey expectations about appropriate behavior and to use rewards and other effective management strategies. By contrast, if Mr. Saunders gives consistent responses of "very unlikely" or "unlikely" to these same items, the response pattern indicates his lack of confidence in his ability to manage students' behaviors.

Caring, compassionate, and positive. Effective teachers respond to students in ways that reflect that they care or are concerned about them, and they interact with students kindly, compassionately, and positively. They foster students' positive self- concepts, and they hold high positive expectations for their students' academic successes. They use encouragement and praise more than reprimands and criticism. Effective teachers convey to students that they have confidence in their abilities. They refrain from sarcasm, ridicule, verbal abuse, and negative comments that only serve to damage a student's self-esteem and reinforce any low opinions that students may have of themselves. When teachers are caring, compassionate, and positive in their interactions with students, they create a motivating, positive, friendly, nurturing, success-oriented classroom atmosphere that is conducive to students' achievement and likely to result in students' appropriate behaviors.

Effective teachers are friendly, and they project understanding, warmth, consideration, and a positive attitude that contributes to students' productive work. Friendliness dispels students' perceptions of feeling threatened or fearful; thus it often increases students' willingness to attempt difficult or intimidating tasks. Effective teachers are understanding and empathetic with those students who are experiencing personal problems, traumatic occurrences, or illnesses.

Effective teachers establish the importance of every student in the classroom by stating and repeating to students that they are worthy, prized, important, and that all students will be treated fairly. They give regular attention to every student by speaking personally and positively with each student every day. Effective teachers do whatever it takes to assist students to feel that they belong in the class as valued and integral participants.

Effective teachers emphasize students' successes. Success is highly rewarding and motivating for building students' positive self-concepts. It is important that every student experience success, especially that which comes from diligent effort. Students' feelings of importance will increase as they experience success, assume responsibilities in the classroom, and receive deserved acknowledgment from others.

Effective teachers establish rapport with students. Effective teachers address students by name and with respect. They are sincere in their attempts to assist students with their problems, and they let students know that they care about and are interested in them. Effective teachers also know that students whose teachers are interested in knowing more about them tend to do better academically than students whose teachers do not know them as well.

Albert (1995) emphasizes the importance of teachers caring about their students, making students feel that they are capable, and helping students to become an integral and important part of the class and school. She indicates that, "Students don't care what you know until they know that you care. Often behind the refusal to learn and disruptive behavior is the perception that nobody cares" (p. 7).

Effective teachers help students feel they are of value, competent, and that they have some control. **To help students feel they are of value, effective teachers do the following**: they listen attentively to what students say; they ask students for suggestions; they help students identify their appropriate behaviors; and they value and celebrate the differences among students.

To help students feel they are competent, effective teachers do the following: they provide activities and experiences that students are successful with; they provide students with challenges and praise their attempts and improvements; they instruct students with strategies that allow them to succeed; and they allow students to carry out and complete tasks by themselves.

To help students feel they have some control, effective teachers do the following: they provide students with opportunities for choice, initiative, and autonomy; they avoid the use of overly competitive activities; they avoid comparing students to each other; and they help students to constructively evaluate their accomplishments.

To create a motivating, positive, friendly, nurturing, success-oriented classroom atmosphere, caring, compassionate, and positive teachers make sure that the assigned work is interesting rather than boring. Effective teachers use teaching methods that accommodate all students' needs; they avoid the use of coercive methods which often fail; they make students feel important; and when criticism is necessary they do it constructively rather than personally or with hostility. Effective teachers consider the needs and abilities of their students when they plan instructional strategies, and they are as concerned about increasing their students' self-esteem as they are about increasing their students' knowledge.

Effective teachers assume a caring and compassionate responsibility for students' learning, and they value academic achievement. They realize that effective teaching is not just a matter of knowing, it is a matter of communicating what is known. Effective teachers are not only well-grounded in their subject area(s), but they also have broad interests and are widely read. Effective teachers are thoroughly prepared; they use well-planned lessons, and they prepare their instructional materials in advance. Their plans are clear, specific, and in writing, and they provide directions for instruction and management for use by substitute teachers.

Effective teachers show students a continual willingness to help them. They are accessible and supportive of students' achievement and their efforts at improvement. **Effective teachers use these techniques to foster students' participation in class**: they encourage students to comment or question; they sincerely and generously praise students' participation; they present challenging and thought-provoking ideas; they use a variety of instructional methods, materials, and media; they ask rhetorical questions; they call on students and acknowledge every student's response; they keep current and relevant on the material presented; and they minimally and constructively criticize students' errors. Effective, caring, and compassionate teachers also refrain from sarcastic, ridiculing, or humiliating comments that serve no positive purpose, often alienating students and resulting in a negative, unpleasant, failure-oriented classroom atmosphere.

Effective teachers make sure that students have ample time to accomplish successfully the learning objectives. They provide appropriate instruction, and they use re-teaching, remedial work, and enrichment activities with all students. Effective teachers also have emergency plans of meaningful and interesting back-up activities that can be used on rainy days or for sudden and unexpected schedule changes.

Carson and Carson (1984) discuss how teachers' expectations, their response styles, and the self-fulfilling prophecy—all of which are related to caring and compassion—should be used to establish a motivating, positive, friendly, nurturing, success-oriented classroom atmosphere. Expectations are thoughts or presumptions about something likely to occur. Expectations impact behavior, and positive expectations are preferable to negative expectations. Teachers' positive expectations for students help students to succeed. Teachers' fatalistic expectations that students will fail or behave inappropriately are often responsible for students behaving in ways that confirm these expectations. Of course, teachers should also refrain from having or conveying confining, unfair sexist, racist, or other stereotyped behavioral expectations. Rationalizing students' behaviors on the basis of their race or sex is discriminatory, unfair to the uniqueness of each student, in direct conflict with the concepts of caring and compassion, and educationally unsound and counter- productive to effective instruction and management.

Effective teachers have high expectations for all students. Effective teachers have realistic and positive expectations about students' behaviors which are conveyed to students with praise, encouragement, and, if necessary, additional reinforcement. Effective teachers sincerely praise students when they have done well, because praise is motivational, and it recognizes students' efforts and improvements. Effective teachers give positive feedback that specifically describes students' accomplishments. Similarly, encouragement motivates students' progress and their efforts at improvement, and it should be used to help students to continue to persist on difficult tasks.

Teachers' response styles to students and their behaviors can foster or impede the establishment of a motivating, positive, friendly, nurturing, success-oriented classroom atmosphere. Canter and Canter (1976), Carson and Carson (1984) and others identify three common teacher response styles, though there are differences in the terminology used. The three teacher response styles are: (1) assertive; (2) aggressive or hostile; and (3) non-assertive or passive. The only response style appropriate for teacher use is the assertive style.

Assertive Teachers

Assertive teachers are neither aggressive towards students nor are they insensitive to students' needs for warmth and positive support. Assertive teachers are caring and compassionate by recognizing students' psychological and emotional needs, yet they also realize that students require adult guidance for proper socialization. Assertive teachers avoid establishing vague and subjective rules and procedures. Assertive teachers set firm and consistent limits while at the same time remaining cognizant of the students' needs for warmth and positive support.

Aggressive Teachers

Aggressive or hostile teachers are harsh with students, and they are viewed by students as insensitive and inattentive to their needs. Aggressive teacher behavior is uncaring and uncompassionate, and it typically stymies or entirely cuts off productive communications and interactions between teachers and students. Aggressive behaviors usually put down or are otherwise abusive of others, and therefore they are totally inappropriate behaviors for teachers.

Non-Assertive or Passive Teachers

Similarly, non-assertive or passive behaviors are inappropriate for teachers to use with students. While non-assertive teachers may appear to be well-meaning in their interactions with students, they often lose control of the classroom to their students because they fail to set proper limits on students' behaviors. Non-assertive teachers often fail to effectively communicate their behavioral expectations to students. Typically, non-assertive teachers also fail to support their words with appropriate actions; if they neglect to provide appropriate consequences for behavior, they will relinquish control of the classroom to the students. Many non-assertive teachers fall victim to their own benign neglect, and they typically spend more time lamenting about students' inappropriate behaviors than they spend taking the initiative to prevent students' inappropriate behaviors.

The Self-fulfilling Prophecy. The self-fulfilling prophecy and one's impression about oneself significantly influence students' motivation, learning, behavior, and the establishment of a motivating, positive, friendly, nurturing, success-oriented classroom atmosphere. The self-fulfilling prophecy quite simply means that people behave the way they do because of the expectations they and others have for their behaviors. The self-fulfilling prophecy establishes an inextricable connection between expectations about behavior and the behavior itself. The self-fulfilling prophecy is responsible for students behaving or performing as expected. For example, if Judy hears her parent or teacher say, "Girls have trouble with arithmetic," she may passively accept her poor performance in arithmetic. This will be especially true if the negative expectations are frequently expressed, and if Judy has a negative sense of self, she may resignedly quit trying to improve. Conversely, if Josh hears his dad say, "I was always good in arithmetic," Josh may be overzealously motivated to meet or exceed his dad's reported arithmetic performances.

Clarity, Firmness, and Communication. Kounin (1970), Evertson and Emmer (1982, 1984), Jones and Jones (1995), and many others have written about the importance of teachers using clarity and firmness to respond effectively to students' inappropriate behaviors which, if not dealt with early on, often lead to further and widening management problems ("desist incidents"). *Clarity* refers to the methods used to explain or communicate content concepts, principles, skills, and ideas. It also refers to the degree to which a teacher specifies what is appropriate or inappropriate behavior. When a teacher says, "Stop that," it is often vague and unclear to students who maybe simultaneously performing a number of behaviors. A better statement, one which has clarity, would be, "Please do not sharpen your pencil while I am talking."

Firmness is the degree to which the teacher communicates, "I mean it." When a teacher says, "Please don't do that," it conveys less firmness than, "I absolutely will not tolerate that (behavior specified) from you." Obviously, the degree of firmness used or required will depend on the age of the students, the frequency with which the inappropriate behavior has occurred, and the seriousness or harmfulness of the inappropriate behaviors. Effective teachers are firm without being rough, hostile, or aggressive.

Effective teachers realize that there are many ways to enhance clarity and to firmly communicate to students about their behaviors. The suggestions that follow are generally effective with all students, but they should be modified as necessary to fit the specifics of a particular classroom, the students, and their behaviors.

How to increase management effectiveness and firmly communicate to students about their behaviors:

- When a student is off task, effective teachers re-direct the student's attention to the task by using a clear and firm statement such as "Gail, you should be writing now." Gail's teacher should check her progress shortly thereafter to be sure that Gail is continuing to write.
- If a student is behaving inappropriately, effective teachers firmly and politely ask the student to stop the inappropriate behavior. They monitor the student until the student stops the inappropriate behavior and begins constructive activity. Effective teachers give students feedback about their behaviors, and they maintain contact with students until they behave appropriately.
- Effective teachers know that clarity, firmness, and communication are enhanced by (1) eye contact with the student whose behavior they are trying to impact, and (2) by moving closer to the student until appropriate behavior occurs.
- Effective teachers also use a signal, such as a finger to the lips or shaking their head, to prompt students to stop an inappropriate behavior and resume an appropriate behavior. Signals also increase the clarity and firmness of their communications. Effective teachers monitor students until they comply.
- If a student is not following a rule or a procedure correctly, effective teachers clarify and firmly remind the student of the rule or the correct procedure. Effective teachers either restate the procedure, have

another student remind the inappropriately behaving student of the correct rule or procedure, or ask the inappropriately behaving student to paraphrase the rule or procedure in his or her own words. When the student understands the rule or procedure and is not complying to receive attention or for some other reason, effective teachers impose a mild penalty, such as withholding a privilege, until the student behaves appropriately. The usual and related consequence for violation of a procedure or rule is to require the student to comply with the rule or to properly perform the procedure.

- Students' off-task behaviors frequently occur when they are engaged too long on unclear, boring, repetitive tasks or aimless recitations. Effective teachers know that sometimes simply clarifying what is expected, changing the activity to one requiring a different form of student response, injecting variety into seat work, or re-focusing a discussion can help stop widespread off-task behaviors.

- Effective teachers also know that clarity and firmness are enhanced by focusing on important rule infractions, such as dangerous or highly disruptive inappropriate behaviors. Effective teachers know the value and necessity of ignoring inappropriate behaviors that are of short duration, that are not likely to persist or spread, and that are only minor infractions of a rule or procedure. Teachers cannot and should not react to every single instance of student misbehavior, because if they do so, they unproductively interrupt the flow or momentum of the lesson, and their reactions to students' inappropriate behaviors often provide unnecessary attention to and reinforcement of those behaviors.

- Sometimes a student refuses to talk, looks angry, upset, anxious, or distracted, disengages from the group, or makes statements like "This is boring. Who need needs to learn this anyway?" Effective teachers clearly, firmly, and thoughtfully respond to such students by actively listening to them, and they identify the feelings students are experiencing. An effective teacher would respond with, "It sounds like you are frustrated with the work," or, "I would be angry too if I thought I was asked to do something I didn't think had been explained very well." If necessary, teachers can offer assistance by saying "Would you like me to explain it again?" Effective teachers also suggest a different learning strategy or a helpful resource when students are experiencing difficulties.

- Clarity and firmness are often enhanced when teachers communicate with an "I-message" to let students know that their behaviors are creating discomfort to the teacher or to the other students. An effective teacher might say, "I expect all students to make only positive comments to their classmates"; clarity is always enhanced when expectations, rules, and procedures are stated in the positive, for example, "We agreed during class discussions that students will talk only when called on so it is easier for everyone to hear and to understand each other."

- Finally, effective teachers clarify to students that it is their choice about how to behave, and they give their students space and time to make a choice. An effective teacher would firmly say, "Jeremy, remember our procedure for sharing ideas. I will call on you soon when your hand is raised, but if you talk out, we'll need to do some practice during recess."

Effective teaching and management requires the explanation of concepts, principles, skills, ideas, and behaviors. **The following strategies are recommended to enhance instructional clarity**. Effective teachers

- provide several clearly articulated examples of each concept.
- use concrete, everyday examples with which students can identify.
- carefully define new, unfamiliar, or complex terms.
- repeat difficult ideas several times with various and different explanations.
- explain key words, write new terms on the board or the overhead, and prepare handouts for complex or especially difficult material.
- emphasize important points through voice changes, such as modulation, inflection, and pausing.
- speak clearly, at an appropriate volume, and without mumbling or slurring their words.
- use graphs, diagrams, charts, pictures, photos, recordings, computer-assisted instruction, and any other media that facilitates transmission of the concept.
- explain the relevancy and applicability of content.
- use peer instruction, webbing, mapping, and other techniques to accommodate students with different learning styles and modality strengths.
- maintain lesson momentum by using appropriate pacing so students stay attentive and interested.
- periodically summarize the points made and review topics previously covered.
- avoid long periods of confusion and delay by using clear, smooth, and brief transitions between lessons and activities.
- avoid meaningless busywork and excessive, unnecessary homework.
- clearly state the objectives of their presentations and assignments.
- organize their presentations and handouts with headings, subheadings,

outlines, italics, emphases, and summaries.
- answer students' questions thoroughly and patiently.
- encourage and stimulate student thinking, problem solving, and questioning.
- refrain from dwelling excessively or over-explaining obvious points.
- avoid rambling and meaningless digressions from major themes, without sacrificing incidental learning opportunities.

Consistency, modeling, enthusiasm, planning, and humor.
Effective teachers are consistent with students so that students know what is expected of them. They follow through on their commitments; if they have promised a reinforcer for students' appropriate behaviors, they deliver the reinforcement as promised or very soon thereafter if circumstances prevent immediate delivery. Effective teachers also deliver punishment as "promised" for students' inappropriate behaviors.

Effective teachers have students make commitments to change their behaviors. The commitments can take the form of a handshake, a verbal agreement or, if necessary, a signed behavioral contract that specifies a behavior and its consequences.

Effective teachers model the behaviors that they expect from their students. Effective teachers model courtesy, good manners, respect, and other appropriate behaviors that they want their students to imitate. Effective teachers also refrain from sarcasm, hostility, favoritism, and other inappropriate behaviors or dispositions that students might imitate. Effective teachers also refrain from using distracting body language and other mannerisms and from dressing in ways that compete for students' attention.

Effective teachers are enthusiastic in a stable and ongoing manner throughout the course of the school day to solicit and maintain student attention and interest. Students of all ages typically react to teacher enthusiasm positively, because enthusiasm is motivating and energizing. Teacher enthusiasm is positively correlated with student achievement.

Teacher enthusiasm is also often contagious, and students become enthusiastic about what they are doing. Teachers' enthusiasm includes, but is not limited to, the following: making the teaching presentation in a dramatic, engaging, or otherwise expressive way; using gestures as appropriate but not as distractions; moving around the room and between the aisles when students are speaking; making eye contact with students; actively engaging students in class discussion; and punctuating academic content with appropriate jokes or humorous anecdotes.

Effective teachers devote time planning for the prevention of students' inappropriate behaviors. They are able to accurately spot students' inappropriate behaviors almost before they start, and they can deal with those behaviors while going right on with the lesson (Kounin's concepts of "with-itness" and "overlappingness," respectively). Effective teachers monitor their students so they are constantly aware of what is happening in all areas of the classroom and with all students.

Effective teachers plan for and teach their students to accept responsibility for their behaviors and for the roles they play in furthering their own learning as well as the learning of the class in general. Effective teachers hold students accountable for knowing what behaviors are appropriate or inappropriate. When students are given responsibilities and held accountable for their behaviors, they find a sense of purpose and often find the motivation to support the group's endeavors.

By planning management as well as instructional strategies, effective teachers can employ fair and realistic standards, rules, and procedures; the resulting classroom atmosphere is positive. Effective teachers consistently, frequently, and without bias or favoritism enforce their standards, rules, and procedures.

Effective teachers accept no excuses for students' inappropriate behaviors, and they do not let students exceed the acceptable limits of behavior. Effective teachers plan for the selection of consequences that are realistic, reasonable, and appropriate for the students' behaviors that they are trying to impact. They inform students of the consequences, and they make sure that students understand what the consequences are for behaving appropriately or inappropriately.

Lastly, effective teachers realize the value of humor to create a pleasant classroom environment. The injection of humor into instruction and into a teachers' interactions with students allows both the students and the teacher to have fun, and it enhances teacher–student rapport. Humor is the trait most often identified by older students when they are asked what they like most about their teachers. (Young children identify "niceness.") Students like to laugh, share jokes, and find humor in situations. The use of humor can diffuse stressful and difficult situations; it is therapeutic, and students appreciate teachers who make a humor a part of the classroom environment.

SPACE, SEATING ARRANGEMENTS, AND FURNITURE LOCATION

The way that space is used affects the learning atmosphere, influences classroom dialogue and communication, has important cognitive and emotional effects on students, and impacts a teacher's ability to manage students' behavior. Where the teacher's chair and desk are located, how and where students are seated for different subjects, assignments, and activities, and where tables, materials, computers, equipment, and bookcases are placed all contribute to facilitating or impeding progress toward a teacher's instructional and management goals.

A commonly used, traditional arrangement of students' desks and chairs is in rows and columns. This arrangement is best suited to situations where the teacher wants attention focused towards the board, the display, the teacher, a student, or another speaker in the front of the room, or in some other direction, towards a display or a video. A variation of the row and column arrangement is the horizontal row formation, where a large number of students sit close to one another in a fewer number of rows. This arrangement is useful for teacher demonstrations to a large group.

Neither one of these arrangements, however, are conducive to class discussions or for small group activities because few students face each other, and there is little eye contact between students. Furthermore, the closer that students are seated to each other, the greater the likelihood of student conversation and cooperative work: behaviors that are desirable in some instances like peer tutoring and laboratory work but not in others, like individual seat work or during examinations.

Students' seating can also be arranged in circles or clusters. Circles allow for class discussion and independent seat work, but they are not suitable for presentations or demonstrations because the teacher is not facing all students, and the teacher is not clearly visible to all the students. Moving students into groups of four or six clusters facilitates group discussion, cooperative learning, and other small group tasks. Effective teachers also plan for students' movement so that it proceeds safely, smoothly, quietly, and efficiently.

A teacher's desk and chair are often placed at the front of the room, but they can be placed elsewhere. Important considerations for the placement of the teacher's desk and chair are visibility, accessibility, and utility. The same considerations impact the placement of work areas for teacher assistants, student teachers, and peer tutors.

Classrooms and the people and materials they contain have to be organized for the desired activities and their purposes. Furniture has to be arranged so there are clearly defined paths for teachers' and students' safe movement, entry, and exit. Storage spaces and cabinets should be easily accessible to all students. The use of space, seating arrangements, and furniture location should enhance visibility, and there should be no vision barriers between the teacher and the students. Effective teachers have a check-in and check-out procedure for the use of materials and equipment; they explain it to students, model it for them, rehearse it with them, and periodically review it with them.

Students' seating should be periodically altered for variety and as a consequence of their behaviors. Appropriately behaving students who are friends can retain the privilege of sitting near each other as long as they continue to behave appropriately. But if the students are off task or talking, those students lose the right to sit near each other. Similarly, students who have a history of fighting with each other should be seated apart rather than close to one another to prevent the occurrence of fighting, an inappropriate behavior. Some teachers find it helpful to designate seats in the front for students' special or exemplary performances or behaviors: "The most improved student of the week," or "The winner of today's brain teaser." Effective teachers also seat students as far away from each other as possible during exams to prevent cheating. The use of alternate forms of examinations which contain the same questions presented in a different order (so that the answer sheets are different) is also effective to prevent cheating.

Effective teachers arrange the students and furniture in their rooms so that they can see and easily move among all students. They maintain awareness of what is going on, and because they are able to move around the room without disturbing students, they can resolve minor problems quickly. Effective teachers scan the classroom frequently to notice and respond to potential problems or minor disruptions before they become more full-blown or problematic. They learn to attend to more than one event or student at a time, and they know the importance of quickly and routinely scanning the room.

Effective teachers thus use space, students' seating arrangements, and the location of furniture in the classroom to minimize the occurrence of students' inappropriate behaviors. Should students' behave inappropriately nonetheless, effective teachers respond to those behaviors calmly and immediately. When such behaviors occur, effective teachers take the first step of quietly making contact with the inappropriately behaving student. This can be done with a glance, by moving closer to the student, by firmly but politely asking the student for an on-task behavior, or by dropping a note on the inappropriately behaving student's desk quietly. The note could simply indicate, "Stop that." This technique does not call other students' attention to the inappropriate behavior, and it allows the teacher to continue instruction without disturbing the momentum of the lesson. Effective teachers remind students of the expected rules and procedures. They re-direct students who are off-task or otherwise behaving inappropriately, and they praise students the moment that they begin to work on the assignment or focus on the class discussion.

SUMMARY OF KEY CONCEPTS IN CHAPTER 8

1. There are numerous traits, human relations skills, dispositions, and behaviors that effective teachers cultivate, refine, and utilize as they attempt to instruct students, effectively manage their behaviors, and establish a motivating, positive, friendly, nurturing, success-oriented classroom atmosphere.
2. Self-efficacy is an expectancy construct of one's ability to accomplish a certain level of performance. Effective teachers expect themselves to be successful in their instructional and management efforts.
3. Effective teachers have positive rather than negative expectations for their own behaviors and for the behaviors of others.
4. Effective teachers respond to students in ways that reflect that they care or are concerned about them, and they interact with students kindly, compassionately, and positively.
5. Effective teachers establish the importance of every student in the classroom by stating and repeating to students that they are worthy, prized, and important and that all students will be treated fairly.
6. Effective teachers emphasize students' successes.
7. Effective teachers establish rapport with students.
8. Effective teachers help students feel they are of value, competent, and that they have some control.
9. Effective teachers make sure that the work they assign is interesting rather than boring.
10. Effective teachers use teaching methods that accommodate all students' needs.
11. Effective teachers avoid using coercive methods that often typically fail.
12. Effective teachers make students feel important.
13. When criticism is necessary, effective teachers do it constructively rather than personally or with hostility.
14. Effective teachers show students a continual willingness to help them.
15. Effective teachers make sure that students have ample time to accomplish successfully the learning objectives.
16. Effective teachers know that students flourish in a motivating, positive, friendly, nurturing, success-oriented classroom atmosphere, and they work to provide such an atmosphere.
17. Effective teachers have high expectations for all students.
18. Effective teachers use praise with all of their students. They use it frequently, and they express, by both their words and their behaviors, their confidence that students can achieve and behave appropriately.
19. Effective teachers are assertive—not aggressive, hostile, non-assertive,

or passive.

20. Effective teachers are assertive, caring, and compassionate about their students' needs for warmth and positive support; they also realize that students require adult guidance for proper socialization.

21 The self-fulfilling prophecy states that people behave the way they do because of the expectations they and others have for their behaviors.

22. Teachers' positive expectations for students' help students to succeed.

23. Effective teachers refrain from having or conveying sexist, racist, or otherwise confining behavioral expectations that are unfair to the uniqueness of each student, that are in direct conflict with the concepts of caring and compassion, and that are educationally unsound and counter-productive to effective instruction and management.

24. Effective teachers use clarity, firmness, and clear communications with students.

25. Effective teachers know the value and necessity of ignoring inappropriate behaviors that are of short duration, that are not likely to persist or spread, and that are only minor infractions of the rules.

26. Effective teachers consistently, frequently, and periodically reinforce, acknowledge, and reward students' appropriate behaviors.

27. Effective teachers model the behaviors they expect from their students.

28. Effective teachers are enthusiastic in a stable and ongoing manner throughout the course of the school day to solicit and maintain students' attention and interest.

29. Effective teachers are enthusiastic.

30. Effective teachers devote time to planning for the prevention of students' inappropriate behaviors.

31. Effective teachers plan for and teach their students to accept responsibility for their behaviors and for the roles they play in furthering their own learning and the learning of the class in general.

32. Effective teachers accept no excuses for students' inappropriate behaviors, and they do not let students exceed the acceptable limits of behavior.

33. Effective teachers realize the value of humor to create a pleasant psycho-social environment.

34. Effective teachers use space wisely so that seating arrangements and placement of the furniture enhance their instructional and management efforts.

35. Effective teachers organize their classroom for maximum accessibility, visibility, and utility.

REFERENCES

Albert, L. (1995). Conferencing with difficult students. *The Cooperative Discipline Connection, 3*(1). Circle Pines, MN: American Guidance Service.

Canter, L., & Canter, M. (1976). A*ssertive discipline: A take-charge approach for today's educator.* Los Angeles: Lee Canter.

Carson, J. C., & Carson, P. (1984). *Any teacher can! Practical strategies for effective classroom management.* Springfield, IL: Charles C Thomas.

Carson, P., & Carson, J. (1982). *Don't say you can't when you mean you won't.* Englewood Cliffs, NJ: Prentice Hall.

Charles, C. M., & Senter, G. W. (1995). *Elementary classroom management.* White Plains, NY: Longman.

Curwin, R., & Mendler, A. (1980). *The discipline book.* Reston, VA: Association for Supervision and Curriculum Development.

Curwin, R., & Mendler, A. (1988). *Discipline with dignity.* Reston, VA: Association for Supervision and Curriculum Development.

Emmer, E. T., & Hickman, J. (1991). Teacher efficacy in classroom management and discipline. *Educational and Psychological Measurement, 51*(3), 755–765.

Evertson, C. M., & Emmer, E. T. (1982). Effective management at the beginning of the year in junior high classes. *Journal of Educational Psychology, 74*(4), 485–498.

Gibson, S., & Dembo, M. (1984). Teacher efficacy: A construct validation. *Journal of Educational Psychology, 76*(4), 569–582.

Glasser, W. (1990). *The quality school: Managing students without coercion.* New York: Harper & Row.

Hamachek, D. (1990). *Psychology in teaching, learning, and growth.* Boston, MA: Allyn & Bacon.

Harlan, G. (1996). Special assistance: The school counselor. In J. C. Harlan, *Behavior management strategies for teachers* (pp. 257–260). Springfield, IL: Charles C Thomas.

Jones, V., & Jones, L. (1995). *Comprehensive classroom management: Creating positive learning environments for all students.* Boston, MA: Allyn & Bacon.

Kagan, S. (1994). The cooperative learning connection. *The Cooperative Discipline Connection, 2*(2), 1–8.

Kindsvatter, R. (1988). The dilemmas of discipline. In P. Wolfe (Ed.), *Catch them being good: Reinforcement in the classroom* (pp. 32–36). Alexandria, VA: Association for Supervision and Curriculum Development.

Kounin, J. S. (1970). *Discipline and group management in classrooms.* New York: Holt, Rinehart & Winston.

Marshall, H. H. (1989). The development of self-concept. *Young Children, 44*(5), 44–51.

Mid-continent Regional Education Laboratory. (1983). Discipline. In P. Wolfe (Ed.), *Catch them being good: Reinforcement in the classroom* (pp. 37–46). Alexandria, VA: Association for Supervision and Curriculum Development.

Page, D. R. (1994). *A study of the differences in efficacy ratings of elementary classroom assistant teachers who did and did not receive training in classroom management strategies.* Unpublished doctoral dissertation, The University of Mississippi.

Raywid, M. A. (1976, February). The democratic classroom: Mistake or misnomer. *Theory into Practice, 27.*

SUGGESTED ACTIVITIES/ASSIGNMENTS

1. Invite a panel of teachers to discuss effective teaching strategies. Include a teacher from K–3, 4–8, and 9–12.
2. Visit the Internet and find suggestions of ways that teachers can establish rapport with students. Summarize and present these suggestions to the class.
3. Prepare a three-page review of literature concerning effective teaching.
4. Reflect on previous teachers who were caring and compassionate and the positive impact of such teachers.
5. Write about positive and negative expectations.
6. Invite a teacher to address the class about the impact of the self-fulfilling prophecy.
7. Invite parents to address the class about their experience with expectations for their children's behaviors.
8. Invite a teacher's aide or a student teacher to address the class about his or her classroom experiences managing students' behaviors.
9. Model the use of enthusiasm and praise.
10. Critique articles concerning traits of effective teachers and effective teaching.

Chapter 9

CONFERENCES, COLLABORATION, AND COMMUNICATION

A large part of a teacher's day may be spent **conferencing, collaborating, and communicating** with students, other teachers, school administrators, parents, caregivers, and others. This chapter includes suggestions and strategies for effective conferences, collaboration, and communication between teachers, parents, students and other education professionals.

CONFERENCES

Teacher–student conferences are often necessary to confer with a "difficult" student in order to negotiate a solution, offer assistance, or establish a consequence for classroom behavior. A teacher–student conference should be carefully planned. The goal of a teacher–student conference is to listen to the student and provide guidance. Canter and Canter (1992) suggest the following guidelines when conducting a teacher–student conference: (1) show empathy and concern, (2) question the student to find out why there is a problem, (3) determine what you can do to help, (4) determine how the student can improve his behavior, (5) agree on a course of action, (6) clearly state to the student that you expect a change in the behavior, and (7) summarize the conference and express confidence that the problem will be solved. Often, during a teacher–student conference certain behaviors may be exhibited. Albert (1995) identifies certain typical behaviors that a teacher may encounter in a conference, along with suggested verbal responses for keeping the dialog on track (p. 6):

    1. The student **stonewalls**, refusing to respond verbally. If there is no response after a few attempts at conversation, say, "Since you're not

ready to talk about it, I'll decide what happens next." Wait a few seconds for a response. Since most students want to be part of the decision-making process, at this point they typically respond. If, however, the student continues to stonewall, thank the student for coming and end the conference.

2. The student gives an **unworkable solution** that you do not feel is appropriate to the situation. Say, "I'm unwilling to try that because. . . . Do you have another idea?" Conferences need to be win–win situations. With continued brainstorming, usually a mutually agreeable solution can be found.

3. The student **promises** not to repeat the misbehavior. As educators, we would love to believe that promises will always be kept, but experience indicates otherwise. In this situation, first acknowledge the positive intention. "I appreciate your promise. That would help a lot." Next, make preparations in case the promise is not upheld. "And what consequence would seem reasonable to you if you should forget?"

4. The student responds with **disrespect**. A firm, direct response is best, offering a simple choice. "You will treat me with respect or you will go to the office. You decide." Clear limits and quick action are best when a student becomes verbally abusive.

5. The student **blames others**. Students are skillful in implicating everyone but themselves. Say, "I'm not interested in fault-finding or in what anyone else did. I'm only interested in finding a solution for the problem we are having."

Notice that these techniques use verbal responses that are delivered in a calm, businesslike manner with a friendly tone of voice. The student will continue the difficult behavior if the student perceives that the teacher's body language or tone of voice is hostile or threatening. Note, too, that the focus is on the future rather than the past, since it is far more productive to focus on what can be done so the same behavior does not reoccur than it is to focus on what has already occurred. The goal is to make concrete plans to eliminate the undesirable behavior, rather than to hear creative student explanations designed to get them off the hook.

Parent–teacher conferences also need to be solutions-oriented, productive, and informative. Effective conferences focus on problem solving, and they help parents and students realize that they, along with school personnel, are a team with common goals. A well-run conference requires planning, preparation, and, occasionally patience. A successful parent–teacher conference ideally informs both parties and puts a plan of action into effect.

Heinrich (1985) suggests that from the first day of school, an anecdotal record on each student be kept which includes student interests, strengths, instances of behavior problems, and academic achievement. Such a record prepares the teacher to attend the conference with written facts, rather than having to rely on memory. She also suggests that it be the student who writes the letter of invitation to parents to attend the conference, and that the teacher send the parents a reminder shortly before the conference. The student may or may not be involved in the conference, depending on the purpose of the conference, the age of the student, and other situational specifics.

In calling a parent–teacher conference and asking parents for assistance, Canter and Canter (1976) remind teachers to **refrain from** the following non-assertive behaviors (p. 157):

- apologizing for bothering the parents ("I'm really sorry for bothering you at home with this. . . .");
- downgrading the problems ("We had a small problem with your child today," when, in reality, he had a violent and disruptive temper tantrum);
- belittling themselves ("I just don't know what to do with your son.") Yes, you do. You need the cooperation of the parents to discipline him at home for his tantrums;
- not clearly stating their needs ("I know you are busy, working and all, but if you could find the time I'd appreciate it if you talked to your son about his tantrums.") You want her to discipline her son at home, period!
- downgrading the consequences of the child's behavior. ("I don't know what will happen if he doesn't change his behavior in class.") Yes, you do. He will need to be suspended.

Planning and preparation for a parent–teacher conference is the key to success. Canter and Canter (1991) suggests three steps for teachers in planning a parent–teacher conference:

1. **Decide who will be involved in the conference.**

   Some teachers may want to include the student in the parent–teacher conference, while others prefer not to include the student. In making this decision, the teacher should consider the student's age and maturity. Including the student in the conference provides input from the student's point of view, makes the student aware of the seriousness of the problem, and demonstrates that parents and teacher are working together. Reasons for not having the student present at a parent–teacher conference include concerns about discussing sensitive matters in front of the student and situations where the student is openly hostile, verbally abusive, agitated, or too young or active to sit still.

2. **Plan and write down what you will say to the parent.**

The key to an effective parent–teacher conference is planning what will be discussed because generally a conference with a parent is called because of a problem. Effective teachers make the parent feel welcome, and they establish a positive atmosphere at the beginning of the conference. This can be accomplished by beginning the conference with a statement of concern: "I wanted to meet with you today because I know both of us want Taylor to be successful in my classroom." The effective teacher then describes the specific problem that is affecting the student's performance, presents documentation of the problem, and describes what has already been done to solve the problem. At this point in the conference, effective teachers get parental input and suggestions on how to solve the problem. Effective teachers reaffirm their commitment to solving the problem. They explain how the parent can help. They express confidence that the problem will be solved, and they let the parent know that they will stay in contact. Finally, effective teachers recap the conference and express their gratitude to the parent for attending.

3. Gather documentation.

Parents often need to see evidence that a problem exists. Effective teachers document student work, behavior, and other relevant classroom information. This documentation can be easily gathered from individual student files, and it should be organized and presented in chronological order when it is explained in detail to the parent.

Carson and Carson (1984) make these suggestions about parent–teacher conferences:

- have an agenda and be prepared;
- schedule the conference at a mutually convenient time;
- keep the conference brief and focused;
- begin and end the conference on a positive note;
- provide specific behavioral information about the student;
- highlight, describe, and emphasize a student's strengths before dealing with weaknesses and inappropriate behavior;
- make the parent feel comfortable at the conference;
- refrain from assessing, blaming, or challenging the parents;
- refrain from making previous teachers look inadequate;
- provide parents with specific, concrete, easy-to-implement suggestions for helping the child improve academic or other behaviors;
- resist the temptation to overpower the parent with complex terminology or test scores;
- be an attentive listener;
- provide many opportunities for the parent to speak and ask questions;
- make the parent feel comfortable about returning, as necessary, for

future conferences;

- use the conference as one opportunity to establish good home–school rapport; and
- write down parents' commitment, if any, and follow up as appropriate.

Teachers should take notes about the conference proceedings immediately after the conference has ended. Note-taking during the conference may intimidate the parent. These notes allow the teacher to follow up on any suggestions, and they provide documentation of the conference as well as the decisions made.

Turnbull and Turnbull (1990) provide questions that teachers should ask themselves regarding parent–teacher conferences. The questions relate to preconference preparation, the conference itself, and postconference follow-up. They are presented below with the authors' recommendation that teachers use them, almost like a checklist, as they prepare and plan for productive parent–teacher conferences.

Preconference Preparation

Notifying Families

- Did I, or did the school, provide parents with written notification of the conference?
- Did I provide a means of determining that the parents knew the date and time?

Preparing for the Conference

- Did I review the student's cumulative records?
- Did I assess the student's behavior and pinpoint areas of concern?
- Did I make notes of the student's misbehavior to show to parents?
- Did I consult with other relevant professionals about the student's behavior?
- Did I mentally rehearse and review what I was going to say at the conference?

Preparing the Physical Environment

- Does the setting provide enough privacy?
- Does the setting provide enough comfort?

Conference Activities

Developing Rapport

- Did I allow time to talk informally before the start of the meeting?

- Did I express appreciation for the parents' coming to the meeting?

Obtaining Information from Parents

- Did I ask enough open-ended questions?
- Did my body language indicate interest in what parents were saying? (Did I maintain eye contact and look attentive?)
- Did I ask for clarification on points I did not understand?

Providing Information to Parents

- Did I speak as positively as possible about the student?
- Did I use jargon-free language?
- Did I use specific examples to clarify my points?

Summarizing and Follow-Up

- Did I review the main points to determine next steps?
- Did I restate who was responsible for completing the next steps and by when?
- Did I end the meeting on a positive note?
- Did I thank the parents for their interest in attending?

Postconference Follow-Up

- Did I consider reviewing the meeting with the student?
- Did I share the results with the appropriate other professionals who work with the student?
- Did I make a record of the conference proceedings?

The importance of parental support and involvement in teachers' instructional and management efforts cannot be overemphasized, and many times parental support and involvement result from a positive parent–teacher conference. Teachers must be willing to "go the extra mile" to obtain parental support and parental. Charles and Senter (1995, pp. 59–61) provide the following suggestions for building and maintaining positive relationships with parents. Effective teachers

- communicate regularly and clearly. The importance of frequent, regular communication cannot be overemphasized, and a system should be implemented at the beginning of the year and followed thereafter.
- describe their programs and expectations early in their communication with parents and repeat them occasionally. Effective teachers inform parents about the daily schedules, the activities they use to accomplish learning goals, the assigned homework, and the grading system to be used.
- emphasize progress when communicating to parents about their child.

Effective teachers soft-pedal, but do not whitewash, the child's difficulties. To dwell on a child's shortcomings is to probe sorely at parents' most sensitive feelings. When discussing the child, effective
teachers use this sequence:
   – mention something positive about the child personally;
   – show progress the child has made and is making;
   – describe plans for producing still greater achievement in the child;
     and finally,
   – mention difficulties that are interfering with the child's progress.
     Effective teachers also assure parents that they have a plan to over-
     come these difficulties, that they need the parent's support at home,
     and that they would appreciate any insights or suggestions parents
     might offer.
- warmly greet the parent and seat the parent beside and not across
  from them. Effective teachers give the parent their child's folder
  which shows progress, strengths, weaknesses, and work samples.
  Effective teachers explain to the parent about the child's strengths,
  progress, and difficulties.

Another opportunity to utilize effective conferencing, collaboration, and
communication skills is during efforts to gain administrator support and
assistance. Many of the suggestions and guidelines in the preceding section
on conferencing apply to **teacher–administrator conferences**. Carson and
Carson (1984) suggest the following guidelines for teacher–administrator
conferences:

- Teachers should document the nature and extent of a problem.
- Teachers should present their "case" in an objective, clear, rational
  manner.
- Principals should be flexible and not arbitrarily deny requests or
  refuse to examine a new or innovative approach.
- Principals should request teacher's input and be responsive to their
  suggestions when they consider solutions and assess the ramifications
  of their decisions.
- Principals should use data for decision making that stem from a variety of sources, and which provide teachers with constructive ideas for
  instructional and management assistance.
- Principals should provide teachers constructive and positive feedback
  about their performance.
- Principals should have administrative policies regarding student
  behavior when students are in groups (cafeteria, restroom, or recess
  time), when students move between classes, and when students travel
  on school buses.

The suggestions and techniques for effective conferencing presented in this chapter depend on collaboration and communication skills. Suggestions for effective collaboration and communication constitute the remainder of this chapter.

COLLABORATION

Collaboration, as used in this section, refers to teachers meeting, conferring, and/or collaborating with various groups: students, fellow teachers, administrators, paraprofessionals, parents, and others. The suggestions given in the previous section on conferencing and the basic principles of communication in the following section are important and relevant when teachers collaborate with students, colleagues, parents, and others. The following roadblocks to communication must be avoided when conferring or collaborating with others (Curwin & Mendler, 1980):

- avoid ordering, commanding, or directing;
- avoid warning or threatening;
- avoid moralizing, preaching, and giving "shoulds" and "oughts;"
- avoid lecturing;
- avoid judging, criticizing, disagreeing, or blaming;
- avoid name-calling, stereotyping or labeling; and
- avoid interpreting or diagnosing.

Charles and Senter (1995) emphasize certain human relations skills that teachers need to have with their colleagues if they expect communication and collaboration to be positive and productive (pp. 57–59). Effective teachers

- support each other in what they are trying to accomplish. The support can be active, as in actual assistance, or more passive, as in acceptance and encouragement. Negativism is detrimental to productive working environments. Furthermore, complainers and back-biters seldom earn the sincere trust of others.
- share the load, whether it is committee work, open houses, school musicals or plays, carnivals, athletic events, safety patrols, and in-service education sessions. Sharing the load builds trust; shirking produces resentment.
- realize that compromise is a way of life. Compromise does not mean giving in to others nor does it mean demanding that one gets his or her way every time. Effective teachers express and abide by what they believe in, and they also try to understand others' feelings and points of view.

Effective collaboration occurs when two or more individuals work to improve their working relationship. Collaboration with colleagues, parents, administrators, students, and others encourages appropriate student behaviors and results in a positive, caring classroom, parental support and involvement, and administrator support.

Charles and Senter (1995, p. 187) describe the expectations that parents and others have of teachers. Teachers are expected to

- care about students and give them attention as people;
- excite students about learning;
- teach the child the basics, such as literacy, something of the human condition, correct ways of behaving, and the good, right and beautiful;
- encourage and support children's efforts by nurturing, prodding, and encouraging;
- control students to prevent self-defeating behavior and especially to prevent mistreatment by others;
- inform parents about their child's educational program and process, emphasizing successes and difficulties that require special attention; and
- be dedicated to doing the best they can for their students.

Like parents, administrators expect these behaviors of teachers, and they therefore need to be kept informed about programs and problems, student achievement, discipline plans, communications with parents, and so forth. Colleagues (fellow teachers, clerical staff, paraprofessionals, librarians, nurses, psychologists, counselors, custodians, lunchroom staff, and others) should also be kept informed of any activities or needs that might impinge on them. When a teacher works at communicating such matters fully, most other colleagues will help willingly, and efforts at communicating will pay off in friendliness, helpfulness, and mutual respect. Hence, collaboration and clear communication enhance collegiality, and they are necessary when teachers interact with administrators, colleagues, students, paraprofessionals, and parents.

COMMUNICATION

One of the most important tasks that a teacher has is communicating effectively with students, parents, fellow teachers, and other individuals involved in the educational process. Teachers' communication skills must be effective in breaking down barriers that would impede student learning and student achievement. Effective classroom communication involves *talking with* students and *listening* to them. Communication skills are critical in establishing and maintaining a positive classroom environment. These same skills are important for building positive relationships with students, parents, colleagues, and administrators.

In today's classrooms, many students exhibit antisocial behaviors toward each other and toward teachers. Teachers who demonstrate effective communication skills and courteous behaviors, such as saying, "thank you," "please," and "excuse me," serve as important role models. While many teacher education programs focus on how to teach academic skills, today's classrooms require teachers to teach basic social skills *and* academic skills in order to promote a positive, caring, classroom environment. Effective communication skills promote a positive classroom environment and build positive relationships with students, parents, colleagues, and others.

Specifying and clearly articulating what is expected, whether for assignments, rules, procedures, routines, or any other behavior is one of the basics of effective communication. To elaborate on what was presented in other chapters, here are some additional examples. Example 1: Any instruction that has more than a few parts has to be taught part by part and rehearsed with students. A teacher cannot simply say, "Come in and get ready to work." It is vague, nonspecific, unclear, uninformative, and subject to various interpretations. An elementary teacher may conceptualize the statement, "Come in and get ready to work," to mean:

1. walk into the room quietly;
2. hang up your coat;
3. take out your books and homework;
4. put your book bag or backpack under your seat;
5. place homework assignments in the bin on my desk;
6. turn in your lunch or milk money to this week's money monitor;
7. go to the pencil sharpener and sharpen your pencils for the day;
8. walk back to your desk;
9. sit down quietly; and
10. silently begin the seatwork assignment that is on the chalkboard.

By contrast, a high school teacher may conceptualize the same statement to mean

1. enter the room quietly;
2. go sit in your assigned seat;
3. take out your notebook and a pen;
4. start to take notes from the chalkboard; and
5. face forward and pay attention to my lecture.

In both cases, each step in the instruction must be taught and rehearsed, although high school students might require fewer instances of practice than elementary students. Effective teachers never assume that students can read their minds.

Example 2: A junior high school teacher who merely indicates, "A term paper about the Civil War is due Thursday," might prompt one student to turn in three pages while another student writes fifteen. If the teacher has not set parameters as to the desired length, how can these widely disparate papers be equitably evaluated? Furthermore, such a vaguely delivered assignment begs clarification relative to these questions, which interested students will likely ask:

- What is the precise topic?
- Is it to be an opinion or a research paper?
- How many supporting references are required?
- What is the required/expected bibliographic style?
- Must it be typed or can it be hand-written?
- Exactly which Thursday will it be due?
- Will it be graded only for content or will there be two separate grades, one for content and one for grammar and style?
- Do we have to have our topic approved in advance by you?
- How much will it count toward the marking period grade? and
- May we work in teams on this report?

Relative to these questions, the effective teacher clarifies in advance the answer to each of these items. If clarification is not given, the teacher can expect to be deluged with continued questions from students, and the teachers is likely to receive vastly different papers, reflecting the different interpretations that result from such vaguely delivered directions.

Example 3: Expectations and procedures for the secondary classroom similarly must also be well articulated, clearly communicated, and rehearsed with students. Wolfe (1988) adapted the work of Evertson et al. (1981) and suggests that there be expectations or procedures for each of the following areas of student behavior (pp. 19–21):

A. **Student use of classroom space and facilities:**
　　1. Administrative matters – Students need to know what is expected of them while teachers handle reporting of absences, tardiness, and other administrative procedures.
　　2. Student behavior before and at the beginning of the period – Students need to know what to do when the tardy bell rings (be seated, stop talking), what to do during public address announcements (no talking, no interruptions of the teacher), what materials to bring to class and how materials to be used during the period will be distributed.

B. **Procedures during whole-class instructional activities:**
　　1. Student talk – Students need to know how and when they may respond (raise hand and wait until they are called on) and

whether choral responding is appropriate.

2. Use of the room by students – Students need to know what the procedures are for using the pencil sharpener, obtaining materials from shelves or bookcases, and if or when it is appropriate to leave their seats to seek help from the teacher or other students.

3. Leaving the room – Students need to know what the procedures are for going to the restroom, the library, the computer lab, the school office, etc. Usually the school will have a specified system concerning hall passes and hall traffic.

4. Signals for attention – Students need to understand what the teachers' signals or cues indicate; cues may be given verbal or by light flashing or bell ringing. When such cues are used consistently, they can be very effective for transitioning between activities or for obtaining student attention.

5. Student behavior during seatwork – Students need to know what kind of talk, if any, may occur during seat work, how to get help, when or if out-of-seat behavior is permitted, how to access materials, and what to do when or if seatwork assignments are completed early.

6. Procedures for laboratory work or individual projects – Students need to know the system for distributing materials, the necessary safety rules, and the clean-up routines.

C. **Expectations regarding student responsibility for work:**

1. Policy regarding form of work – Students need to know how to place headings on paper, whether to use pen or pencil, what the neatness requirements are and so forth.

2. Policy regarding completion of assignments – Students need to know whether and under what conditions late or incomplete work is acceptable and how such work will be graded. There also need to be some procedures for informing students of due dates for assignments along with procedures for make-up work for absent students.

3. Communicating assignments to students – Students need to know what is expected and when. An effective procedure for communicating assignments is to post a list of each period's work assignments for a two or three week period of time, thus allowing students who were absent to easily identify make-up work. This also allows students to work ahead if they desire.

4. Checking procedures – Students need to know what the procedures are for exchanging and checking papers (provides immediate feedback), how errors are to be noted, how papers are to be returned, and how papers are to be passed to the teacher for

recording purposes.

5. Grading policy – Students need to know what components comprise their grade and the weight or percentage given to each component.

D. Other procedures:

1. Student use of teacher's desk or storage areas – These areas are generally off-limits except for when the teacher gives special permission.

2. Fire and disaster drills – Students need to know what the school's master plan is for such drills and how to respond in an emergency.

3. Procedures for ending class – Students need to know what is expected of them relative to cleaning up the room, returning to seats, noise level, and the signal for dismissal.

4. Interruptions – Students need to know whether they are required to sit quietly and continue working or allowed to stop working and talk when an interruption occurs.

Effective teachers convey sincerity, warmth, caring, and compassion while at the same time developing **a command presence**. A command presence allows a teacher to gain the respect of and take positive control of a class. A modification of the hints given by Chernow and Chernow (1981, pp. 22–23) appears below. These hints can help teachers to develop a command presence and thus gain the immediate respect of the class. Effective teachers

- speak in short sentences with emphasis on the verbs. "You will **walk** to the end of the hall." This erases from the students' minds any images they may have had of running, sliding, skipping, hopping, jumping, or pushing.
- stand up to their full height even if some of their pupils are taller than they are.
- are omnipresent so students sense their presence everywhere and walk around the room as they speak. Effective teachers occasionally stand in the rear of the room as they give directions for seat or board work, getting a different perspective from that vantage point, and where the pupils seated in the rear will also sense their control.
- use their eyes as well as their voices. Effective teachers, when speaking to one student, make eye contact with that student, and when addressing the whole class, move their eyes from face to face.
- use the "Tower of Pisa" approach. Effective teachers, when talking to an individual student about some misbehavior, **lean toward the student** as physical proximity is an important control tool. Effective teachers never fold their arms across their chest while correcting a stu-

dent; this is a self-protective gesture that is read as a sign of weakness.
- do not turn their backs on a situation too soon. Effective teachers stay with a problem situation long enough to be sure that it is resolved before they turn their backs and move away. Effective teachers do not have their backs to their students for any lengthy period of time.
- use "I" messages and speak in a forceful, "I mean what I say and I say what I mean" tone.

Effective teachers utilize these suggestions when planning conferences, when collaborating with other school personnel, and when they are communicating with students, teachers, parents, and others.

SUMMARY OF KEY CONCEPTS IN CHAPTER 9

1. Teacher–student and parent–teacher conferences need to be solution-oriented, productive, and informative.
2. Effective conferences require planning and preparation.
3. Effective teachers are assertive and good listeners.
4. Effective teachers assure parents and students, even difficult ones, of their interest and support of each and every student.
5. Many of the conferencing strategies and techniques may be used with school administrators.
6. Roadblocks to communication and collaboration must be avoided.
7. Effective communication requires talking with people and listening to people.
8. Expectations and routine procedures must be clearly articulated and communicated to all students.
9. A command presence is important in order to gain respect and take positive control of a classroom.
10. Developing a command presence includes speaking in short sentences with emphasis on the verbs, standing up to your full height, walking around the room, using your eyes as well as your voice, using the "Tower of Pisa" approach, facing toward students, and using "I" messages to communicate with students.

REFERENCES

Albert, L. (1995). Conferencing with difficult students. *The cooperative discipline connection, 3*(1), 6–7.

Canter, L., & Canter, M. (1992). *Lee Canter's assertive discipline: Elementary workbook.* Santa Monica, CA: Lee Canter & Associates.

Canter, L., & Canter, M. (1991). *Parents on your side.* Santa Monica, CA: Lee Canter & Associates.

Canter, L., & Canter, M. (1976). *Assertive Discipline: A take-charge approach for today's educator.* Los Angeles, CA: Lee Canter & Associates.

Carson, J. C., & Carson, P. (1984). *Any teacher can! Practical strategies for effective classroom management.* Springfield, IL: Charles C Thomas.

Charles, C. M., & Senter, G. W. (1995). *Elementary classroom management.* White Plains, NY: Longman.

Chernow, & Chernow. (1981). *Classroom discipline and control.* Parker.

Curwin, R., & Mendler, A. (1980). *The discipline book: A complete guide to school and classroom management.* Reston, VA: Reston.

Evertson, C. M., Emmer, E. T., Clements, B. S., Sanford, J. P., & Worsham, M. E. (1984). *Classroom management for elementary teachers.* Englewood Cliffs, NJ: Prentice Hall.

Heinrich, L. B. (1985, October). Parent teacher conferences: Include the student, please. *Learning,* 87.

Homme, L. (1973). *How to use contingency contracting in the classroom.* Champaign, IL: Research Press.

Jones, V., & Jones, L. (1995). *Comprehensive classroom management: Creating positive learning environments for all students.* Boston, MA: Allyn & Bacon.

Turnbull, A. P., & Turnbull, H. R. (1990). *Families, professionals, and Exceptionality: A Special Partnership* (Second Edition). Columbus, OH: Merrill/Macmillan.

Wolfe, P. (1988). Expectations and procedures for the secondary classroom. *Classroom management: A proactive approach to creating an effective learning environment.* Alexandria, VA: ASCD.

SUGGESTED ACTIVITIES/ASSIGNMENTS

1. Script and role-play a effective teacher–student conference and an effective teacher–parent conference based on the techniques and strategies from this chapter.

2. Script and role-play an ineffective teacher–student and/or teacher–parent conference. Identify how conferences can be counterproductive, based on techniques and strategies from this chapter.

3. Invite a teacher and/or principal to address the class about the importance of planning teacher–student and parent–teacher conferences.

4. Invite an administrator to address the class about his or her expectations for teacher behaviors.

5. Invite a parent to address the class about his or her experience with

successful or unsuccessful parent–teacher conferences.

6. Invite a paraprofessional and/or a student teacher to address the class about their classroom experiences.

7. Role-play effective and ineffective communication skills.

8. Critique journal articles concerning effective parent–teacher conferences

9. Critique journal articles concerning collaboration with colleagues.

10. Critique journal articles concerning effective communication skills with students, parents, and colleagues.

Chapter 10

TEACHER–STUDENT INTERACTIONS: WHAT EFFECTIVE TEACHERS SHOULD DO AND WHAT THEY SHOULD NOT DO

T his chapter provides suggestions that can help teachers effectively interact with their students. The content of this chapter is closely related to the contents of other chapters concerning effective teaching, motivational, and management practices; working with special populations; and how effective teachers can establish a motivating, positive, friendly, nurturing, success-oriented classroom atmosphere. This chapter explores a variety of approaches that effective teachers use and behaviors they should model to enhance teacher–student interactions. It also explores approaches and behaviors that effective teachers refrain from which are harmful to teacher–student interactions.

WHAT EFFECTIVE TEACHERS SHOULD DO

Effective teachers realize the value of play, and they make learning activities fun, interesting, and meaningful. Effective teachers use praise, and when they have to deliver criticism, they do so constructively and in conjunction with the "sandwich technique," as explained below. Effective teachers work at getting their students' parents involved in school activities. They treat all of their students equally, and they do not erroneously equate being kind and caring with being too permissive. Effective teachers utilize behavioral techniques. They capably and equitably respond to all of the special populations of students in their classroom, and they utilize the expertise of other professionals. As explained in great detail in the second portion of this chapter, effective teachers and administrators refrain from the use of physical punishment because it is a highly aversive procedure fraught with numerous drawbacks.

Use games and play activities. *Play* denotes amusing oneself as by taking part in a game or sport or to engage in recreation. As a verb it implies activity–physical or mental–whose sole aim is diversion or amusement. Whether students play a game, competitively participate in an organized sport, or more informally interact during a "friendly" game of any type, they remain focused on the activity, learn about rules and strategies, are involved in social interactions, and learn to deal with competition. Furthermore, when students are engaged with a task, they are less likely to misbehave. Thus, it is our perspective that play, enjoyment, learning, and achieving are inextricably tied to one another, and we use the idea of *play* in this general sense, more synonymous with a task's appeal.

Effective teachers use games and traditional play activities as part of their instructional strategies. The games used can be teacher-made or purchased. Teacher- made games are often more specific to the teacher's learning objectives and students. Teacher-made games should be simple, and they often are a variation of established commercially available board games (e.g., "Sorry" and "Tic-Tac-Toe") or popular television games (e.g., "Wheel of Fortune" and "Concentration"). Effective teachers also use modifications of crossword puzzles, moderately competitive activities between groups of students, and commercial brain teasers and word, number, and problem solving games as part of their instruction.

Beyond games and traditional play activities, effective teachers strive to increase the intrinsic appeal of all of the learning tasks required of their students. Effective teachers are knowledgeable about and carefully select from the multitude of available audio–visual media and instructional computer software. They select these and all of the instructional materials that they use in accordance with their learning objectives and the needs of their students.

Praise, constructive criticism, and the "sandwich technique." Praise was discussed in detail in Chapter 5, and that content will not be repeated here. However, within the context of striving for more effective teacher–student interactions, we make the following observations about praise.

Some teachers acknowledge that they have difficulty being sincerely positive, encouraging, and giving praise comfortably and easily, even though they recognize the tremendous value that sincere praise has for maintaining and increasing students' appropriate behaviors. These teachers should practice praising. Many teachers find it helpful to practice in front of a mirror, to talk into a tape recorder and then evaluate the results, or to be videotaped and then critique the tape for improvement. Effective teachers practice being positive, and they practice using praise.

Constructive criticism is helpful, evaluative, focused commentary about someone's behavior. In the classroom, effective teachers know that constructive criticism is not simply a criticism of what a student has done; rather it provides some guidance and instruction about how a student could improve. Constructive criticism focuses on a behavior and not on the student personally.

Communicating to a student merely that his or her report is "poor" or "needs work," is vague. It provides no guidance or instruction about how the report could be improved, and it conveys the idea that the student's work is devoid of any merit whatsoever. Such a communication is de-moralizing. It often negatively influences the student's motivation, and it is counter-productive to a teacher's attempts to enhance teacher–student interactions. An effective teacher, one who is trying to keep students motivated and who wants to enhance teacher–student interactions, would instead use constructive criticism: "Your title is excellent because it is focused and reflects the content of the report. The organization of the report is a bit illogical because what you indicate in the third and fourth paragraphs is unclear until the reader gets to the sixth paragraph. Your closing summary paragraph is very well-structured."

We recommend that constructive criticism be delivered with the "sandwich technique." Like a traditional sandwich with two pieces of bread and a filling, the sandwich technique involves enfolding a criticism or a negative comment (the filling), between two sincere laudatory or praising comments (the two pieces of bread). At first glance, the sandwich technique may seem like a mixed message. But a mixed message usually contains only one positive and one negative message, and so the negative component often cancels out the positive component. By contrast, with the sandwich technique, the positive initial and closing comments serve to soften the impact of the critical comment.

Constructive criticism can be of any length, and different teachers will phrase their comments differently. In the example of constructive criticism given above, there are three sentences. The first and last sentences are positive statements that recognize something in the report that the student did well. The middle or second sentence, the "filling," contains the criticism which is constructively phrased so it provides guidance to the student about how the student can improve the report.

As indicated with the use of praise, some teachers may have to practice the sandwich technique until they are comfortable delivering constructive criticism with it. Delivering constructive criticism with the sandwich technique enhances students' motivation and significantly improves teacher–student interactions.

Parental involvement. Effective teachers find creative ways to involve their students' parents in school activities. They contact parents by mail, e-mail, or phone. They encourage parents to become actively involved with their children's academic work, and they provide parents with specific suggestions about how they can help. They explain their management plan to parents so that parents are supportive of the teachers' efforts with their children at home.

Effective teachers do not limit their involvement with parents to the traditional "open-school nights" which usually leave little time for teachers to have lengthy enough and hence meaningful conversations with parents about their children. Effective teachers have a positive written or oral communication with each student's parent(s) at the beginning of the school year to establish rapport, and they inform parents of their philosophies, strategies, and expectations. Such initial contact also smooths the way for later conferences that may have to be called for students' academic or disciplinary problems.

Effective teachers also realize that there are numerous reasons why some parents refrain from school involvement: intimidation, lack of transportation, inflexible work schedules, frustration, competing commitments to other children or activities, or the fear of losing wages. Effective teachers help parents to overcome these obstacles, and they help parents understand the absolute necessity of a school–home partnership for the effective instruction and management of students. More information on parental involvement is provided in Chapter 13.

Permissiveness and equity. Effective teachers relate to all students fairly, equally, and without prejudice or malice. Effective teachers refrain from thinking that they must "police" their students since that is a harsh way to interact with them, and they do not equate being kind and caring with being too permissive.

Effective teachers establish a classroom environment and create an atmosphere so that students' interactions with each other and with them are mutually respectful. Effective teachers establish a classroom atmosphere where the focus is on students' appropriate rather than their inappropriate behaviors; namely, they work at "catching the students being good" rather than anxiously, vigilantly, and often counter-productively trying to catch every instance of students' inappropriate behaviors.

Effective teachers also realize that they cannot, will not, and do not have to like every student equally, but they nonetheless diligently work to treat all students with caring, courtesy, respect, and equity. Effective teachers find something good about every student's behavior that they can focus on and reinforce. If an effective teacher does recognize that he or she has difficulty interacting with a student, especially a student who is repeatedly or frequently problematic or disruptive, he or she finds ways to interact more positively with that student.

Two additional comments relative to permissiveness, equity, and how teachers can improve on their interactions with students. Effective teachers focus on the group of students that they currently have rather than comparing them to previous students. Living in the past by dwelling on the so-called "good old days" is self-defeating, demoralizing, and counter-productive to a proactive approach to managing students' behaviors. Effective teachers refrain from thinking about "how students used to behave." Effective teachers refuse to waste time and effort lamenting about, "how better-behaved students were years ago," or, "if today's students were only more like previous students," because such thinking distracts them from the more important task of functioning in a situation as it is presently. Effective teachers do not pre-judge students on the basis of their family or background.

Effective teachers also refrain from comparing their students with their siblings or with other teachers' students. Effective teachers do not pre-judge students based on hearsay and gossip about students' and their families that is often repeated and/or generated in the teachers' lounge. It is inherently unfair to judge one student on the basis of his or her siblings' performance, regardless of whether it is in the same or a different situation and in the past or the present. A student who behaves inappropriately with one teacher may not do so with another teacher. Students interact in ways that are unique and specific to each of their teachers and to the specific dynamics of a particular classroom.

Behavioral techniques. Throughout this text, we have emphasized the use of a proactive behavioral approach to prevent the occurrence of students' inappropriate behaviors, and we have encouraged the use of classroom management techniques. We make these additional observations about behavioral techniques and classroom management techniques relative to improving teacher–student interactions.

Some teachers erroneously believe that behavioral techniques are difficult to learn and use. With practice, effective teachers can consistently reinforce students' appropriate behaviors. With restraint and the realization that every student's inappropriate behavior cannot and should not be acknowledged, effective teachers learn to ignore students' harmless or minimally disruptive inappropriate behaviors. With diligence, effective teachers learn to use non-physical forms of punishment or to deny reinforcement for students' harmful or potentially injurious inappropriate behaviors.

The behavioral techniques and strategies suggested have been utilized for many years by astute behavior managers in schools, businesses, industries, homes, and other settings, although admittedly, they were not codified, identified, publicized, or empirically tested until relatively recently. The value of praise and other reinforcers for maintaining and increasing productivity and appropriate behavior has long been recognized in the business world through the use of rewards, perks, incentives, bonuses, and other such acknowledgments. The techniques and strategies are not complex, nor are they artificial or contrived.

The Premack Principle and the contingency contracting/behavioral contracting strategies were informally used by our ancestors long before Premack or Homme formalized them as strategies. For example, when our great, great grandparents first required that chores, a less preferred and hence lower frequency behavior, be completed before play, a more preferred and hence higher frequency behavior, they were using what is now known as **The Premack Principle**. When parents require their children to eat their vegetables (a less preferred and hence lower frequency behavior) before they allow them to have their dessert (a more preferred and hence higher frequency behavior), they are using The Premack Principle (Homme, 1973).

When teachers and parents use written, formal descriptions of expected behaviors and specify what the consequences will be for performing those behaviors, they are using contingency contracting. Clearly communicating behavioral expectations and delivering the appropriate consequences are techniques that have been informally used for many years by successful teachers and parents in their disciplinary efforts. More formalized job descriptions and outcome statements, similarly, have been used for years by successful business managers and leaders.

Behavioral techniques and classroom management strategies are not complex; rather, they require a reversal of traditional reactive thinking where the focus is on punishing students' inappropriate behaviors to a commitment to pro-actively acknowledge and otherwise reinforce students' appropriate behaviors. The management of students' behaviors, like instruction, should be a dynamic and changing process. The true hallmark of professionals is their ability to accept change, grow, and improve rather than stagnate.

Effective teachers are amenable to experimenting with changing, tested, non-trendy, and otherwise sound approaches to instruction and management, and that is precisely what behavioral techniques and classroom management strategies are. Furthermore, effective teachers thoroughly communicate to their curriculum supervisors and principals why they are using innovative, different, or non-traditional management strategies, and they inform them of their successes with behavioral techniques.

Special populations. Classrooms nationwide contain students from a variety of socio-economic, linguistic, racial, cultural, ethnic, and religious backgrounds. Our classrooms contain motivated and unmotivated students, students with different abilities and with learning disabilities, and students with attention-deficit or hyperactivity disorders. Effective teachers use a variety of instructional and management strategies so that they are successful in their interactions with all students. Effective teachers convey to all students that they expect them to succeed and to behave appropriately, and that such behaviors will have more desirable consequences than will failure and inappropriate behavior.

Effective teachers refrain from labeling, typecasting, or stereotyping their students on the basis of any characteristic, and they do not pre-judge their students on the basis of their backgrounds or any other factors, all of which are largely out of the students' control. Additional information on working with diverse learners and with students with disabilities appears in Chapters 11 and 12, respectively.

Working with other professionals. Effective teachers assume responsibility for contacting and working with other professionals to enhance their management and instructional efforts and to improve their interactions with students. They know how to access other professionals for assistance, and they interact comfortably with them. Effective teachers respect and value the input of professionals from all disciplines, and they realize the power and efficacy of an inter-disciplinary approach to instruction and management.

Effective teachers thoroughly explain their instructional philosophies and management strategies to teaching assistants, student teachers, and classroom volunteers. While the certified and licensed teacher is the one who is officially in charge and ultimately responsible for the instruction and management of students' behaviors, teaching assistants, student teachers, and volunteers often have good ideas, different strategies, and a wealth of experiences that effective teachers consider, refine, and adopt.

Effective teachers have their instructional plans and their management plans in writing for substitute teachers' use so there is continuity relative to which behaviors should be reinforced, ignored, or punished. Effective teachers know that there must be consistency between the regular teacher and the substitute teacher regarding the behaviors that are allowed or disallowed and regarding the delivery of appropriate consequences for both types of behaviors.

Effective teachers realize that they are not alone in their instruction and management efforts, and they avail themselves of the services of other professionals to enhance their interactions with students. Effective teachers approach their instructional and management tasks as a cooperative endeavor among school, district, and community professionals, and they are amenable to accepting and refining the recommendations of others. Furthermore, many specialists—like counselors, psychologists, nurses, and speech therapists—are available on-site for all kinds of assistance: counseling; testing; test construction and interpretation; the derivation of treatment and behavior change plans; the implementation of suicide prevention, substance abuse, or other specialized programs; the treatment of minor health problems; and speech therapy.

Effective teachers refrain from resorting to corporal or physical punishment. The next section focuses on the myriad of problems associated with the use of physical punishment and on how even the infrequent use of physical punishment impedes effective interactions with students. Additional content on legal issues associated with the use of physical punishment appears in Chapter 14.

EFFECTIVE TEACHERS AVOID PHYSICAL PUNISHMENT

Punishment in its various forms was discussed extensively in Chapter 7, and we encourage readers to review that content prior to reading this section. In this section, we present the many reasons why public school personnel–teachers and administrators alike–should avoid the use of physical punishment. Physical punishment is sometimes also referred to as *corporal punishment*. Both terms denote "chastisement inflicted on the body in order to modify behavior." Both connote a painful penalty that is inflicted as a consequence of the performance of a forbidden behavior.

In an informal or colloquial sense, parents, lay people, and others sometimes refer to physical punishment as *a whipping, a switching,* or *a spanking,* each of which has somewhat different connotations. *Whipping* implies a physical punishment of great severity if not barbarity. *Switching* refers to the use of a hickory branch or a stick of some sort to deliver physical punishment. *Spanking* often connotes the use of a hand, a paddle, a belt, or some other instrument to deliver physical punishment.

There are numerous drawbacks associated with public school personnel's use of physical punishment. The drawbacks and reasons why school personnel should not use physical punishment are not presented in any order of priority. They are presented with the sole intention of discouraging all public school personnel from ever using corporal punishment with their students. It is our hope that school personnel will review the numerous drawbacks and reasons presented and then thoughtfully and professionally conclude that use of physical punishment with inappropriately behaving students is fraught with far more problems than any temporary advantages it may appear to yield.

It needs to be understood that these drawbacks and reasons are most relevant within the context of public school personnel in those states and school districts where the use of physical punishment is permitted. The drawbacks and reasons presented are based on three assumptions that we make about school personnel's use of physical punishment, assumptions that may not always be true, further adding to the volatility and problems associated with the use of physical punishment. It is assumed that physical punishment (1) is delivered in strict accordance with prescribed and often complex local school district policies; (2) is delivered only with the use of a paddle; and (3) is applied only to a student's clothed rear end/buttocks. (Additional content on legal issues associated with the use of physical punishment, and the current status of where physical punishment is prohibited or permitted in public schools appears in Chapter 14.)

Physical punishment typically suppresses rather than eliminates students' inappropriate behaviors. As is true for non-physical forms of punishment, physical punishment may influence the inappropriately behaving student to stop the behavior momentarily, but it also teaches the student to become increasingly adept at avoiding detection and hence avoiding punishment for the inappropriate behavior. It is precisely because punishment serves to suppress rather than eliminate a student's inappropriate behavior that some school personnel resort to its use; it provides school personnel with immediate, but often temporary, relief from the student's inappropriate behavior.

Physical punishment may decrease students' inappropriate behaviors, but this usually occurs only with those students who are infrequently physically punished. For those students who are rarely physically punished, physical punishment may appear to be effective, but it is often at a great cost. School personnel who resort to the use of physical punishment often find themselves ineffective when they attempt to deliver reinforcement.

Conversely, physical punishment is often ineffective with inappropriately behaving students who are frequently physically punished. Many school personnel lament the fact that physical punishment is used repeatedly with the same few inappropriately behaving students. These school personnel resort to the use of physical punishment often out of desperation or because they are unaware of other, more powerful punishment options available to them. These school personnel also fail to recognize the irony of their repeated use of physical punishment with the same few inappropriately behaving students; they think they are punishing, but if the same students are continuing their inappropriate behaviors, punishment has not, by definition, occurred. Furthermore, in many cases when students are given a choice between physical punishment and another punishment, like detention or a parental conference, they often select physical punishment, indicating that they perceive the physical punishment as more perfunctory and less punitive than other punishment options. That there is a high rate of recidivism among students who are physically punished clearly indicates the futility of using physical punishment with students.

Physical punishment may decrease or eliminate students' inappropriate behaviors, but typically only if it is very severe. If the physical punishment that is used is very harsh or excessive, it might constitute child abuse or battering. McFadden (1987), Rich (1989), and others characterize physical punishment as "legalized child abuse," an abusive procedure that compounds problems by escalating a student's anger. Admittedly, most school personnel initially employ physical punishment with no intention of abuse, but if they escalate the severity of the punishment after routinely administered physical punishments have failed, it may be tantamount to child abuse. Furthermore, while any policy can be abused if people act inappropriately, unprofessionally, or out of anger and retaliation, in situations when school personnel are allowed to use physical punishment, serious transgressions can result: students have been shaken, choked, kicked, kneed, stomped, thrown against desks and walls, locked in a dark closet, and subjected to nasty personal indignities (Maurer, 1994).

School personnel's use of severe physical punishment can cause the very real possibility of litigation, suspension, or termination. Effective and professional school personnel realize the serious ethical, moral, philosophical, and possibly legal ramifications associated with the use of severe or harsh physical punishment, and they avoid the use of physical punishment entirely.

Physical punishment is an unreliable procedure for decreasing students' inappropriate behaviors, and, ironically, it is often responsible for the inadvertent reinforcement of the very behaviors that school personnel target for elimination. When teachers send inappropriately behaving students to the principal's office for physical punishment, the process often backfires because many students perceive the sequence of events as more reinforcing than punishing. Many students enjoy getting out of class and having time away from the expected academic activities. Many students enjoy observing the personnel and activities that occur in the principal's office.

Many students also consider it a badge of distinction, a reinforcer rather than a punisher, if they get the reputation as "the class clown" or "the holy terror." For junior high and high school students, the peer groups' attention positively acknowledges anti- establishment behavior. For these older students, the reinforcement they receive from their peers is far more influential on their behaviors than the negative labels that school personnel (whom the students often dislike or otherwise have little respect for) impose directly or otherwise imply.

When school personnel resort to the use of physical punishment,

it often results in a power struggle between school personnel and the student. The use of physical punishment often tests an inappropriately behaving student's obstinacy or prowess. Some students attain status and bravery for enduring the punishment. Older students often proudly show off in front of their peers when they receive physical punishment, since they have lived to tell about the "ultimate test." These students demonstrate to their peers that they are tough enough to withstand the process and that they survived the physical punishment without displaying noticeable duress or discomfort. School personnel should question whether the paddles they wield are not, in fact, catalysts to students' disruptive behaviors.

Physical punishment focuses on students' inappropriate behaviors, and thus it is an inefficient way to teach students how to behave appropriately. Students will not learn appropriate behaviors if the focus is only on their inappropriate behaviors.

Physical punishment often leads to students disliking or fearing school personnel. Respect is earned, and it cannot be aggressively commanded. School personnel who administer physical punishment and even those who refer inappropriately behaving students for its administration become disliked. School personnel may then find themselves the targets of students' retaliatory aggressive or violent behaviors.

When school personnel resort to the use of physical punishment, they often find an increase in students' avoidance behaviors. Avoidance behaviors, like lying, evasion, misrepresentation, sneaking, hiding, concealing, or even skipping school entirely, are unacceptable outcomes of school personnel's use of physical punishment. Further alienating students to the school environment often propels those students most estranged from the system and those students who find school unrewarding to passively withdraw from or to actively drop out of school.

When school personnel use physical punishment, it frequently increases students' behaviors that are counter-productive to school personnel's goals and expectations for students. Physical punishment is an invasive procedure. It often angers students, and its use often results in students becoming angry, sullen, negative, or hostile. Students who have been physically punished typically manifest passive–aggressive behaviors that are a direct result of having been physically punished. School personnel's use of physical punishment often results in some students' passive withdrawal from academic and social activities. Some students feign sickness or helplessness. Some students opt to become lethargic, unmotivated, and uninterested. Some students become even more unresponsive, uncooperative, or noncompliant than they were prior to being punished. It should further disturb school personnel that some students continue these counter-productive behaviors in schools whose state law requires that they remain in school until they reach a certain age or in order to retain their drivers' licenses.

Yet other students angrily choose to actively engage in potentially very disruptive and harmful behaviors as a result of school personnel's use of physical punishment with them. Some students engage in serious retaliatory behaviors, like vandalism, antagonism, or even potentially deadly assaults on students and school personnel. When students passively or actively respond to school personnel's use of physical punishment by displaying these undesirable behaviors, everyone's safety and well-being are at stake, and school becomes a negative, unsafe, and less productive environment.

Physical punishment is often unjustly administered and inequitably delivered. Boys, minorities, students from low socioeconomic groups, young children, and others who are the least powerful and the most vulnerable are the most likely to receive physical punishment in public schools. That certain groups of students receive a disproportionate share of physical punishment leaves school personnel subject to criticisms of discrimination, racism, sexism, inconsistency, and unfairness, and it may result in painful, costly, and prolonged litigation.

Furthermore, many school districts under-report embarrassing statistics relative to the use and administration of physical punishment. This can be problematic for school personnel if physical punishment has been delivered unjustly or in a discriminatory manner, if parents opt to seek legal remedy and the required records or paperwork are inaccurate or nonexistent.

When school personnel resort to the use of physical punishment, their behaviors model as appropriate the use of physically aggressive ways of interacting with others. School personnel should manage students' behaviors assertively, not aggressively. When school personnel resort to the use of physical punishment, their behaviors imply that "might makes right." When school personnel resort to using a physically aggressive method to eliminate a student's physically aggressive behavior, they are behaving inconsistently. Students often identify this inconsistency, and they rightly challenge the teacher or the administrator who is dispensing physical punishment with, "If it is not okay to hit someone else, how come you are hitting me?" It is our position that school personnel can fashion no satisfactory, no professional, and no research-supported response to this question. Not surprisingly, both school personnel and parents who were frequently subjected to physical punishment themselves use physical punishment more frequently than those who were not.

When school personnel use physical punishment, they may be unwittingly getting themselves involved with parents' abusive behaviors towards their children. Some parents are physically and/or emotionally abusive of their children. If school authorities use physical punishment with students who are concurrently paddled or perhaps even beaten at home, those parents may try to cover-up their abusive behavior towards their children by shifting the blame to school authorities.

When school personnel use physical punishment the process sometimes degenerates into a chaotic and uncontrolled scenario wherein school professionals perform additional unprofessional behaviors causing unforeseen harmful and problematic outcomes. Some students are humiliated, intimidated, and feel bullied by the process of physical punishment. Some students actively refuse to be subjected to physical punishment. If such students are forcibly positioned or actively restrained so that they can be physically punished, school personnel are acting in a physically aggressive, unprofessional, and unseemly manner. School personnel should not place themselves in any physical jeopardy because they use physical punishment, nor should they engage in the unprofessional and certainly stressful behaviors of fighting with students under the guise of administering physical punishment. (Note: Some districts anticipate these problems by having policies about what will happen, like the automatic delivery of additional penalties, if students refuse to submit peacefully to physical punishment or if they fight back or hit others during the administration of the punishment.)

Many school personnel report thwarted attempts with the administration of physical punishment, and some report being attacked by angered students who retaliate with physical methods. School personnel who use physical punishment may be forced to endure prolonged threats of legal action against them. The professional literature is replete with examples of physical punishment unintentionally causing atrocious injuries to one or both of the parties involved in the process. The issue is further compounded when physical punishment is repeatedly used with young children whose vulnerable bodies make them more susceptible to severe injuries like hematomas, ruptured blood vessels, massive fat emboli, sciatic nerve damage, muscle damage, and brain hemorrhages. School personnel using physical punishment may find themselves liable for injury, damage, and touching the students in places other than the students' clothed rear ends/buttocks.

When school personnel use physical punishment, there are many decisions to be made which often take more time and attention than the entire process warrants. School personnel have to comply with all laws, policies, and requirements concerning the type and size of paddle used. School personnel have to be sure that the paddle used conforms to requirements about its size, thickness, what it can be made from, and what it cannot contain, such as purposeful grooves or attached spikes. School personnel have to determine how many "swats" or "licks" are appropriate for different rule infractions. School personnel have to make decisions about which offenses will result in paddling.

When school personnel deliver physical punishment, they have to be knowledgeable of and abide by all school, district, and state laws and policies, and they have to deliver physical punishment in accordance with the many, often conflicting, court decisions and guidelines. School personnel also have to make decisions about where and when the physical punishment will occur so that it proceeds smoothly and so that the process is not disruptive to others.

To further compound the complexity of using the seemingly simple process of physical punishment, many school personnel are unaware of or are misinformed about the necessary rules and procedures that govern its use. Many school personnel are unfamiliar with the correct rules and procedures because they change with new court decisions and because there are widely varying rules, procedures, and requirements between schools, between school districts, and across state lines.

When school personnel use physical punishment, they incur many problems relative to using a witness to the procedure. Physical punishment should be administered in the presence of a witness. The presence of a witness serves to protect both parties involved in the process. The witness should be a licensed teacher or administrator—not a staff member.

Some teachers are willing to witness to the administration of physical punishment. Some teachers agree to witness because they feel a professional responsibility to their colleagues and to protect students. Some teachers agree to serve as a witness because they are intimidated by their administrators into doing so. Some teachers fear a loss of collegiality if they turn down their fellow teachers' requests that they be a witness to the use of physical punishment.

But many, many teachers and administrators report difficulties finding licensed school personnel who are willing to serve as witnesses. Many teachers and administrators themselves, even if they utilize physical punishment, do not want to serve as witnesses when other school personnel administer physical punishment. There are numerous reasons why teachers do not want to function as a witness to the administration of physical punishment.

Some teachers are unwilling to serve as a witness because if they serve as a witness and do not intervene on the student's behalf when or if the teacher or administrator is purposefully or accidentally abusive, they (by their inaction) have incurred liability. Some teachers are unwilling to serve as a witness for fear that they may have to help restrain a student who is refusing to receive the punishment and that in the process they may accidentally incur liability or be hurt. Some teachers resist serving as a witness because it takes them away from their classroom. Being a witness is also stressful for many teachers. Some teachers refuse to serve as a witness because it typically requires the completion of precise and often lengthy paperwork. Some teachers refuse to be a witness to the use of physical punishment because they philosophically object to the use of physical punishment, and they want no involvement whatsoever with its use.

When school personnel use physical punishment, they typically incur additional and often burdensome paperwork. School personnel's use of physical punishment with students at school invariably requires a "paper trail" to protect all parties. Well-run school districts require that some written record, such as a form or a report, be completed that contains the specifics of the disciplinary incident: the names of the teacher, the student, and the witness; the age, race, and sex of all parties; a specific description of the infraction; a specific description of the number of "licks" or "swats"; specifics about where, when, and how the punishment occurred; specifics about what other disciplinary strategies were attempted for the same inappropriate behavior before physical punishment was selected; and proof that physical punishment was used as a last resort. Some districts require that the paperwork be sent to parents, some require that the paperwork be filed with the central office, and some require that a copy of the paperwork be kept in the student's folder for a specified period of time.

The form or the report detailing the specifics about the use of physical punishment should be completed very soon after the administration of physical punishment. If there is a lengthy delay between the incident and the completion of the required paperwork, there is a distinct possibility that there will be errors that can come back to haunt the teacher or the administrator. For example, if a teacher or administrator frequently uses physical punishment but delays completing the required paperwork, he or she is likely to make mistakes in the reported data, and if litigation does result, those errors could be financially quite costly, and such errors are both personally and professionally embarrassing.

To further complicate the issue, there is no statute of limitations concerning how long after the use of physical punishment a parent may request a copy of the paperwork. If the report or form has not been completed in a timely manner and it is then hastily prepared for parents, the possibility of memory lapses that result in entering erroneous data increases exponentially and, again, can cause problems for the teacher or administrator.

When school personnel use physical punishment, they may incur expenses for optional insurance coverage. Many insurance companies offer school personnel insurance coverage that they can purchase to protect them from liability that they might incur as a result of their use of physical punishment. Some professional organizations and unions offer, as part of the services provided for dues, somewhat minimal coverage for school personnel who become involved in litigation concerning their use of physical punishment.

Like all insurance coverage, different policies provide varying amounts of coverage, and the coverage may or may not sufficiently protect school personnel from additional financial obligations if they are found liable for a large award for damages. While the cost of annual coverage is moderate, it is an additional but optional expense for school personnel. There are also "umbrella coverage" policies that are available for all professionals. We neither advocate nor argue against the necessity of these kinds of insurance coverage; rather, we obviously recommend that all public school personnel simply refrain from ever using physical punishment.

While some parents might advocate the use of physical punishment with their children by their teachers or administrators at school, school personnel should make the decision about the use of physical punishment on a professional basis and in accordance with school, district, and state laws, rules, procedures, and regulations. School personnel are professionals who, by definition, have been schooled in the use of appropriate, professional, tested, and successful instructional and management strategies. School personnel should not be pressured into using physical punishment because of parents' arguments in favor of it, their anecdotal or religious-based support of it, or their tenacity about its supposed effectiveness.

The different rules and procedures for the delivery of physical punishment vary widely between school districts, and compliance with them is often confusing to, and stressful for, school personnel. In some districts, the rules specify that only administrators–not classroom teachers–can administer corporal punishment. In other districts, parents are allowed to, but are not required to, come to school, and they are allowed to deliver, but not exceed, the required physical punishment for their child's inappropriate behavior. In yet other school districts, parents are required to give school personnel permission for the use of physical punishment with their children before they can be physically punished. If the parents do not give the school authorities permission to use physical punishment with their children, then district policies specify what will occur. (In many school districts that allow the use of physical punishment, parents do not have to give school personnel permission to use physical punishment with their children.) In some districts, teachers who decide to use physical punishment are required to administer the punishment themselves, and they cannot pass the onerous task on to others. The myriad of rules, procedures, and policies for the use of physical punishment is thus often confusing and burdensome for school personnel.

All policies governing the use of physical punishment should be, but often are not, sufficiently specific, so sometimes they are interpreted subjectively, inconsistently, or in a discriminatory way. All policies should be reviewed annually, although many are not.

Teaching is the only profession that allows the practicing professionals to strike their clients. School personnel need to examine whether they are using physical punishment out of desperation, for retribution, for deterrence, for reform, or because its use gives them a sense of power and control over students who are smaller, weaker, and more helpless than they are. Public schools are the only public institution in which battery and assault are legally accepted forms of discipline (Owens, 1991). It is against the law to beat or to physically punish inmates in Federal, state, or local correctional institutions, patients at public psychiatric hospitals, and members of the armed forces. When school personnel resort to the use of physical punishment, it keeps them from finding and utilizing better approaches to managing students' behaviors.

When teachers refer students to others for physical punishment, they often worry if the physical punishment will be delivered inappropriately, harshly, or in a cursory manner. Irate parents who have to take time off from work to come to school to discipline their children may be angry and therefore excessively or unduly harsh in their administration of the punishment. Administrators or other teachers who have been pressed into service to deliver the physical punishment may do so in such a routine and rote manner that its delivery is ineffective, too mechanical, or merely perfunctory. If physical punishment is dispensed without any counseling or instructional commentary about students' appropriate behaviors, it is likely to be effective only temporarily and probably a waste of everyone's time and effort.

Physical punishment is an artificial form of punishment because typically the punishment is not logically related to the misbehavior. As noted previously, effective management requires the use of natural, related, and logical consequences. It is not a logical consequence to use physical punishment with a student who is off task or talking inappropriately. While there may be a bit of logical connection for the administration of physical punishment to a student who has been fighting, it is inconsistent because it teaches that "might makes right." Furthermore, there is no satisfactory, professional, research-supported response to a student's question, "If it is not okay to hit someone else, how come you are hitting me?"

The frequent use of physical punishment places students at increased risk for many dysfunctional behaviors, for adolescent antisocial aggressiveness, for various criminal and abusive behaviors, and for vandalism and delinquency. Students who are frequently physically punished are much more likely to be physically aggressive with others. Young children who receive a lot of physical punishment often experience sleep disturbances, problems with wetting the bed, anxiety, and learning problems; they also may become juvenile delinquents in their adolescent years. Students of any age who receive a lot of physical punishment often lose self-esteem. They may suffer from impaired ego function. They may experience stifled relationships with others, and they may engage in self-destructive behaviors or behaviors that are harmful to others.

When school personnel use physical punishment with students, the process sends a mixed message to students, namely that those who care about them and for them are using violent methods and hurting them. The use of physical punishment conveys to students, "Those who love you, hurt you. Therefore love hurts," and the confusion of love and violence can precipitate students abusing others and can even extend to spousal abuse in adulthood. When parents use a lot of physical punishment with their children, the same message is conveyed: the parents, a child's primary source of protection and security, now become a source of fear and pain.

Physical punishment may evoke a sense of humiliation, which can lead to dehumanization. Humiliation can damage a student's sense of dignity, even if it is only temporary. Humiliation is not merely a cause of embarrassment and shame, it also constitutes a blow to one's dignity and self-respect. If the humiliation is severe enough to be traumatic, it approaches brutalization. Students need to have a sense of dignity to maintain self-respect and their feelings of personal worth, and each instance of humiliation damages students' self-respect and their feelings of personal worth.

Many school personnel report that when they deliver physical punishment, it is a tension-ridden, emotional, and often psychologically unpleasant experience. There is a lot of stress and perhaps guilt when teachers and administrators wield the paddle with students, especially with young students. The use of physical punishment requires physical exertion, and it often is a distasteful experience for all parties.

The research and data in the professional literature are clear. The best ways for public school personnel to teach and manage students and to develop an optimal classroom and school atmosphere is through the proactive and frequent use of positive strategies to encourage students' appropriate behaviors, the consistent use of nonphysical punishment methods for students' severely inappropriate or dangerous behaviors, and refraining from the use of physical punishment. A list of resources to help educators end physical punishment follows.

RESOURCES TO HELP EDUCATORS END THE USE OF CORPORAL PUNISHMENT IN SCHOOLS

End Violence Against the Next Generation
977 Keeler Avenue
Berkeley, CA 94708

Louisiana Coalition Against Corporal Punishment in Schools
Louisiana School Psychological Association
4213 Linstorm Drive
Baton Rouge, LA 70814

National Center for the Study of Corporal Punishment and Alternatives in the Schools
Temple University
251 Rutter Annex
Philadelphia, PA 19122

National Coalition to Abolish Corporal Punishment in Schools
155 W. Main Street #100-B
Columbus, OH 43215

National Committee for Prevention of Child Abuse
332 S. Michigan Avenue, Suite 1600
Chicago, IL 60604

People Opposed to Paddling Students, Inc. (P.O.P.S.)
P.O. Box 19045
Houston, TX 77224

SUMMARY OF KEY CONCEPTS IN CHAPTER 10

1. Play and enjoyment of school are not incompatible with learning and achieving; rather, they are inextricably tied to one another.
2. Effective teachers work towards increasing the inherent or intrinsic appeal of all of the learning tasks that they require of their students.
3. Effective teachers are knowledgeable about and they select and use games, traditional play activities, audio-visual media, and instructional and recreational computer software to increase the effectiveness of their instruction.

4. Effective teachers recognize the tremendous value that sincere praise has for maintaining and increasing students' appropriate behaviors.

5. Effective teachers practice praising sincerely and enthusiastically.

6. Constructive criticism is helpful, evaluative, focused commentary about somebody's behavior.

7. Constructive criticism is not simply a criticism of what a student has done, but it also provides some guidance to the student, some instruction about how the student can improve or perform otherwise.

8. The "sandwich technique" involves to the enfolding of a criticism or a negative comment (the filling) between two sincere laudatory or praising comments (the pieces of bread) so that the impact of the critical comment is softened.

9. Effective teachers deliver constructive criticism using the sandwich technique.

10. Effective teachers find creative ways to involve their students' parents in school activities.

11. Effective teachers celebrate, rather than merely tolerate, the many differences among their students, and they relate to all students fairly, equally, and without prejudice or malice.

12. Effective teachers refrain from thinking that they must "police" their students since that is a harsh way to interact with them, and they do not equate being kind and caring with being too permissive.

13. Effective teachers establish a classroom environment and create an atmosphere so that students' interactions with each other and with them are mutually respectful.

14. Effective teachers refrain from comparing students to others, to their siblings, or to students they have had in the past.

15. Effective teachers refrain from participating in or allowing teachers' lounge gossip to impact their interactions with students or to mold the expectations they have about students' behaviors.

16. Effective teachers realize the efficacy and value of behavioral techniques.

17. Effective teachers practice and consistently reinforce students' appropriate behaviors.

18. Effective teachers realize that they cannot and should not acknowledge students' harmless or minimally disruptive inappropriate behaviors.

19. Effective teachers vigilantly and consistently punish or deny reinforcement for students' more severe inappropriate behaviors.

20. Effective teachers use The Premack Principle and contingency/behavioral contracting.

21. The Premack Principle requires that a student perform a less pre-

ferred and lower frequency behavior before they may perform a more preferred and higher frequency behavior.

22. When other more informal approaches have been unsuccessful, effective teachers use contingency/behavioral contracting. Effective teachers use written, formal descriptions of expected behaviors, and they specify what the consequences will be when students perform those behaviors.

23. It is not bribery when teachers contingently dispense reinforcement to maintain or increase the frequency of occurrence of students' appropriate behaviors.

24. Effective teachers refrain from labeling, typecasting, or stereotyping their students on the basis of any characteristic.

25. Effective teachers refrain from having confining, unfair, or sexist behavioral expectations abut their students' behaviors.

26. Effective teachers know how to access and interact comfortably and professionally with experts from other disciplines.

27. Effective teachers have their instructional and management plans in writing so that there is continuity with respect to which student behaviors are reinforced, ignored, or punished.

28. Effective public school personnel, both teachers and administrators, avoid the use of physical punishment altogether because there are so many drawbacks associated with its use.

29. Physical punishment typically suppresses, rather than eliminates, students' inappropriate behaviors.

30. Physical punishment may decrease students' inappropriate behaviors, but this decrease usually occurs only with students who are infrequently physically punished.

31. Conversely, physical punishment is often ineffective with inappropriately behaving students who are frequently physically punished.

32. Physical punishment may decrease or eliminate students' inappropriate behaviors, but typically, only if it is very severe.

33. Physical punishment is an unreliable procedure for decreasing students' inappropriate behaviors and, ironically, it is often responsible for the inadvertent reinforcement of the very behaviors that school personnel target for elimination.

34. When school personnel resort to the use of physical punishment, it often results in a power struggle between school personnel and the student.

35. Physical punishment focuses on students' inappropriate behaviors; therefore, it is an inefficient way to teach students how to behave appropriately.

36. Physical punishment often leads to students disliking or fearing

school personnel.

37. When school personnel resort to the use of physical punishment, they often find an increase in students' avoidance behaviors.

38. When school personnel use physical punishment, it frequently increases students' behaviors that are counterproductive to school personnel's goals and expectations for students.

39. Physical punishment is often unjustly administered and inequitably delivered.

40. When school personnel resort to the use of physical punishment, their behaviors model the appropriateness of physically aggressive ways of interacting with others.

41. When school personnel use physical punishment, they may be unwittingly getting themselves involved with parents' abusive behaviors towards their children.

42. When school personnel use physical punishment, on occasion the process degenerates into a chaotic and uncontrolled scenario wherein school professionals perform additional unprofessional behaviors, and there are other unforeseen harmful and problematic outcomes.

43. When school personnel use physical punishment, there are many decisions to be made that often take more time and attention than the entire process warrants.

44. When school personnel use physical punishment, they incur many problems relative to using a witness to the procedure.

45. When school personnel use physical punishment, they typically incur additional and often burdensome paperwork.

46. When school personnel use physical punishment, they may incur expenses for optional insurance coverage.

47. While some parents might advocate the use of physical punishment with their children by their teachers or administrators at school, school personnel should make the decision about the use of physical punishment on a professional basis and in accordance with school, district, and state laws, rules, procedures, and regulations.

48. The different rules and procedures for the delivery of physical punishment vary widely among school districts, and compliance with them is often confusing to, and stressful for, school personnel.

49. School personnel's use of physical punishment infringes on parental rights to discipline their children the way that they want to.

50. Teaching is the only profession that allows practicing professionals (school personnel) to strike their clients.

51. When teachers refer students to others for physical punishment, they often worry if the physical punishment will be delivered inappropriately, harshly, or in a cursory manner.

52. Physical punishment is an artificial form of punishment because the punishment is typically not logically related to the misbehavior.

53. The frequent use of physical punishment with students places them at increased risk for many dysfunctional behaviors, for adolescent antisocial aggressiveness, for various criminal and abusive behaviors, and for vandalism and delinquency.

54. When school personnel use physical punishment with students, the process sends a mixed message to students, namely that those who care about and for them are using violent methods and hurting them.

55. Physical punishment may evoke a sense of humiliation which can lead to dehumanization.

56. Many school personnel report that when they deliver physical punishment, it is a tension-ridden, emotional, and often psychologically unpleasant experience.

REFERENCES

Baker, J. N., Shapiro, D., Wingert, P., & Joseph, N. (1987, June 22). Paddling: Still a sore point. *Newsweek*, 61.

Butterfield, G. E. (1991, Spring). Landmark decisions: A balance of rights. *School Safety*, 16–17.

Carson, J. C., & Carson, P. (1984). *Any teacher can! Practical strategies for effective classroom management.* Springfield, IL: Charles C Thomas.

Carson, P., & Carson, J. C. (1982). *Don't say you can't when you mean you won't.* Englewood Cliffs, NJ: Prentice Hall.

Cella, C. (1995). You don't have to spank. *The Last Resort, 23*(4), 5.

Elrod, W. T., & Terrell, S. M. (1991). Schools without corporal punishment: There are alternatives. *Contemporary Education, 62*(3), 188–193

Evans, E. E., & Richardson, R. C. (1995, Winter). Corporal punishment: What teachers should know. *Teaching Exceptional Children*, 33–36.

Hamachek, D. (1995). *Psychology in teaching, learning, and growth.* Boston: Allyn & Bacon.

Hindman, S. E. (1986, August). The law, the courts, and the education of behaviorally disordered children. *Behavioral Disorders*, 280–289.

Homme, L. (1973). *How to use contingency contracting in the classroom.* Champaign, IL: Research Press.

The last resort. (1994, Winter). Newsletter of the Committee to End Violence Against the Next Generation, Vol. 2, Berkeley, CA.

Mauer, A. (1990). Corporal punishment. *End Violence Against the Next Generation,* 1–2.

Maurer, A. (1974). Corporal punishment. *American Psychologist, 29*(8), 614–626.

McFadden, M. (1987, Fall/Autumn). Corporal punishment: Legalized child abuse. *Education Canada*, 5–6.

National Coalition to Abolish Corporal Punishment in Schools, 750 Brooksedge, #107, Westerville, OH 43082, pp. 1–2 (includes comments by Fathman, R.).

Novelli, J. (1993, July/August). Better better. *Instructor,* 74–77.

Orentlicher, D. (1992, June 17). Corporal punishment in the schools. *The Journal of the American Medical Association, 267,* 3205–3208.

Owens, M. R. (1991, March 21). Outlaw corporal punishment. *Congressional Record,* 12–13.

Rich, J. M. (1989). The use of corporal punishment. *The Clearing House for the Contemporary Educator in Middle and Secondary Schools, 63*(4), 149–152.

Rich, J. M. (1991). Should students be punished? *Contemporary Education, 62*(3), 180–184.

Richardson, R. C., & Evans, E. D. (1993, Winter). Empowering teachers to halt corporal punishment. *Kappa Delta Pi Record,* 39–40.

Squires, S. (1995, March 24). Despite advice, spanking still common. *The Commercial Appeal,* C4.

Stark, E. (1985, April). Taking a beating. *Psychology Today,* 16.

West, N. (1994, April 17). Should a child be spanked? P*arade Magazine,* 12–14.

SUGGESTED ACTIVITIES/ASSIGNMENTS

1. Research the different forms of play and make a presentation to the class.

2. Select a subject and grade level. Use the Internet or peruse educational materials and computer software catalogs to identify five pieces of instructional software that would help make the selected subject more interesting to learners. Provide the rationale(s) for the selection and for why the selections are developmentally appropriate to the grade level they identified.

3. Work in pairs to practice the effective delivery of praise.

4. Work in teams and practice the use of the sandwich technique for the effective delivery of constructive criticism.

5. Interview teachers and administrators for their ideas on how to get parents involved with schools and their children's activities at school.

6. Interview teachers about their perceptions of what *permissiveness* means. Compare and contrast responses from teachers who are new to the profession with those who have been teaching for 10 or more years.

7. Read and critique two or more journal articles from the professional literature about The Premack Principle.

8. Role-play the use of The Premack Principle. Specify the targeted behavior and the grade level of the children.

9. Read and critique two or more journal articles from the professional

literature about Homme's process of contingency/behavioral contracting.

10. Design a contingency or behavioral contract. Make sure that students specify the targeted behavior and the grade level of the students.

11. Interview teachers, administrators, counselors, and some non-school professionals (such as nurses, dentists, psychologists) concerning how often they work with experts from other disciplines.

12. Interview a teacher or administrator who experienced legal problems relative to the administration of physical punishment.

13. Compose a panel of parents to address them concerning the parents' perspectives on public school personnel's use of physical punishment with inappropriately behaving students. Be sure that the panel includes both parents who are in favor of the use of physical punishment and those who are opposed to its use.

14. Review school handbooks and district policies relative to the administration of physical punishment.

15. Be involved in two debates on the issues related to public school personnel's use of physical punishment with students. Be "pro-physical punishment" in one debate and then "anti-physical punishment" in the other debate.

16. "Shop around" various insurance companies to research the coverage and costs of malpractice coverage and umbrella coverage policies for school personnel. The coverage investigated should relate to school personnel's liability arising out of the use of physical punishment.

17. Invite students from all grade levels to address the class about their reflections and feelings when school personnel used physical punishment with them in school.

18. Critique journal articles in the professional literature concerning the legal implications of physical punishment. Present the findings to the class.

19. Contact the resources/organizations listed at the end of Chapter 10 to find out ways that school personnel can work to end the use of physical punishment in the public schools.

20. Invite an attorney, a judge, a police officer, or a probation officer to address the class about legal issues surrounding the use of physical punishment and students' violent behaviors. Doctors, dentists, and nurses could also be invited to address the class about medical issues, and psychologists, social workers, and counselors could be invited to address the class about the emotional, social, and psychological issues surrounding the use of physical punishment.

Chapter 11

TEACHING DIVERSE LEARNERS:
THE THREE R'S
RECOGNIZE, RESPECT, AND RESPOND

As discussed in Chapter 1, today's classrooms are filled with diverse learners. This diversity includes differences in socioeconomic status, ethnicity, gender, family structure, language, exceptionality, religion, and learning styles. Effective teachers work to create culturally responsive, inclusive classrooms where collaboration and communication promote the academic, social, and behavioral skills of all students. Current demographic trends suggest that teachers will increasingly work with students who exhibit numerous differences. Hoover and Kindsvatter (1997) cite statistics that indicate that by the year 2035, the majority of the American school population will belong to minority groups, and less than 6% of students will be in a family where dad works and mom stays at home.

Teachers can expect students to represent a range of cultures and family structures, to have a variety of learning styles and special educational needs, and to come from a wide range of background experiences. The increase in diversity requires that teachers **recognize** the differences among students, **respect** these differences, and **respond** to those differences in a positive and proactive manner. This chapter provides information and suggestions for creating a classroom community where diversity is respected, recognized, and responded to so that all students feel valued, accepted, and included.

RECOGNIZING DIVERSITY

Individual personal and cultural experiences serve as a baseline for how diversity is perceived. Montgomery (2000) suggests that to create culturally responsive, inclusive classrooms, teachers need to look first at their own attitudes and current practices. A diversity self-assessment, based on the work of Bromley (1998), can assist teachers to productively examine their assumptions and biases. Effective teachers question themselves about the following:

- What is my definition of diversity?
- Do the students in my classroom and school come from diverse cultural backgrounds? If yes, what are these backgrounds?
- What are my perceptions of students from different racial, ethnic, and cultural groups?
- How were these perceptions formed?
- Have I identified my students' different learning styles?
- How do I address my students' different learning styles?
- What are my perceptions of students with disabilities?
- How were my perceptions formed?
- How do my perceptions affect my interactions with my students?
- How can I foster social relationships among my diverse learners?
- How can I make my instruction responsive to the needs of diverse learners?
- What skills do I need to teach diverse learners?
- How can I collaborate with others such as school personnel, family members, community groups, to create a culturally responsive classroom?

Participating in a self-evaluation is the first step effective teachers take to create a classroom environment that actively recognizes diversity and, thus, provides the framework for creating the culturally responsive, inclusive classroom. Self-evaluation allows teachers to examine their beliefs, assumptions, and perceptions related to diversity so that they that can improve their classroom environment and enhance their instructional and management effectiveness.

Individualization of instruction to accommodate each student's **learning styles** and **modality strengths** is another integral component of recognizing diversity. As Midkiff and Thomasson (1993) indicate in their review of Dunn and Dunn's early 1979 pioneering research on learning styles, "Extensive data verify the existence of individual differences among youngsters–differences so extreme that identical methods, resources, or grouping procedures can prevent or block learning for the majority of students" (p. 9).

A *modality* is the way that an individual receives and retains information. A *modality strength* or a *dominant modality* is the sensory channel by which incoming information is most efficiently received, processed, and stored. While one can gain information from any of the five senses, three senses are more readily identified as modalities of learning. Carson and Bostick (1988), Midkiff and Thomasson (1993) and others indicate that there are **visual learners, auditory learners,** and **kinesthetic–tactile learners.** Students who are visual learners need to see the information, and they prefer to watch demonstrations. Students who are auditory learners need to hear the information, and they learn through auditory repetition. Students who are kinesthetic learners need more involved body movement as an aid to acquiring information, while tactile learners need to touch to learn best.

Carson and Bostick (1988) characterize each of these as follows (pp. 21–29):

- The **visual learner** depends on sight and learns best by seeing and watching. Verbs that could be used to describe the visual learner are behold, glance, look, picture, see, show, view, visualize, and watch. Visual learners
  - like to take notes and then review them;
  - are distracted by visual disorder or movement but are not easily distracted by sounds;
  - show intense concentration during reading;
  - respond well to visual displays, pictures, reading from or writing on the chalkboard, filmstrips, slides, and other visual media;
  - write things down and take notes to enhance remembering; and
  - can visualize in detail, and they often think in terms of pictures and what they look like.
- The **auditory learner** understands the world by hearing about it and then by talking about it. Verbs that could be used to describe the auditory learner are converse, discuss, explain, hear, listen, remark, say, speak, and talk. Auditory learners
  - benefit from oral instruction and auditory repetition;
  - prefer to hear or recite information that is presented;
  - think in terms of sounds and are easily distracted by sounds;
  - frequently move their lips or speak under their breaths when they read or count;
  - have better recall when the material is presented orally;
  - respond well to lectures, discussion, tapes, records, radio, and other audio media;
  - respond more favorably to music than to the visual arts; and
  - are typically not concerned with details.
- The **kinesthetic–tactile learner** depends on movement and learns best by touching and manipulating. Verbs that could be used to describe the kinesthetic–tactile learner are do, draw, feel, grasp, hold, make, shape, smell, taste, and touch.

Kinesthetic–tactile learners:
- fidget and move around a great deal;
- benefit from hands-on activities with real objects that can be touched and otherwise sensed;
- like stories with lots of action;
- benefit from direct sensory involvement with objects;
- benefit from making and using various types of media;
- respond well to activities which involve movement and action;
- like to try things out, touch, feel, and manipulate;
- quickly lose interest in lengthy verbal discussions;
- do not respond well to lengthy auditory or visual presentations; and
- communicate kinesthetically often with touching and gesturing.

In addition to these learning styles, characterized as modality strengths, there are other learning styles that need to be recognized in a classroom. Midkiff and Thomasson (1993) describe some categories of learning styles that relate to **environmental stimuli, emotional stimuli, sociological stimuli,** and **physical stimuli**. A brief analysis of each of these categories is presented below to assist teachers in recognizing diversity and improving instructional effectiveness and classroom management.

Environmental stimuli include **noise,** quiet, and sound, cool or warm **temperatures,** bright or dim **lighting,** and formal or informal **design**. While the sound, temperature, and lighting levels are relative, individual student's preferences profoundly impact their attention and learning. Similarly, in terms of classroom design, some students prefer lounging on the floor, others are more comfortable sitting at a desk, and yet others may choose to curl up on a couch or a recliner. Therefore, the effective teacher surveys, either formally or informally, individual student preferences and makes accommodations for those preferences and variations accordingly.

Emotional stimuli are related to **motivation, persistence, responsibility,** and **structure**. Motivation, as discussed previously, is essential for attention, achievement, and retention. Showing students the applications of what they are learning and using real-life experiences enhance students' motivation. Effective teachers enhance students' persistence on a task until it is completed by designing interesting assignments, by giving students short breaks, and by restructuring lengthy assignments into smaller more manageable ones. Such teacher behavior encourages responsible students to follow through with a given task, to complete a task to the best of their abilities, and to do so without direct or frequent teacher supervision. Effective teachers let nonconforming students, know that the task is important. They talk diplomatically rather than talking down to or dictating to these students, and they give the students a choice of how they will demonstrate that they are learning. *Structure* refers to the establishment of specific rules for working on and completing a task. Here again, different students have different needs for structure that should be surveyed and accommodated for instructional and management effectiveness.

Sociological stimuli are factors that relate to how students are **grouped** for instruction. Students learn in a variety of sociological patterns that include working alone or with one or two friends, working within a small group or a large group, working with or without adults, and/or working in some combination of these patterns depending on the task. Grouping students based on ability is not suggested as an effective management technique.

Physical stimuli are related to students' preferences about **time of day, intake,** and **mobility**. These stimuli profoundly impact how and if students learn and behave. Virtually everyone has a time of day preference, and some individuals have a need to nibble, drink, or otherwise snack while working and learning. Because of the variety of mobility needs, some students, especially kinesthetic learners or students with attention deficit disorder, need the freedom to get up and move about during the course of the school day. Assessing these perceptual preferences and accommodating them enhances teachers' instructional and management effectiveness.

Gardner (1983) defines *intelligence* as the human ability to solve problems or to make something that is valued in one or more cultures. According to Gardner, everyone has various combinations of eight basic intelligences: linguistic, logical–mathematical, spatial, bodily–kinesthetic, musical, interpersonal, intrapersonal, and naturalist. Effective teachers should use Gardner's theory to design classroom management techniques that accommodate the diverse students in today's classrooms. For students who are strong in language, effective teachers have students talk about feelings, cooperation, and respect for others. Students who have a strength in logical–mathematical intelligence may respond positively to the use of logical consequences for behaving a certain way. Drawing pictures or making images of desired behaviors may assist the student who has a strong spatial intelligence. Role-playing appropriate and inappropriate behaviors may help a student who has a strong bodily–kinesthetic intelligence. Students who have strong musical intelligence may respond positively to creating songs, raps, and other musical presentations about appropriate behavior. Effective teachers provide group meetings for students who have a strong interpersonal intelligence, and they schedule time to work alone or time away from the group for students who have strong intrapersonal intelligence. The students who have the naturalist intelligence may enjoy investigating how species get along with their families.

Planning for classroom management involves recognizing the diversity within classrooms. Using a variety of techniques that meet the needs of all learners creates a classroom environment where behavior problems are minimal, differences are recognized, respected, and accommodated, and positive learning experiences occur.

RESPECTING DIVERSITY

Jones and Jones (1995), in their review of extensive research by Dunn and Dunn (1983, 1987), Gregoric (1982), and others, indicate that,

> Writers disagree on how effectively teachers can diagnose students' learning styles. Knowing the quality of knowledge available in this area and the demands individualization places on teachers, it seems reasonable that rather than attempt to individualize according to each student's preferred learning style, we should use instructional methods that respond to obvious differences in students' learning styles." (pp. 191–192)

Their suggestions, with parenthetical comments from the authors, appear below. They suggest that teachers incorporate a **variety of instructional techniques**, and they make these suggestions relative to **adjusting environmental factors to meet students' learning needs** (pp. 192–193):

- When presenting material, use visual displays, such as writing on the overhead projector, to assist students who are visual learners. (Chalkboards, bulletin boards, computer-assisted instruction and other visual displays are also suitable. Similarly, audio cassettes and multimedia materials should be utilized for auditory learners, and hands-on kinesthetic and tactile materials should be utilized for auditory and kinesthetic learners, respectively.)
- Allow students to select where they will sit. (This accommodates individual student preferences about light, sound, and temperature, and it personalizes the learning environment.)
- Permit students to choose where they wish to study. (Some may prefer to work at a table, at a traditional school desk, in a soft chair, on a couch, or on a bean bag. Student abuse of the privilege of where to sit and where to study is minimized if students are taught the concept of learning styles and if such privileges are presented as part of a planned process to make learning more personalized and thus effective for every student.)
- Be sensitive to individual student's needs to block out visual or auditory distractions. (Certain areas of the room, such as near the teacher's desk or the windows, are typically more distracting than others, and student needs differ based on students' preferences and the demands of the task.)

- Make healthy snacks available to students or allow them to bring their own. (Effective teachers secure parental permission for teacher- or school-provided snacks such as juice, crackers, fruit, and carrot or celery sticks. Effective teachers are aware of students' food allergies, and they establish procedures for safe handling, storage, and clean-up of snacks and edibles.)
- Provide opportunities for students to select whether they will work alone, in pairs, or in a small group. (Students' selection of how they prefer to work will vary with the individual student and with the nature of the task.)
- Provide adequate structure for both short-term and long-range assignments. (Effective teachers periodically check students' progress, and they make provisions for students to assist each other, especially with lengthy and complex tasks.)
- Give students instruction in study skills. (All students need to learn how to organize material prior to writing and how to effectively study, review, and research material. Furthermore, right brain students may prefer to organize by **mapping**–making connections in a nonlinear fashion–while visual and kinesthetic learners profit from learning how to take notes.)
- Provide learning activities that require the use of both sides of the brain. The left brain learner responds well to workbooks, worksheets, drill, repetitive learning games and activities, and demonstrations. The left brain learner typically enjoys copying, following directions, collecting facts, computing, and record keeping. The right brain learner responds well to creative art activities, guided imagery, creative writing, the use of metaphors and symbols, designing, solving old problems in new ways, mythology, open-ended discussions, and self-expressive activities. (Learning activities suitable for both types of learners should be provided since hemispheric dominance implies preference but not exclusivity.)
- Employ individual goal-setting, self-monitoring, and contracts. (Such activities empower students, enhance motivation, and show students that they have responsibilities and choices.)
- Realize that some students require more frequent breaks than other students. Effective teachers instruct students about how to take short breaks without disrupting the class. (Provisions should also be made to have all students productively engaged, with little "down" or wasted time, time which only encourages the occurrence of inappropriate behavior. Accommodation of students' different needs for breaks increases the likelihood of their meeting and exceeding academic goals and behavioral expectations.

- Consider that students doing poorly in a subject might perform better if that subject were taught at a different time of day. (This will be easier to accomplish in a self-contained elementary classroom than with junior high and high school classes. Administrative difficulties aside, adjusting when different subjects are taught is essential for motivation, learning, and management. Interestingly, college and graduate students often arrange their course schedules according to the time of day when they learn best, and they are students who have successfully navigated their way through the K–12 curriculum.)
- Increase the length of time they wait before they call on students to answer questions. This added time assists students who are more reflective learners. (Explain and teach this procedure to the students, call on all students, and do not, even inadvertently, be punitive towards the slower responding or less verbally articulate student.)
- Create learning centers with a variety of materials to accommodate all students' learning modalities. (Effective teachers use a variety of instructional materials and techniques, and they utilize emerging research and technologies.)

How activities are scheduled has a significant impact on different students and their various learning styles and modality preferences. In scheduling classroom activities, effective teachers make decisions about which activities to start and end the day with, which subjects to teach in the morning and the afternoon, which activities should be consecutive, adjacent, and/or integrated with each other, and about the pacing of activities. Axelrod (1983) provides these suggestions for scheduling activities (p. 83):

- Begin each day with an activity that students prefer. This reinforces students for coming to school promptly.
- Alternate the least preferred activities with more preferred activities. This reinforces students for completing less-desirable work because of the opportunity to enjoy a more preferred activity.
- In many cases it is better to schedule two medium-length assignments during the day than to have one large one.
- It is often helpful to publicly post each day's schedule. This is particularly important when the schedule changes daily.

Scheduling, using a variety of instructional techniques, and adjusting classroom environmental factors are important in creating a classroom that respects the diversity of each student within the classroom.

RESPONDING TO DIVERSITY

Creating a classroom that responds to diversity in a manner that acknowledges and respects differences takes careful planning. The use of classroom management techniques that enhance students' self esteem is one way to respond to student diversity. Culturally responsive classrooms have an atmosphere that respects and recognizes individual differences in socioeconomic status, ethnicity, gender, family structure, language, exceptionality, religion, and learning styles. Schlosser (1992) studied 31 culturally diverse high school students who had been identified as potential dropouts. Students who were interviewed indicated that good teachers displayed the following behaviors:

- Noticing you and asking if you're in trouble;
- Including topics of interest to students in classroom discussions;
- Telling you that you can come back after class if you want to talk more; and
- Listening to what you say without jumping at you. (Schlosser, 1992, p. 133)

These four relatively simple behaviors can create a classroom that responds to differences in a positive, proactive way. When problems arise, teachers need to feel that they know how to approach problems with diverse students, especially those from different cultures. It is important to remember that respecting the culture of all students does not include ignoring the rules of the school and the classroom. Students, regardless of their differences, can be taught appropriate behaviors. Helping students to understand and appreciate diversity creates a positive, safe, and caring classroom environment.

SUMMARY OF KEY CONCEPTS IN CHAPTER 11

1. Today's classrooms are filled with diverse learners. This diversity includes differences in socioeconomic status, ethnicity, gender, family structure, language, exceptionality, religion, and learning styles.
2. Demographic trends suggest that diversity in classrooms will increase.
3. By the year 2035, the majority of the American school population will belong to minority groups.
4. Teachers must recognize, respect, and respond to diverse classroom in a positive way.
5. A self-assessment will assist teachers in examining beliefs, assump-

tions, and perceptions related to diversity.

6. A *modality* is the way an individual receives and retains information. A *modality strength* or a *dominant modality* is the sensory channel by which incoming information is most efficiently received, processed, and stored.

7. There are visual learners who learn best by seeing, auditory learners who learn best by hearing, and kinesthetic–tactile learners who learn best by touching, manipulating, and moving.

8. Environmental stimuli may impact student behavior and learning. Sound, temperature, and lighting are environmental stimuli that influence behavior.

9. Motivation, persistence, responsibility, and structure are emotional stimuli that influence behavior.

10. Students learn in a variety of sociological patterns that include working alone, with one or two friends, within a small group, within a large group, with adults, or in some combination of these patterns.

11. Modality strength differences, time of day preferences, intake needs, and mobility preferences are physical stimuli that influence behavior.

12. Gardner defines intelligence as the human ability to solve problems or to make something that is valued in one or more cultures.

13. Effective teachers use Gardner's theory to design classroom management plans that meet the needs of diverse learners.

14. Planning for effective classroom management involves recognizing the diversity within classrooms.

15. Allowing students to select where they will sit accommodates individual learner preferences in light, sound, and heat and personalizes the learning procedure.

REFERENCES

Axelrod, S. (1983). *Behavior modification for the classroom teacher.* New York: McGraw Hill.

Bandura, A. (1986). *Social foundations of thought and action.* Englewood Cliffs, NJ: Prentice-Hall.

Bromley, K. D. (1998). *Language art: Exploring connections.* Needham Heights, MA: Allyn & Bacon.

Brophy, J. (1987). Synthesis of research on strategies for motivating students to learn. *Educational Leadership, 45,* 40–48.

Carson, J. C., & Bostick, R. N. (1988). *Math instruction using media and modality strengths.* Springfield, IL: Charles C Thomas.

Charles, C. M., & Senter, G. W. (1995). *Elementary classroom management.* White Plains, NY: Longman.

Emmer, E. T., & Hickman, J. (1991). Teacher efficacy in classroom management and discipline. *Educational and Psychological Measurement, 51*(3), 755–765.

Gibson, S., & Dembo, M. (1984). Teacher efficacy: A construct validation. *Journal of Educational Psychology, 76*(4), 569–582.

Goodlad, J. (1984). *A place called school: Prospects for the future.* New York: McGraw Hill.

Gardner, H. (1983). *Frames of Mind: The theory of multiple intelligences.* New York: Basic Books.

Hoover, R. L. & Kindsvatter, R. (1997). *Democratic discipline: Foundation and practice.* Upper Saddle River, NJ: Merrill/Prentice Hall.

Jones, V. F., & Jones, L. S. (1995). *Comprehensive classroom management: Creating positive learning environments for all students.* Boston: Allyn & Bacon.

Kounin, J. (1970). *Discipline and group management in classrooms.* New York: Holt, Rinehart & Winston.

Midkiff, R. N., & Thomasson, R. D. (1993). *A practical approach to using learning styles in math instruction.* Springfield, IL: Charles C Thomas.

Montgomery, W. (2000). Creating culturally responsive, inclusive classrooms. *Teaching Exceptional Children, 33,* 4–9.

Richardson, V. (1984). Time and space. In *Learning to Teach* (pp. 73–197). New York: McGraw Hill.

Rowe, M. (1978). Wait, wait, wait. *School Science and Math, 78,* 207–216.

Rosenthal, R. (1973). The Pygmalion effect lives. *Psychology Today, 7,* 56–63.

Tobin, K. (1987). The role of wait time in higher cognitive level learning. *Review of Educational Research, 57,* 69–95.

SUGGESTED ACTIVITIES/ASSIGNMENTS

1. Administer a learning styles inventory to students in a classroom. Report and discuss the results.
2. Complete the diversity assessment in this chapter. Discuss the results in class.
3. Invite culturally diverse parents, teachers, or community leaders to share information about their culture, beliefs, values, food, dress, religious practices, family structure, traditions and customs.
4. Create a bulletin board that involves culturally diverse themes. Present it to the class.
5. Graph the diversity/differences in your classroom. Examine the differences based on learning styles, gender, ethnicity, family structure, and other differences.
6. Select a children's book that addresses diversity/differences. Explain

and/or demonstrate how you would use this to create a lesson that would recognize, respect, and respond to diversity.

7. Search the Internet for information on diversity in today's class-rooms. Create a resource file of 5 or more ideas that could be used to celebrate diversity.

8. Critique journal articles related to diversity in today's classrooms.

Chapter 12

STUDENTS WITH DISABILITIES: MANAGEMENT AND MOTIVATION

Meeting the needs of students with disabilities in today's classrooms requires that regular education and special education teachers work as partners in providing appropriate services to these students. Identification and assessment of students with any of the disabilities described within this chapter is the responsibility of teachers, parents, administrators, and others. Medical treatment and/or intervention may be necessary in some cases, and this must be determined and frequently re-assessed by a competent health-related professional. This chapter includes information regarding legislation pertaining to students with disabilities, describes inclusive education and categories of students with disabilities, discusses attention deficit hyperactivity disorder (ADHD), and suggests strategies for the accommodation, management, and motivation of students with disabilities.

MAJOR LEGISLATION THAT PERTAINS TO STUDENTS WITH DISABILITIES

A number of federal laws mandate that students with disabilities be educated in "the least restrictive environment," which may be the regular classroom. In 1975, The Education for All Handicapped Children Act (Public Law 94-142) was passed. This was the first federal law requiring school districts to provide a free, appropriate education for children with disabilities. This landmark legislation revolutionized schools and the services provided to children with disabilities. PL 94-142 guaranteed a free, appropriate public education (FAPE) to all students with disabilities, regardless of the severity of the disability. Other provisions included parental notification, procedural rights, related services, individual assessment, individual education program (IEP) programs, and education in the least restrictive environment (LRE). The law has been reauthorized and revised several times since 1975 with the basic requirements essentially remaining the same. In 1990, the name was changed to Individuals with Disabilities Education Act (IDEA). Other revisions included a change in language from "handicapped children" to "children with disabilities." Two categories were added (autism and traumatic brain injury), and schools were required to develop transition plans for students by age 16. Currently, IDEA requires that a program of special education and related services be provided to all eligible students with disabilities between the ages of 3 and 21. Additionally, states are required to identify and evaluate children from birth to age 21. Regulations regarding IDEA may be found at the following web site: http://www.ideapractices.org/law/IDEA97A.HTM.

Some students who require special assistance and services do not necessarily fit into the categories defined by IDEA. These students may qualify for services under *Section 504 of the Rehabilitation Act of 1973* and/or the 1990 *Americans with Disabilities Act (ADA)*. Section 504 requires that schools provide a guarantee of the basic right of accommodation to individuals with disabilities. The greatest benefit of this legislation may be to those students who do not qualify for services under IDEA but still have very special needs. Section 504 provides accommodations for students with physical disabilities, sensory impairments, special health needs such as asthma, diabetes, attention deficit hyperactivity disorder (ADHD), and other disabilities. The Americans with Disabilities Act (ADA) is considered a civil rights and antidiscrimination law, and it provides access to employment and participation in the workplace and community. Under Section 504 and ADA, an individual is considered to have a disability if that individual (a) has a physical or mental impairment that substantially limits one or more of the person's major life activities; (b) has a record of such an impairment, or (c) is regarded as having such an impairment. These two acts do not specify a list of "impairments." They do require the functional criterion of "substantial limitation" to the qualifying element. Educators and parents should be aware of these two important pieces of legislation as well as IDEA in meeting the needs of students with disabilities and other students who need accommodations and modifications (Smith & Patton, 1998).

Most students with disabilities will be included in the general education classroom for a significant portion of the day. Therefore, it is imperative that regular and special education teachers communicate, cooperate, and collaborate to ensure the success of all students.

INCLUSIVE EDUCATION

Approximately 70% of all students with disabilities are included for a substantial part of the day in general education classrooms and are taught by general education teachers (Schnailberg, 1994; U.S. Department of Education, 1995). The issue of where students with disabilities should be educated is still a much discussed and debated topic. *Inclusive education* and *inclusion* are terms that are used to explain the movement toward providing services to students with disabilities in the general education classroom. Smith (1995) states that *inclusion* means (a) every student should be included in a regular classroom to the optimum extent appropriate to the needs of the student; (b) education of students with disabilities is viewed by all educators as a shared responsibility; (c) there is a commitment to include students with disabilities in every facet of the school; and (d) every student must have a place and be welcome in the regular classroom. Inclusive education means that special education personnel and general classroom teachers will work more closely than ever to develop strategies that will facilitate success for all students with disabilities.

The role of the special education teacher in a successful inclusion program is very important. The special education teacher provides instructional support to the general classroom teacher and assistance to students, including those having difficulties but not identified specifically as having a disability. In the inclusive classroom, the general classroom teacher assumes a major responsibility for the education of all students, including those with disabilities. The key to providing effective instruction for all students is the feeling of "shared responsibility" that must occur among classroom teachers, special educators, and other education personnel. According to Hobbs and Westling (1998), classroom teachers play an important role in educating students with disabilities in inclusive classrooms. Classroom teachers must be able to:

- act as a team member on assessment and IEP committees;
- advocate for students with disabilities in general classrooms and special programs;
- counsel and interact with parents of students with disabilities;
- individualize instruction for students with disabilities;
- understand and abide by the due process procedures required by federal and state regulations; and
- provide innovative educational opportunities for all students.

All teachers should be knowledgeable about special education laws, disabilities, characteristics of students with disabilities, instructional strategies, and management strategies so that they can effectively work with all students. All teachers should also have a positive attitude toward students with disabilities so that appropriate educational services can be provided to all students.

GENERAL CLASSROOM MANAGEMENT STRATEGIES FOR STUDENTS WITH SPECIAL NEEDS

All teachers should:

- teach, practice, and reinforce the behaviors desired;
- use teacher proximity to improve on-task behavior and activity level of students;
- use private conferences with students to discuss problems and set goals;
- define objectives and obtain the support needed to reach the objectives;
- seat good role models near the students who have special needs;
- use peer tutors;
- use learning styles information to teach to students using their modality strength(s);
- build a strong, positive relationship with students who have special needs;
- use behavioral and/or academic contracts;
- teach students organization skills; and
- modify lessons and requirements to build in success.

CATEGORIES AND DISABILITY TYPES: ACCOMMODATIONS AND MODIFICATIONS

A brief description of the categories of disabilities that are served in schools by the provisions of the Individuals with Disabilities Education Act (IDEA) is included with examples of suggested accommodations and modifications for each category.

Specific Learning Disabilities

Learning disabilities are indicated by deficits in reading, math, written expression, speaking and/or listening. Other problems may be present in social interactions, emotional maturity, attention, hyperactivity, memory, cognition, metacognition, motor skills, and perceptual abilities (Mercer, 1997).

Teachers should make these accommodations and modifications:

- check to be sure student understands and is able to do assignments;
- have students use a peer partner;
- develop a behavior management plan, and reinforce students' on-task behaviors;
- provide extra time to complete assignments, tests, and projects;
- allow tests and assignments to be read to the student;
- modify the curriculum;
- teach appropriate social skills;
- provide taped textbooks;
- consider the use of alternative assessment (projects, presentations, portfolios);
- allow student to respond orally to classroom tests and exams;
- use a note taker or provide copies of the teacher's notes to the student;
- permit the use of a tape recorder, laptop computer, and other assistive devices.

Speech or Language Impairment

Speech disorders include impairments of voice, articulation, and fluency. Language disorders are impairments in comprehension or use of language.

Teachers should make these accommodations and modifications:

- build a positive classroom environment;
- allow students the time they need to express themselves;
- encourage students to use communication skills;
- structure activities for success;
- pair students with peers for support and modeling;
- allow conversation time so students can share ideas and information;
- encourage students to participate in group responses;
- be specific in giving directions;
- use age appropriate games and music to improve language skills;
- collaborate, consult, and communicate with speech–language pathologists; and
- use assistive technology and augmentative communication systems (communication boards, communication books, sign language, and computerized voices). These devices may be simple or complex with the purpose being to augment oral or written language production.

Mental Retardation

Students with mental retardation are usually identified through intelligence tests and measures of adaptive behavior. Mental retardation begins before age 18 (Luckasson, et al., 1992) and is manifested by significantly subaverage intellectual functioning with related limitations in two or more adaptive skill areas (communication, self-care, home living, social skills, community use, self-direction, health and safety, functional academics, leisure, and work).

Teachers should make these accommodations and modifications:

- create a classroom community where all individuals are welcomed and involved;
- model acceptance by teaching all students awareness, sensitivity, acceptance and how to build friendships;
- emphasize content material that is meaningful and relevant;
- teach social skills;
- use technology to enhance curriculum and learning;
- provide support (peers, volunteers, special educators);
- reinforce appropriate behaviors;
- provide concrete examples;
- encourage speech and active participation; and
- otherwise modify the curriculum as appropriate.

Emotional Disturbance

Students who have emotional and behavior problems exhibit inappropriate behaviors or emotions that result in disruption for themselves or others in their environment (Kauffman & Wong, 1991). Students may refuse to follow directions, use inappropriate language, exhibit aggressive behaviors, appear to have an inability to learn, show signs of severe depression and isolation, and fail to interact with peers, teachers, and others.

Teachers should make these accommodations and modifications:

- build on the student's strengths and interests;
- teach appropriate social skills;
- arrange space in the classroom where students can do quiet work;
- create a motivating reward system;
- use positive reinforcement and peer tutoring;
- build cooperation and trust;
- develop classroom rules and procedures with students;
- structure the classroom curriculum and environment;
- be consistent;

- enlist the help of school counselors, school psychologists, and mental health service providers; and
- collaborate, communicate, and cooperate with others.

Orthopedic Impairments

Some students experience problems related to their physical abilities. Examples include, but are not limited to, cerebral palsy, epilepsy, spina bifida, amputations, and muscular dystrophy.

Teachers should make these accommodations and modifications:

- modify the classroom environment to ensure safety and accessibility;
- develop an effective system for organizing schoolwork;
- provide extra help and time to complete assignments;
- use computer technology and other assistive devices;
- collaborate closely with school nurse and other health-related professionals;
- encourage peers to assist and tutor;
- provide opportunities for the student to engage in social interactions and games;
- allow extra time for students to move from class to class;
- adjust classroom furniture for students who use wheelchairs; and
- plan ahead for field trips, checking to be sure that transportation and sites are accessible.

Autism

Students with autism may have deficits in communication and social interactions. Other characteristics include engagement in repetitive activities, stereotyped movement, resistance to change, and unusual responses to sensory experiences.

Teachers should make these accommodations and modifications:

- collaborate with inclusion specialists to understand autism;
- communicate with specific directions and questions;
- break learning tasks into small steps;
- promote involvement in social activities;
- teach social skills;
- use functional activities to teach skills;
- use visual images and music to teach abstract concepts;
- help peers to understand the behaviors of students with autism and encourage students to be supportive and accepting;

- develop a peer assistance program; and
- use a team approach to meet the needs of students with autism.

Visual Impairments

This category includes students who are partially sighted and those who are blind. Even with correction, these students' educational performance may be adversely affected, and services and accommodations may be needed.

Teachers should make these accommodations and modifications:

- seat students away from bright light and glare;
- teach students board or card games so that they may interact with other students;
- call the student by name and speak directly to the student;
- reinforce the student for effort;
- arrange for tests to be read;
- allow extra time;
- teach peers to say both the student's name and their name in greeting the student with a visual impairment;
- team the student with a sighted peer;
- utilize technology by allowing note-taking devices;
- provide reading list, syllabi, or notes in advance to allow for taping;
- obtain texts on tape or in braille;
- make the classroom accessible; and
- use tactile materials when presenting graphs or illustrations

Hearing Impairments

Students who have permanent or fluctuating hearing impairments that adversely affect their educational performance may require a variety of special education services and classroom accommodations. A hearing impairment may be severe, moderate, or mild. Teachers will need to rely on support from special educators, interpreters, and others in meeting the needs of these students.

Teachers should make these accommodations and modifications:

- include an interpreter as a member of the team;
- make an effort to learn sign language;
- encourage peers to learn sign language;
- speak clearly and audibly;
- check student understanding frequently;

- provide written directions;
- give adequate time for students to respond;
- if hearing aids are used, check that they are working properly;
- encourage small group work;
- confirm students' understanding of rules and classroom procedures;
- seat students near orally presented information;
- provide visual reminders, organizers, and planners for homework assignments;
- repeat the comments of other students who speak;
- use a variety of instructional techniques; and
- allow students to use computers and other technology devices.

Traumatic Brain Injury

Students who have an acquired injury to the brain (caused by an external force) that results in a total or partial functional disability may receive special education services. Students with traumatic brain injury (TBI) may experience impairment in cognition, language, memory, attention, reasoning, abstract thinking, judgment, problem-solving, and sensory, perceptual, and motor abilities. Other impairments may be present in psychosocial behavior, physical functions, information processing, and speech.

Teachers should make these accommodations and modifications:

- provide predictable routines;
- reward positive behaviors;
- structure activities for successful social interactions;
- prepare classmates for the re-entry of the student and discuss changes that may be present (reduced stamina, confusion, frustration, seizures, headaches, hearing loss, vision problems, behavior problems, and reduced self-esteem);
- capitalize on what is familiar to retrieve and develop memory, organization, and cognitive processes;
- prioritize the academic skills that the student needs to learn;
- allow frequent rest periods;
- modify the amount and intensity of assignments;
- allow flexibility in scheduling;
- implement positive behavior management techniques to eliminate inappropriate behaviors; and
- plan together, set goals, and report and evaluate progress.

Other Health Impairments

Students who have limited strength, vitality, or alertness due to chronic or acute health problems are included in this category. Examples include asthma, cystic fibrosis, diabetes, epilepsy, hemophilia, AIDS, and leukemia. Students with attention deficit hyperactivity disorder (ADHD) are included in this category based on the 1999 IDEA regulations.

Teachers should make these accommodations and modifications:

- communicate regularly with parents, health professionals, and other related service providers;
- ensure that students take medications at appropriate times;
- allow frequent rest periods;
- work on building the student's self-image;
- provide extra support and help during times of absence;
- encourage student to develop a cueing system to signal when they are not feeling well;
- use peers as a support system; and
- reduce the length of assignments and provide extra time, if needed.

STUDENTS WITH ATTENTION DEFICIT HYPERACTIVITY DISORDER (ADHD)

Perhaps more than any other group within our schools, students with ADHD seem to present many classroom and administrative challenges. The growing numbers of students with ADHD and recent changes in IDEA regarding ADHD suggest the importance of general and special education teachers understanding this disorder. Estimates of the prevalence of ADHD range from 2% to 30% with 3%–5% being the most probable (American Psychiatric Association, 1994). More important than numbers is the fact that teachers must recognize and implement effective strategies that promote success in the classroom for students with attention deficit hyperactivity disorder.

Teachers are often the first to notice the characteristics of ADHD. These characteristics include difficulties in: attention span, impulse control, and hyperactivity in some cases. Unfortunately, these characteristics are often misinterpreted and misunderstood by classroom teachers and school personnel. Typical teacher comments include "he is very smart, but he is so lazy," "she could do the work, but she just doesn't pay attention," "his behavior keeps him in trouble all the time," "she is so disorganized," "he loses his home work every day," and "if she would just think before she acts."

According to the criteria in the *Diagnostic and Statistical Manual of Mental Disorders* (Fourth Edition; DSM-IV; American Psychiatric Association, 1994), attention deficit/hyperactivity disorder may be diagnosed by a clinician if six or more symptoms are identified from the following.

Attention Span Criteria

- pays little attention to details; makes careless mistakes;
- has a short attention span;
- does not listen when spoken to directly;
- does not follow instructions; fails to finish tasks;
- has difficulty organizing tasks;
- avoids tasks that require sustained mental effort;
- loses things;
- is easily distracted; and/or
- is forgetful in daily activities.

Hyperactivity Criteria

- fidgets; squirms in seat;
- leaves seat in classroom when remaining seated is expected;
- often runs about or climbs excessively at inappropriate times;
- has difficulty playing quietly; and/or
- talks excessively.

Impulsivity Criteria

- blurts out answers before questions are completed;
- has difficulty awaiting turn; and/or
- often interrupts or intrudes on others.

It is important to remember that not all students with ADHD behave in the same way. Classrooms with even one or two students with ADHD can be a challenge and difficult to manage. Effective classroom management, a combination of effective educational accommodations, counseling and medication (if appropriate) are important in reaching and teaching students with ADHD. Students with ADHD, like all other students, respond to positive reinforcement, the Premack Principle, and individual contracts as discussed in previous chapters. Another technique that works is the use of cueing or signaling when the student with ADHD is on the verge of inappropriate behavior. The teacher and student decide on a cue or signal to be used when the behavior begins or is about to begin. This technique helps to establish a positive relationship between the teacher and student, and it sends a message of working together to solve a problem.

Between 60% and 90% of students with ADHD are treated with some form of medication. Teachers should not recommend medication nor attempt to diagnose ADHD. Teachers should work with a team of parents, special educators, administrators, school psychologists, and health care professionals to develop specific plans and accommodations for students with ADHD. Collaboration, communication, and cooperation will increase the likelihood that students with ADHD will be successful in the general classroom.

There are many critical factors to consider when teaching students with ADHD. The following suggestions are not intended to be comprehensive, but will give teachers, administrators and parents ideas about what works with students with ADHD.

Effective teachers

- are flexible, committed and willing to work with students, parents, caregivers, and others involved;
- learn about ADHD and how to meet the needs of student with ADHD;
- request that their school district provide staff development to educate teachers about ADHD, the effect of ADHD on student learning, and appropriate accommodations and modifications for students with ADHD;
- establish regular communication with parents and/or caregivers for success with students with ADHD;
- provide clarity and structure through clear communication, expectations, rules, and consequences;
- engage students with ADHD by using effective, innovative teaching strategies, and avoid lecture as a teaching method;
- limit, prioritize, and modify homework assignments (Parents report that homework is a "nightmare" for students with ADHD.)
- document specific behaviors and communicate with parents, especially if the student begins or changes medication;
- give the student extra time to complete assignments, especially those that require a lot of writing.
- accept alternate methods of presenting and sharing knowledge and encourage the use of computers for word processing; and
- build the self-esteem of students with ADHD and never embarrass or ridicule any student.

Students with ADHD often experience behavior problems in the classroom. The suggestions in Chapter 4 and elsewhere throughout this text may be used with all students, including those who have ADHD. Remember, there is no substitute for positive reinforcement. The authors agree that positive reinforcement is the best behavior management and motivational strategy for all students for building self-esteem and increasing appropriate classroom behavior. The following suggestions for accommodations and modifications for students with ADHD may increase appropriate behavior.

- Seat the student with ADHD near the teacher's desk.
- Surround students with ADHD with good role models.
- Encourage peer tutoring and cooperative learning.
- Avoid distracting stimuli.
- Maintain eye contact during verbal instruction.
- Make directions clear and concise.
- Repeat instructions when needed.
- Enforce classroom rules consistently.
- Have pre-established consequences.
- Administer consequences immediately.
- Reward more than punish.
- Change the rewards offered if they are not effective in motivating a behavioral change.
- Use time out and time away to help students calm down and regain self-control.
- Use cues to stop disruptive behaviors before they begin.
- Write a contract specifying what behavior is expected and what reinforcement will be used.
- Develop an IEP or a Section 504 accommodation plan if needed.

HOME MANAGEMENT TECHNIQUES FOR STUDENTS WITH ADHD

The following suggestions may be helpful for parents of students with ADHD. Parents and teachers must work together to improve academic success and appropriate behavior of students with ADHD.

- Establish clear rules when the child is young and be consistent.
- When possible, consider the child's opinion and allow the child to make some decisions.
- Use a reward system to establish and maintain appropriate behaviors.
- Give the child responsibilities (tasks) at home.
- Create a short list of tasks to help the child remember. The child will gain satisfaction by checking the tasks off as they are completed.
- Be sure you have the child's attention before giving directions and commands. Make eye contact, state the directions slowly, and have the child repeat what was said.
- Do not permit the child to be unduly loud and noisy in a public place.
- Set up a routine for meals, homework, TV, getting up, and going to bed.

- Help others to understand the child with ADHD.
- Use incentives before punishment.
- Avoid physical punishment.
- Reward for compliance with privileges, tangibles, money, activities, praise.
- Punish for noncompliance with loss of privileges and time-out.
- Design the punishment to "punish behavior," not the child.
- Practice forgiveness.

Children with ADHD require a lot more monitoring and supervision than other children. Parents, teachers, school administrators, and other professionals must work together so that all students with ADHD can experience success academically and behaviorally.

For more information on ADHD, visit the world wide web at www.chadd.org.

SUMMARY OF KEY CONCEPTS IN CHAPTER 12

1. Providing appropriate services to students with disabilities requires that general education teachers and special education teachers work as partners.
2. The first federal law that addressed students with disabilities in schools was The Education for All Handicapped Children Act (Public Law 94-142), passed in 1975.
3. The basic provisions of EHA included a free, appropriate public education for all students with disabilities, procedural rights, related services, individual assessment, parental notification, IEPs, and education in the least restrictive environment.
4. The original law has been revised, re-authorized, and amended. The name was changed to Individuals with Disabilities Education Act (IDEA) in 1990.
5. In 1990, two new categories of disability were added: autism and traumatic brain injury.
6. In 1990, the terminology changed from "handicapped children" to "students with disabilities."
7. Schools are required to provide transition plans for students with disabilities by the age of 16.
8. Final regulations regarding IDEA may be found at: http://www.idea practices.org/law/IDEA97A.HTM.
9. Section 504 of the Rehabilitation Act of 1973 and the Americans with Disabilities Act (ADA) may provide services for students who may

not be served by IDEA.

10. Inclusive education provides support and services to students with disabilities in the general education classroom, when appropriate.
11. It is imperative that regular and special educators communicate, collaborate, and cooperate for inclusive education to be successful and to ensure the success of all students.
12. Special educators must provide instructional support to the general classroom teacher and to students who need assistance.
13. The general classroom teacher must assume a major responsibility for the education of all students, including those with disabilities.
14. A feeling of "shared responsibility" must be present in inclusive education.
15. Suggestions for accommodations and modifications for each type of disability will enable students with disabilities to be successful in the classroom.
16. The estimated prevalence of students with ADHD is 3%–5%.
17. Teachers are often the first to notice the characteristics of students with ADHD; these include inattention, impulsivity, and hyperactivity.
18. Suggestions for management and motivation of students with ADHD include providing extra time to complete assignments, accepting alternate methods for completing assignments, and limiting homework assignments.
19. Effective teachers of students with ADHD are flexible and willing to learn how to meet the needs of students with ADHD.
20. Suggestions for classroom accommodations and modifications for students with ADHD include preferential seating for students with ADHD; clear, concise directions; consistently enforced rules; pre-established consequences; and the use of positive reinforcement.
21. Home management strategies for parents include establishing clear rules, using a reward system to establish and maintain behaviors, setting up a routine for the child with ADHD, avoiding physical punishment, and helping others to understand the child with ADHD.

REFERENCES

American Psychiatric Association. (1994). *Diagnostic and statistical manual of mental disorders (DSM-IV)* (Fifth Edition). Washington, DC: Author.

Hobbs, T., & Westling, D. L. (1998). Promoting successful inclusion. *Teaching Exceptional Children, 34*, 10–14.

Kauffman, J. M., & Wong, K. L. H. (1991). Effective teachers of students with behavioral disorders: Are generic teaching skills enough? *Behavioral Disorders, 16,* 225–237.

Luckasson, R., Schalock, R., Snell, M., & Spitalnik, D. (1996). The 1992 AAMR definition and preschool children: Response from the committee on terminology and classification. *Mental Retardation, 34,* 247–253.

Mercer, C. D. (1997). *Students with learning disabilities* (Fifth Edition). New York: Merrill.

Schnailberg, L. (1994, October 19). E. D. report documents "full inclusion" trend. *Education Week,* p. 8.

Smith, T. E. C., Polloway, E. A., Patton, J. R., & Dowdy, C. A. (1998). *Teaching students with special needs in inclusive settings,* (Second Edition). Boston: Allyn & Bacon.

U.S. Department of Education. (1999). *Annual report to Congress on the implementation of the Individuals with Disabilities Education Act.* Washington, DC: Author.

SUGGESTED ACTIVITIES/ASSIGNMENTS

1. Individually or as partners review two films that include a character with a disability. Identify the title of the film, the character, and the type of disability. Evaluate the accuracy or appropriateness of the characterization of the disability. Share this "review" with the class.

2. Interview an individual with a disability. Identify what the individual's experiences have been academically, socially, vocationally, and personally.

3. Search the Internet for books, stories, poems, films, and other resources for children ages 4–16 that provide information regarding types of disabilities. Provide an annotated bibliography of this information to share with your class.

4. Search the Internet for laws/legislation that relate to students with disabilities (IDEA, Section 504, ADA). Report on your findings.

5. Interview a special education teacher and a general education teacher. Find out how they meet the needs of students with disabilities in the classroom.

6. Search the Internet for categories/types of disabilities. Select one category or type that you want to know more about. Write a paper that defines and describes the category, describes the characteristics of the category, and suggests educational accommodations and modifications that may be used to meet the needs of students with that type of disability.

7. Search the Internet for current information on students with ADHD.

Present to classmates strategies for classroom management, effective accommodations, and modifications for students with ADHD.
8. Organize a panel of parents, teachers, and other professionals to discuss students with disabilities.
9. Critique journal articles related to the pros and cons of inclusive education.
10. Critique journal articles related to students with ADHD.

Chapter 13

PARENTAL INVOLVEMENT: A KEY TO EFFECTIVE CLASSROOM MANAGEMENT

The importance of parental involvement in managing the behavior of students and increasing achievement cannot be over emphasized. Research indicates a strong link between parental involvement and student achievement (Hester, 1989). Teachers have identified the importance of strong parental involvement as an issue that should receive the highest public education policy priority. A 1993 Metropolitan Life survey of teachers found that a large majority believed that the nation's schools could be improved by the federal government if parents were encouraged to be more involved in their children's education (Richardson, 1993). Yet effective parental involvement is not easily accomplished. This chapter describes types of parental involvement, possible barriers to parental involvement, and suggestions, techniques, and strategies that teachers may use to increase cooperation and parental involvement in schools and classrooms.

As the structure of the family has changed, so has parental involvement within schools. The rise in families with two working parents, one-parent families, and the need for family members to hold more than one job has changed many aspects of parental involvement in schools. The diversity among families requires that educators develop creative plans and programs that will promote parental involvement. Liontos (1992) suggests a positive approach for recognizing the strengths of all parents and families:

- all families have strengths,
- parents can learn new techniques,
- parents have very important perspectives about their children,
- most parents really care about their children,
- cultural differences are valid and valuable, and
- many family forms exist and are legitimate.

TYPES OF PARENTAL INVOLVEMENT

The National PTA Board of Directors (1993) has endorsed three types of parental involvement:

- Parents as the first educators in the home,
- Parents as partners with the schools, and
- Parents as advocates for all children and youth in society.

Parents are truly the first teachers of their children. A growing number of programs called Parents as First Teachers has sprung up throughout the country, and these programs assist parents in understanding how they can be effective "first teachers." Many school districts provide resources, materials, and information to parents by establishing parent resource centers in the community and school. This type of resource center provides training and materials for parents in learning and implementing effective parenting skills early in their child's life.

Parent resource centers and other programs encourage parents to become involved as active partners in their child's education. School administrators and teachers recognize that parental involvement increases achievement and has positive effects on student attitudes and behavior. Research has indicated time and time again that students' attitudes towards school, their achievement, attendance, motivation, self-concept, and behaviors are directly influenced by the attitudes of their parents towards learning and school. Parents want their children to succeed in school as a preparation for success in life, and this success will occur if teachers, parents, and students work together as partners in schools and classrooms.

Schurr offered 16 "proven parent involvement strategies" (1992, pp. 4–9). She suggested that schools:

1. involve parents in mutual goal setting, contracting, and evaluating;
2. involve parents in assessment of school policies, practices, and rituals;
3. open a parent lounge, center, or resource room;
4. develop public information displays, public service messages, and work site seminars;
5. develop a parent handbook of guidelines and tips;
6. hold a weekend or evening public information fair;
7. have a student and parent exchange day;
8. award extra academic credit for parent involvement;
9. have an old-fashioned family night at school (ice cream party, potluck dinner, etc.);
10. develop a school-wide communications plan;
11. keep parent–teacher dialog journals for communication;

12. praise parents' efforts;
13. assemble monthly home achievement packets;
14. conduct home visits for a special bond;
15. enact a school wide homework policy; and
16. plan a meet-and-greet program for involvement.

Recognizing parent efforts, making parents feel welcome in the school and classroom, communicating effectively with parents, and organizing special events will build a strong partnership between parents, teachers, and students, thus increasing the likelihood that students will be successful academically and behaviorally.

The importance of parents as advocates for all children and youth in society cannot be overemphasized. Parents are often the best educational advocates for their children. True parental advocacy is a positive process that benefits parents, teachers, students, and in many cases the entire school district. The following suggestions may help parents to become effective advocates:

1. Know the policies, rules, and regulations that schools must abide by. Contact the local school district office or State Department of Education regarding specific laws and parental rights.
2. Get to know school personnel. Communicate concerns or problems through appropriate channels.
3. Maintain an organized file of educational records. Take notes during telephone conversations and conferences with teachers.
4. Join a parent support group, read books and articles related to education issues, and attend conferences.
5. Know your child's strengths and interests. Assist professionals in identifying appropriate learning accommodations.
6. Focus on the big picture.

When parents are advocates, they may work at the local, state, and national levels to impact legislation and policies that directly impact children.

Parental involvement can mean many different things and can take many different forms. Parents may be supporters of school and classroom activities, active partners, volunteers, facilitators of children's development, and/or collaborative decision makers. The following suggestions may help focus parental involvement efforts:

- define what your school district or classroom means by parent "involvement";
- provide examples of how parents can be involved in the school and classroom;
- remove possible barriers; and
- identify possible community interest in increasing the parents' role in the school and classroom.

POSSIBLE BARRIERS TO PARENTAL INVOLVEMENT

A number of barriers may exist between educators and parents. These barriers can originate from beliefs, perceptions, and attitudes of teachers, parents, and administrators. A substantial barrier to parental involvement is the firmly rooted belief that education is best run by professionals rather than as a democratic process that involves all parties with a vested interest. Perhaps, Ferr (1992) said it best: "Parents are like shareholders in a company without the opportunity to attend the shareholders' meeting." Recognition of barriers is an important step when planning effective parental involvement programs. The following barriers may be present:

- past negative experiences in school,
- poor communication between school and home,
- personal circumstances of parents,
- defensiveness on the part of both teachers and parents,
- educators may not know how to involve parents,
- lack of time and opportunity,
- fear of conflict,
- mistrust,
- insecurity, and
- disinterest.

Ferr (1992) suggests the following ways to reduce barriers:

- School boards may consider inviting parents to express views and suggestions regarding education programs;
- Administrators could appoint committees to develop policies and guidelines for parental involvement programs;
- Administrators may consider parent–school communication throughout the school district;
- Classroom teachers could be strongly encouraged to fully and effectively communicate pertinent classroom information to parents; and
- A district-wide philosophy should be developed with an array of activities that will bring parents, teachers, students, and administrators together.

Successful parental involvement is encouraged when a welcoming climate is present in schools and classrooms, creating a sense of mutual respect. A welcoming climate allows parents, teachers, administrators, and students to share a common cause and a meaningful reason for being involved. Again, parent involvement must be viewed by all as a positive partnership that benefits the school district, educators, parents, and students.

TECHNIQUES FOR INCREASING PARENTAL INVOLVEMENT

There is no shortage of research or suggestions for improving parental involvement in schools and classrooms. It is important to note that there is no one best way for schools to develop and implement parental involvement programs. Each school district and its community will need to develop, implement, revisit, and refine parental involvement strategies to meet their unique needs. Fredericks and Rasinski (1990) identified 14 ways to involve parents. They are:

1. flood parents with information;
2. make parent involvement a school-wide effort;
3. recognize students and parents;
4. involve students in recruiting parents;
5. conduct projects and activities that include the entire family;
6. recruit community members;
7. make classrooms and the school a welcoming and comfortable place;
8. use the telephone as an instrument of good news;
9. find out why parents are not involved;
10. have a variety of events to involve parents;
11. operate a parent hotline for concerns, homework, and other issues;
12. use community members to endorse the parental involvement program;
13. videotape programs for parents; and
14. provide support services for parents (e.g., child care).

Teachers who are successful in involving parents in the classroom begin **before** the first day of school. Typically, teachers receive the names of students who will be in their class before the students actually arrive. This first opportunity for parental involvement may be one of the most important contacts a teacher can have. As soon as a class roll is available, the teacher should make a phone call or write a short note to the parents or guardians. This first contact should be a brief introduction and should express a positive and enthusiastic tone to parents. Effective teachers let the parent know that they are excited and enthusiastic about the upcoming school year, and they communicate their excitement and enthusiasm to parents. For example, a note or phone call could include the following greeting and information.

Mr. & Mrs. Fox:
I am so happy to have Tucker in my classroom this year, and I look forward to meeting both of you. I have an exciting year planned for my students, and I want both of you to be involved in our classroom community. Please

feel free to call me if you have questions, concerns, or suggestions for our classroom.
Mrs. Fleming
Third Grade Teacher

The goal of this first communication is to establish a positive tone with the parents and to let them know that you are a caring, concerned professional. A phone call could include the same information with a slightly different format. Be sure to plan your call or letter so that a positive communication is established early. Positive phone calls and notes are proven techniques for getting and maintaining parental support and involvement. Remember, this is most effective when done **before** the students actually arrive in the classroom.

Following the first communication with parents, a letter of introduction to the parents is suggested. This letter, usually written during the first week of school, gives the parents an opportunity to get to know their child's teacher early in the year. The letter should be brief, express confidence that their child will be successful in your classroom, and tell parents something about you as the classroom teacher. Many teachers take this opportunity to describe their classroom management/discipline plan and homework policy. Explain to the parents how they can help with homework, convey confidence that the child will be successful, invite parents to visit the classroom, and explain that you will continue to communicate throughout the year in various ways. This communication should convince parents that they are the most important people in their child's life, and that they will be working as partners with their child's teacher to ensure academic and behavioral success. It is suggested that parents sign and return this letter indicating that they understand and support the teacher's classroom management plan, homework policy, and other classroom routines.

As the school year progresses, effective teachers continue to make positive phone calls, write positive notes, and communicate with parents on a regular basis. Many teachers create parent handbooks to be given to parents. A parent handbook could include the following items:

- names of students in the class;
- list of faculty, school address, phone number, school hours;
- a map of the school;
- daily classroom schedule;
- grade level curriculum (objectives/goals for the year);
- school calendar showing holidays;
- classroom policies regarding absences, homework, and makeup work;
- suggested reading list;
- suggestions for how parents can help students at home; and
- request for parent volunteers to help in the classroom.

An invitation for parents to visit the school and classroom should occur early in the school year. Canter (1991) suggests a "back to school" night as a way to involve parents and begin building a strong partnership. Canter suggests the following ideas for making this time successful:

- Create a welcoming environment. Display a "Welcome Parents" poster on the door or in the classroom. Have students sign it.
- Prepare name tags for parents or provide blank name tags. Leave space for "parent of_____" for students who may have a different last name from their parents.
- Display a class schedule and your classroom management plan.
- Display work completed and work in progress.
- Provide a tour of your classroom.
- Explain the different areas in your classroom and why you have them. Show your classroom library and different centers in the classroom; point out how they are used to enhance learning.
- Present special activities or a program that involves students. Present a slide show or a video showing students in the classroom working in small groups or independently. Be sure that all students appear in the presentation.
- Tape record a song and play for parents while they are visiting the classroom.
- Have student write notes to parents and leave them in their desk.
- Display a variety of student work. Provide folders for parents to see student 's work.
- Provide materials for parents to take home.
- Send materials to parents who did not attend.

The excitement and enthusiasm that is shown during "back to school" night is an excellent way to gain and maintain parent support. The results of establishing a positive relationship with parents early in the year will be increased student achievement and appropriate behavior. Positive parent communication builds and maintains parental involvement throughout the entire school year. Effective teachers take advantage of the many occasions throughout the year that can provide parents with positive feedback concerning their child. Ongoing positive communication also makes communication about a problem much easier, and increases the likelihood of its success.

Parental involvement is a valuable, sometimes largely untapped, resource for teachers. Effective teachers will use this resource to increase student achievement and appropriate behavior, build positive partnerships with parents and caregivers, and create a classroom community that values and promotes success.

SUMMARY OF KEY CONCEPTS IN CHAPTER 13

1. Research indicates a strong link between parental involvement and student achievement.
2. The changing structure of the family has changed the level of parental involvement within the school.
3. All families can be involved in schools and classrooms.
4. Three types of parental involvement are discussed: parents as first educators, parents as partners within the school, and parents as advocates for all children and youth in the society.
5. Schurr (1992) suggests strategies for involving parents, including developing a parent handbook, involving parents in assessment of school policies, developing a school- wide communication plan, and planning a school-wide parent involvement plan.
6. Parental advocacy is a positive process that can benefit parents, teachers, students and entire school districts.
7. Parental involvement may take many different forms.
8. Barriers to parental involvement include past negative experiences in school, poor communication between school and home, personal circumstances of parents, defensiveness on the part of both teachers and parents, and lack of time and opportunity.
9. Suggestions for reducing barriers to parental involvement include appointing parents to serve on policy and procedure committees, inviting parents to act as volunteers, encouraging teachers to communicate regularly with parents, and developing district- wide parental involvement programs.
10. Techniques for increasing parental involvement include using the telephone as an instrument of good news; operating a parent hotline for concerns, homework, and other issues; and providing support services for parents.
11. Effective teachers communicate with parents before the first day of school.
12. Positive communication continues throughout the school year.
13. An invitation for parents to visit the school and classroom should occur early in the school year.
14. A "back to school" night is a way to involve parents and build a strong parental involvement partnership.

REFERENCES

Canter, L., & Canter, M. (1991). *Parents on your side.* Santa Monica, CA: Lee Canter & Associates.

Ferre, D. (1992). *Parental involvement in school decision making.* Unpublished Masters Thesis: University of Saskatchewan.

Fredericks, A. D., & Rasinski, T. V. (1990). Working with parents: Involving the uninvolved: How to. *The Reading Teacher, 43*(6), 424–425.

Hester, H. (1989). Start at home to improve home–school relations. *NASSP Bulletin, 73*(543), 23–27.

Liontos, L. B. (1992). *At-risk families and schools: Becoming partners.* Eugene, OR: ERIC Clearinghouse on Educational Management.

National PTA. (1993). *The heart of the PTA: Parent and family involvement.* Chicago: Author.

Richardson, J. (1993). Teachers in poll seek greater push for parent involvement. *Education Week,* p. 10.

Schurr, S. L. (1992). Fine tuning your parent power: Increasing student achievement. *Schools in the middle, 2*(2), 3–9.

SUGGESTED ACTIVITIES/ASSIGNMENTS

1. Write a letter of introduction to parents that could be sent before school starts. Explain your classroom rules, procedures and other information. Share a copy of this letter.
2. Make of list of activities explaining how parents could be involved in your classroom as active supporters, volunteers, or resource persons.
3. Role-play a telephone call that could be made to parents before the school year begins.
4. Role-play a telephone call sharing "good news" to parents.
5. Create a parent handbook for your classroom. Share a copy with classmates.
6. Create a list of websites for parents to visit that would provide information on effective parenting skills.
7. Write a list of suggestions explaining how parents can help their child study at home.
8. Plan a "back to school' night. Include an invitation, activities that you will present, and information that you want to share with parents.
9. Design five positive notes to parents to be used during the school year.

10. Prepare a classroom newsletter. Share with classmates.
11. Critique journal articles related to parental involvement.

Section IV

LEGAL ISSUES
AND SCHOOL VIOLENCE

Chapter 14

LEGAL ISSUES ASSOCIATED WITH THE USE OF CORPORAL PUNISHMENT

This chapter contains a brief analysis of some of the legal issues related to the use of corporal punishment in the public schools by school personnel. Many of the legal issues are also relevant to personnel in private schools.

The material presented in this chapter is included to further emphasize the inappropriateness of school personnel's use of corporal punishment. The inclusion of this chapter should in no way be construed to be an endorsement of the practice which we consider to be always inappropriate for the many reasons presented in Chapter 10.

This chapter's content is not exhaustive, and it should not be used as a substitute for legal advice. Readers who elect to administer corporal punishment should thoroughly familiarize themselves with building, district, and state policies concerning the use of corporal punishment, and they should seek legal advice for interpreting and conforming to the numerous and often conflicting building, district, and state policies governing the use of corporal punishment.

NATIONAL ORGANIZATIONS THAT OPPOSE CORPORAL PUNISHMENT AND SUPREME COURT DECISIONS

In February of 1995, the National Education Association specifically advised its members that, "The best legal advice is simply not to use corporal punishment at all since expert testimony about the effects of 'educator-induced post-traumatic stress disorder leading to lifelong psychological damage' has been successful in pressuring schools to settle out of court in the victims' favor" (Gootman, 1991, p. 180). Additional compelling evidence of professionals' disapproval of corporal punishment can be noted from the list below, which is not exhaustive but which nonetheless clearly indicates national organizations that oppose corporal punishment in the schools:

American Academy of Pediatrics
American Association of Counseling and Development
American Association for Protecting Children
American Association of School Administrators
American Bar Association
American Civil Liberties Union
American Humane Association
American Medical Association
American Nurses Association
American Orthopsychiatric Association
American Psychiatric Association
American Psychological Association
American Public Health Association
American Society of Dentistry for Children
American Speech-Language-Hearing Association
Association for Childhood Education International
Association for Humanistic Education
Association for Junior Leagues International
Association of State Departments of Education
Council for Exceptional Children
Defense for Children International USA
Dental Coalition to Combat Child Abuse and Neglect
National Association for the Advancement of Colored People
National Association of Elementary School Principals
National Association of Elementary School Principals
National Association of School Psychologists
National Association of Social Workers
National Association of State Boards of Education
National Black Catholic Congress
National Committee for Citizens in Education
National Committee for the Prevention of Child Abuse
National Congress of Parents and Teachers
National Council of Teachers of English
National Education Association
National Foster Parents Association
National Indian Education Association
National Mental Health Association
Network of Runaway and Youth Services

Parents Anonymous
Pediatric Nurses Association
Society for Adolescent Medicine
Society of Friends (Quakers)
Unitarian Universalist General Assembly
U.S. Department of Defense: Office of Dependents' Schools
Overseas

As Evans and Richardson (1995) indicate, there are

Two significant cases (that) have caused many school districts to support and maintain the use of corporal punishment in their discipline code. The U.S. Supreme Court affirmed that corporal punishment in the school neither violates the Eighth Amendment protection against cruel and unusual punishment, nor does it breach the Fourteenth Amendment due process guarantees. (*Baker v. Owen*, 1975; *Ingraham v. Wright*, 1977; p. 34)

In *Baker v. Owen* (395 F. Supp. 294, 1975), though the court recognized the parents' basic rights in the upbringing of children, the Court considered the "legitimate and substantial interest" of the state "in maintaining order and discipline in the public schools." If a state allows corporal punishment, parental objections to the practice will not prevail (school officials had corporally punished the plaintiff, Russell Baker, even though his mother had previously expressed her opposition to such punishment). Furthermore, the court ruled that minimal procedural safeguards must be provided and established specific guidelines must be followed when administering corporal punishment:

1. Students must be warned that a specific misbehavior will result in a spanking.
2. Spanking is to be used only as a last resort after less drastic measures have failed. In effect, physical punishment should never be used as a first line of punishment for a misbehavior. However, neither of these principles apply if "the student's behavior is so antisocial or disruptive in nature as to shock the conscience."
3. Physical punishment has to be administered in the presence of another staff member who has been informed beforehand, in the student's presence, of the reason for the punishment; and
4. A written report detailing the reasons for using physical punishment must be made available to parents if they so request.

The guidelines from *Baker v. Owen* can be problematic for school personnel if they face a legal challenge of their use of corporal punishment. Accurate written documentation is required to prove that the first two guidelines have been satisfied, although in practice school personnel rarely document when and how they warned students that a specific misbehavior will result in a spanking (Guideline 1). While Guideline 2 may be easier to document than Guideline 1, the decision gives little, if any, definition of *antisocial or disruptive behavior,* thus making it highly subjective and vulnerable to varying interpretations. Guideline 3, about a witness, is a bit easier to document, but only if accurate records about who witnessed and what was specifically said and done are kept at or shortly after the administration of corporal punishment (true also for Guideline 4). With guideline 4, there is no time period specified concerning how much time after the administration of corporal punishment a parent can request a written report, and if a report is generated at a much later date and from memory, there may be significant and embarrassing errors of fact reported.

In *Ingraham v. Wright* (430 U.S. 651, 1977), the United States Supreme Court ruled that the use of corporal punishment in schools does not violate the Eighth Amendment nor the Fourteenth Amendment, due process guarantees. The court concluded that the Eighth Amendment was never intended to apply to schools but was designed to control the punishment of incarcerated criminals, since the openness of the public schools and its supervision by the community affords enough safeguards to prevent the type of abuse from which the Eighth Amendment protects the prisoner (Rich, 1989, p. 149). In comparing the Ingraham and Baker cases, Hindman (1986) draws this conclusion: "The Court altered its position when it deliberated the case of *Ingraham v. Wright* (1977). In a narrow 5–4 decision, the justices ruled that punishment was merely a routine disciplinary measure which did not affect a student's liberty. In so doing, the Court not only refused Constitutional protection for children, it also held that the due process clause of the Constitution does not require notice and hearing prior to the imposition of corporal punishment" (p. 281).

As Hindman (1986) observes, "Schools have the power to administer corporal punishment under the common law doctrine of *in loco parentis,* where parental power traditionally reserved to discipline the child is transferred to school personnel while the child is under their supervision" (p. 281). Butterfield (1991) indicates that "The reasoning behind the *in loco parentis* doctrine is contrary to compulsory education laws because school officials do not merely exercise voluntary parental authority. Instead, they must adhere to and promote publicly mandated educational and disciplinary policies (p. 16). The discretionary power of *in loco parentis,* questionably applied in many cases, has resulted in modern courts applying the standard of "reasonableness"; punishment is excessive when it is not reasonable. Four tests decide the issue of reasonableness:

1. Was the rule being enforced reasonably?
2. Was the form and extent of the force used reasonable in light of the type of offense committed by the pupil?

3. Was the form and extent of the force used reasonable in light of the pupil's age and known physical condition? and

4. Did the teacher act without malice or personal ill will toward the pupil?

Butterfield (1991) comments that two other major court decisions have an impact on school discipline. "The landmark decisions in 1975 and 1985 (*New Jersey v. T.L.O.* 469 U.S. 325, 1985, and *Goss V. Lopez,* 419 U.S. 565, 1975) had these three significant outcomes:

1. reasoned that school officials are state agents subject to the strictures of the Fourth Amendment (the Fourth Amendment provides "the right of the people to be secure in their persons, houses, papers, and effects, against unreasonable searches and seizures, shall not be violated, and no warrants shall be issued, but upon probable cause . . .");

2. previous application of the *in loco parentis* doctrine to student searches was held to be in "tension with contemporary reality and the teachings of the court"; and

3. searches of students at school require only "reasonable suspicion." The standard for reasonable suspicion is met by a two-fold test: it must be reasonable both at inception (are there reasonable grounds for suspecting that the search will turn up evidence that the student has violated either the law or school rules?) and scope (were the search measures reasonably related to the objectives of the search, and were they not excessively intrusive in light of the age and sex of the student and the nature of the infraction?) (pp. 16–17).

No attempt at an exhaustive legal literature review will be made here. However many cases and changing legal perspectives about everything from the *in loco parentis* doctrine to what constitutes an "appropriate" paddle and "reasonableness" serve to confuse the issues surrounding the use of corporal punishment. From a legal perspective, therefore, school personnel are advised to follow the guidelines set down by legal precedents and to abide by building, state, and district policies concerning due process relative to corporal punishment (as well as with suspension, detention, and expulsion).

Carson and Carson (1984) indicate that,

Educators talk of the inhumane treatment of people in Communist countries and the advantages of living in a democracy compared to other societies. However, physical punishment is prohibited in the Soviet Union and in almost all other Communist Block countries. Physical punishment in schools has been banned in Poland since 1783, in the Netherlands since 1850, in France since 1887, in Finland since 1890, and in Sweden since 1958. (p. 200)

A review of recent issues of the periodical, *The Last Resort,* published by The Committee to End Violence Against the Next Generation, and publications from Epoch World Wide, a federation of organizations committed to ending physical punishment of children world- wide, indicates that most civilized nations have abolished the practice. In addition to the countries mentioned above, corporal punishment is outlawed in: Argentina, Austria, Belgium, China, Cypress, Denmark, Ecuador, Germany, Holland, Iceland, India, Ireland, Israel, Italy, Japan, Jordan, Luxembourg, Mauritius, New Zealand, Norway, Philippines, Portugal, Qatar, Rumania, Spain, Switzerland, Turkey, and the United Kingdom (England, Scotland, Wales, and Northern Ireland). Corporal punishment remains in use in some parts of the United States, in the Australian outback, in portions of Canada, and in Iran.

In 1988, Robert Fathman, the Chairman of the Coalition to Abolish Corporal Punishment in Schools, characterized corporal punishment as "a barbaric carryover from the days of Charles Dickens that has been abandoned by the rest of the world. American school children are being legally assaulted. . . ." (National Coalition to Abolish Corporal Punishment in Schools, p. 1). The American Medical Association calls the use of corporal punishment an anachronism and notes that "The schools are the only public institution in which corporal punishment is still permitted" (Orentlicher, 1992).

Because the Constitution of the United States leaves the regulation of corporal punishment in schools totally to the states, parents have no federal recourse on constitutional grounds. Rich (1991) indicates that,

> Local school boards cannot prohibit corporal punishment if a state law authorizes its use. Corporal punishment is permissible in states without statutory language to the contrary, but local boards may develop policies restricting or banning its use. Educators who use excessive force may be dismissed or be charged with unprofessional conduct by the school district, may be subject to a tort suit for assault, or may be subject to criminal penalties if the force is especially excessive. (p. 181)

STATES WHERE CORPORAL PUNISHMENT IS BANNED OR PERMITTED

Corporal punishment has been abolished by state law or regulation in 27 states as of mid-2001, with 21 of the 27 states abolishing the practice between 1985–1995. **Corporal punishment is banned in these 27 states** (the date the ban was implemented is indicated parenthetically):

Alaska (1989)	Maryland (1994)	New Hampshire (1975)	Utah (1992)
California (1987)	Massachusetts (1971)	New Jersey (1967)	Vermont (1985)
Connecticut (1989)	Michigan (1988)	New York (1985)	Virginia (1985)

Hawaii (1973)	Minnesota (1989)	North Dakota (1989)	Washington (1994)
Illinois (1994)	Montana (1991)	Oregon (1989)	West Virginia (1995)
Iowa (1989)	Nebraska (1988)	Rhode Island (1975)	and
Maine (1975)	Nevada (1994)	South Dakota (1990)	Wisconsin (1988).

Corporal punishment is also banned in the District of Columbia (1988).

Corporal punishment is permitted in these 23 states:

Alabama	Georgia	Mississippi	Pennsylvania
Arizona	Idaho	Missouri	South Carolina
Arkansas	Indiana	New Mexico	Tennessee
Colorado	Kansas	North Carolina	Texas
Delaware	Kentucky	Ohio	and
Florida	Louisiana	Oklahoma	Wyoming.

Within the 23 states that permit corporal punishment, however, corporal punishment is forbidden by regulation in many major cities and large population areas, and in hundreds of smaller cities and school districts. Some of those cities/districts are: Atlanta, Albuquerque, Austin, Birmingham, Cincinnati, Cleveland, Columbus, Dayton, Hilton Head, Houston, Huntsville, Kansas City, Laramie, Little Rock, Miami, Montgomery, New Orleans, Oklahoma City, Philadelphia, Phoenix, Pittsburgh, St. Louis, Topeka, Tulsa, and Wichita.

However, there are still large numbers of school personnel using corporal punishment with students in rural areas and in southern states. As the National Coalition to Abolish Corporal Punishment (1988) indicates, "There are 'striking' regional differences in school corporal punishment, with children attending schools in southern states nearly 4,000 times more likely to be hit by teachers wielding boards than the students attending schools in the Northeast, where the practice is almost extinct" (p. 1). Data from the seventh annual National Conference to Abolish Corporal Punishment in Schools indicate that "Only a handful of states still paddle children as a common practice. Arkansas, Mississippi, Alabama, Tennessee and Texas still hit more than 50,000 children a year (Committee to End Violence Against the Next Generation, p. 2).

Rich (1989) makes this compelling point: "Various evidence and arguments have been advanced against corporal punishment. Perhaps the most convincing is that none of the leading theories or disciplinary models advocates corporal punishment" (p. 151). Hunches, folklore, conjecture, and anecdotal evidence as to the efficacy of corporal punishment, rather than scientific research support, are often used to justify continuation of the practice. Baker, Shapiro, Wingert and Joseph (1987) indicate that corporal punishment and paddling continue because adults remember being paddled and believe that what was right for them is right for their children (p. 61). Furthermore, giving up corporal punishment may seem like betrayal to such adults as it forces them to face difficult questions about their own childhood experiences (Squires, 1995):

> We are so desperate to believe that our own parents loved us and had our best interests at heart, even though they used violence on us, that we do the same to our own children as if to remove any shred of doubt. The more I paddle or spank my own children, the more it must be true that this is what a loving parent does. It is a very troubling argument. (p. C4)

ARGUMENTS AGAINST CORPORAL PUNISHMENT

1. It perpetuates a cycle of child abuse. It teaches children to hit someone smaller and weaker when angry.
2. Injuries occur. Bruises are common. Broken bones are not unusual. Children's deaths have occurred in the U.S. due to school corporal punishment.
3. Corporal punishment is used much more often on poor children, minorities, children with disabilities, and boys.
4. Schools are the only institutions in America in which striking another person is legally sanctioned. It is not allowed in prisons, in the military, or in mental hospitals.
5. Educators and school boards are sometimes sued when corporal punishment is used in their schools.
6. Schools that use corporal punishment often have poorer academic achievement, more vandalism, truancy, pupil violence, and higher drop out rates.
7. Corporal punishment is often not used as a last resort. It is often the first resort for minor misbehaviors.
8. Many alternatives to corporal punishment have proven their worth. Alternatives teach children to be self-disciplined rather than cooperative only because of fear.

Alternatives to corporal punishment include emphasizing positive behaviors of students, realistic rules consistently enforced, instruction that reaches all students, conferences with students for planning acceptable behavior, parent–teacher conferences about student behavior, use of staff such as school psychologists and counselors, detentions, in-school suspension, and Saturday school.

That school personnel who are professionals even contemplate the use of corporal punishment is indeed a troubling argument to many professionals across various and respected disciplines. It is our hope that the next generation of school personnel will elevate the status of the teaching profession by refraining from the use of corporal punishment in schools.

SUMMARY OF KEY CONCEPTS IN CHAPTER 14

1. The use of corporal punishment by both public and private school personnel is inappropriate.
2. Specific guidelines must be followed when administering corporal punishment.
3. Thousands of professionals across many disciplines, as represented by professional organizations, formally oppose the use of corporal punishment in schools.
4. Corporal punishment does not violate the Eighth Amendment's prohibition against cruel and unusual punishment, nor does it breach the Fourteenth Amendment's due process guarantees.
5. The 1975 *Baker v. Owen* case provides four minimal procedural safeguards and establishes specific guidelines that must be followed when administering corporal punishment.
6. School personnel have the power to administer corporal punishment under the common law doctrine of *in loco parentis*, where parental power traditionally reserved to discipline a child is transferred to school personnel while the child is under their supervision.
7. Most civilized nations have abolished the practice of corporal punishment in their schools.
8. Corporal punishment remains in use in 23 states in the United States, in the Australian outback, in portions of Canada, and in Iran.
9. Within the 23 states that permit the use of corporal punishment, it is forbidden by regulation in many major cities and large population areas.
10. Students in rural areas and in southern states receive a disproportionately large amount of corporal punishment.
11. American schools are the only public institution in which corporal punishment is still permitted.

REFERENCES

Baker, J. N., Shapiro, D., Wingert, P, & Joseph, N. (1987, June 22). Paddling: Still a sore point. *Newsweek.*

Butterfield, G. E. (1991, Spring). Landmark decisions: A balance of rights. *School Safety,* 16–17.

Carson, J. C., & Carson, P. (1984). *Any teacher can! Practical strategies for effective classroom management.* Springfield, IL: Charles C Thomas.

Committee to End Violence Against the Next Generation. (1994, Winter). *The Last Resort, 2,* 3.

Evans, E. E., & Richardson, R. C. (1995, Winter). Corporal punishment: What teachers should know. *Teaching Exceptional Children,* 33–36.

Gootman, M. (1988, October). The teacher hit me, Mommy! *Redbook, 131,* 176–180.

Hindman, S. E. (1986, August). The law, the courts, and the education of behaviorally disordered students. *Behavioral Disorders,* 280–289.

National Coalition to Abolish Corporal Punishment in Schools. (1988). Available at: 750 Brooksedge, #107, Westerville, OH 43081, pp. 1–2.

Orentlicher, D. (1992, June 17). Corporal punishment in the schools. *The Journal of the American Medical Association, 267,* 3205–3208.

Rich, J. M. (1989). The use of corporal punishment. *The Clearing House for the Contemporary Educator in Middle and Secondary Schools, 63*(4), 149–152.

Squires, S. (1995, March 24). Despite advice, spanking still common. *The Commercial Appeal,* C4.

SUGGESTED ACTIVITIES/ASSIGNMENTS

1. Invite an attorney or an expert on school law to address the class about the use of corporal punishment in schools.
2. Debate the issues related to the use of corporal punishment by teachers in schools.
3. Examine malpractice insurance policies for school personnel, with particular attention to the coverage provided or excluded with respect to the use of corporal punishment.
4. Invite an attorney or a judge to address the class about the legal issues surrounding the use of corporal punishment in school.
5. Review school handouts and codes of conduct about the required, forbidden, or permissible use of corporal punishment.
6. Invite parents to address the class about their perspectives and experiences with school personnel using corporal punishment with their children.
7. Interview a teacher or administrator who experienced stress or legal problems relative to the administration of corporal punishment.
8. Poll school personnel about their perspectives concerning the use of corporal punishment and/or about witnessing the use of corporal punishment.
9. Research 10 different websites concerning public school personnel's use of corporal punishment.
10. Critique articles related to the legal, ethical, and moral implications of using corporal punishment in school.

Chapter 15

STRATEGIES FOR PREVENTING VIOLENCE IN SCHOOLS

This chapter will explore various issues related to violence in schools. The information in each section is not intended to be comprehensive, but rather to give readers some ideas about these topics so that a safe school environment is created and maintained. Furthermore, because violence occurs in contexts unique to each school and community, a one-size-fits-all approach is impossible. The suggestions and strategies provided will need to be adjusted to the specifics of the school situation. Additionally, school communities could do everything that is recommended herein and still experience violence in schools.

VIOLENCE AND CRIME: A SOCIETAL PROBLEM

Many experts who perceive violence and crime as societal problems consider our nation's schools to be a microcosm of an inattentive, unaccountable, violent, and irresponsible society. Violence and crime are community problems that have entered schools at all grade levels. Much of the violence and many crimes, both at school and elsewhere, are committed by young people, and school-based violence is no longer prevalent in only the junior high and high schools.

Today's school personnel are expected to solve the problems of violence, a problem that has its roots outside of school classrooms. The fraying of the fabric of the family and the resultant breakdown of traditional family values causes a lack of respect for authority at all levels and is a large part of the problem. Further compounding the problem are irresponsible parents, the availability of guns and other deadly weapons, and numerous socio-cultural elements: the devastating influences of unemployment, illiteracy, and poverty; the violent videos, games, music lyrics, movies, television programs, and news media coverage which glorifies gangsterism and desensitizes children to violence; boxing, wrestling, and other "sports" whose roots are in physically aggressive behaviors; unsupervised Internet use; children who feel isolated and have difficulty understanding how their actions affect others because they come from broken and scattered families, single-parent households, or homes where parent(s)/caretaker(s) feel inadequate to do anything about their children's aggression, depression, psychological and emotional problems, drug use, suicidal or violent tendencies, and children with other aggressive or violent interpersonal behaviors.

Today's students have lived with and learned about violence from families with histories of violent behaviors and other crimes. Many students have grown up to the sounds of sirens and gunshots and the sight of blood and death, both in inner city neighborhoods as well as in small town gathering places. Furthermore, virtually all children are exposed to or at least hear about other societal adult expressions of violence: students paddled at school and at home, bullies' behaviors, aggressive drivers with road rage, and airline passengers physically or verbally venting their rage when they encounter flight problems.

School authorities, students, staff, parents, and members of the community face gangs and ritualistic groups who promote violence and crime as a way of life. There are drug dealers and drug and alcohol abusers. There are teens bearing children and children bearing children. There are fights, assaults, homicides, felonies, knifings, stabbings, clubbings, drive-by shootings, robberies, and rapes. Compounding the problem is the fact that students receive little, if any, formal education or preparation to resolve conflicts non-violently, to raise and discipline children without resorting to physical punishment, and for non-aggressively dealing with the aggressive behavior of others.

But, just as violence and crime in the schools is a societal problem, the prevention of violence and crime in the schools is a societal responsibility. The necessary interventions and the following suggestions for creating a safe school environment are everyone's responsibility: all school personnel, parents, students, and members of the community. Everyone has a responsibility for reducing the risk of violence and crime in schools. Everyone must demonstrate and model mutual respect and caring for one another, and ensure that students who are troubled get the help that they need. Everyone should have an understanding of the early warning signs that help identify students who may be headed for trouble. Everyone should participate in the development of a comprehensive plan to combat school violence and crime, and everyone must be prepared to respond appropriately to a school's crisis situation.

PREVENTING VIOLENCE IN SCHOOLS

Many of the following suggestions are school-wide measures for preventing violence in schools. They are drawn from the emerging literature on preventing violence in schools, and are not presented in any order of importance. While many of the suggestions appear to be common-sense based, they are nonetheless necessary. Furthermore, some of the suggestions are costly and/or controversial or unpopular, but we believe that virtually all of them are necessary for creating a safe school environment and for preventing, at any cost, violence and the loss of human life.

Schools that are responsive to all students. Well-functioning schools foster learning, safety, and socially appropriate behaviors. Well-functioning schools have a strong academic focus and support all of their students to achieve high academic standards. Well-functioning schools foster positive relationships between all school personnel and students, and they promote meaningful parent and community involvement. School personnel in well-functioning schools know that safety and order are necessary for students' social, emotional, and academic development. Effective school personnel also know that few students relish the monotony, boredom, and frustration characteristic of much of the routine drill and recitation activities and assignments, and they strive to make schooling a challenging and interesting experience.

The following are characteristics of schools that are safe and responsive to all students:

- Schools that are safe and responsive to all students focus on academic achievement. Effective school personnel clearly communicate to all students that they can achieve academically and behave appropriately. The expectations are the responsibility of the student, school personnel, and parents. Students who do not receive the support that they need are less likely to behave in socially desirable ways.
- Schools that are safe and responsive to all students promote good citizenship and character. In addition to a school's academic mission, effective school personnel help students to become good citizens. Effective teachers teach and recognize the shared values of their local communities, such as honesty, kindness, responsibility, and respect for others.
- Schools that are safe and responsive to all students assure that school personnel treat all students with equal respect. Conflict in schools often arises because of the perceived or real problem of bias and/or unfair treatment because of race, gender, ethnicity, religion, social class, nationality, disability, sexual orientation, or some other factor.

Effective school personnel communicate to students that they are all valued and respected, and they establish a climate that demonstrates caring and a sense of community.

- Schools that are safe and responsive to all students emphasize positive relationships between school personnel and all of their students. Effective school personnel encourage students to help each other. They establish positive relationships with all students, and they are comfortable assisting others in getting help when needed. Effective school personnel create ways to safely protect those students who know in advance about potential school violence and report the violence, and they help all students to safely express their needs, fears, and anxieties.

- Schools that are safe and responsive to all students involve families in meaningful ways. Effective school personnel actively work to make parents feel welcome in their children's school, and they work toward keeping families positively engaged with their children's education. Effective school personnel also address barriers to parents' participation, and they support families in getting the help they need to address behaviors and other concerns that they have about their children.

- Schools that are safe and responsive to all students train school personnel to discuss safety issues openly, identify problems, and assess progress toward solutions. Effective school personnel teach students about the dangers of firearms, about how to deal with feelings and appropriate non-violent and non- aggressive expressions of anger, and about how to resolve conflicts without resorting to violence or other aggressive behaviors. Effective school personnel also objectively and continuously examine circumstances that are potentially dangerous, and then develop, periodically assess, and refine a plan of action for dealing with those situations where students or school personnel feel intimidated, threatened, or otherwise uncomfortable.

The safe school environment. Prevention of violence in schools begins when school personnel take the necessary steps to make the school campus a safe and caring place. The physical condition of the school buildings and the school grounds impacts students' behaviors, attitudes, and motivation to achieve. There typically tend to be more incidents of fighting and violence in school buildings that are dirty, too cold or too hot, filled with graffiti, in need of repair, unsanitary, physically unappealing, or where students and school staff do not have a rightful pride in their shared environment.

School personnel can enhance school safety and minimize the likelihood of crime and violence in the school by doing the following:

- Supervise access to the building and grounds;
- Monitor the parking lots and bus stops;
- Install locked gates at all school entrances and exits;
- Reduce class size and school size;
- Install solid doors and replace glass inserts with unbreakable glass;
- Replace existing windows with a plexiglass or poly-carbon material;
- Install bullet-proof windows in school buildings that are adjacent to high-crime areas;
- Install additional lighting of the school grounds;
- Alter landscape foliage and design to maximize security, minimize visibility obstacles, and to remove any areas of concealment;
- Schedule classes to minimize the time that students are in the hallways or other potentially dangerous locations;
- Modify traffic patterns to limit potential conflicts;
- Arrange for supervision of students at critical times, like in the hallways between classes;
- Devise a plan to deploy supervisory staff or specially trained security personnel to areas where crimes or violence are likely to occur;
- Prohibit students from congregating in areas where they are likely to engage in aggressive or other inappropriate behaviors;
- Position school personnel with high visibility throughout the school building and on the campus;
- Have adult "greeters" (school personnel and parents who have been screened and trained) at school entrances to welcome visitors and control access;
- In schools where crime and violence are prevalent, station uniformed and armed police officers or security personnel in school hallways, and station plain-clothed or uniformed trained security personnel on other parts of the campus;
- Have teachers place their desks to assist surveillance and escape;
- Have teachers keep all aisles and passage ways traffic-friendly and uncrowded;
- Have school supplies in locked cabinets and remove any supplies that could become potential weapons;
- Stagger dismissal times and lunch periods;
- Conduct a building safety audit in consultation with school security personnel and/or law enforcement experts;
- Ensure that the buildings and grounds are in compliance with guidelines set by the State Department of Education and with federal, state, and local public safety and non-discrimination laws;
- Coordinate with local police to ensure that there are safe routes to and from the school;

- Install an alarm security system with sound and motion detectors;
- Close the school grounds during lunch and recess periods;
- Install walk-through metal detectors;
- Purchase hand-held search wands;
- Establish a system for legal and appropriate car searches;
- Employ drug-sniffing and weapons-searching trained dogs whose use are under the supervision of appropriately trained personnel and in compliance with students' constitutional rights;
- Develop awareness programs that encourage the prevention of crime and violence. Such programs stress locking automobiles, securing personal valuables, engraving and registering costly items like computers, televisions, and VCRs, and securing other costly items to discourage thievery for pawn or re-sale;
- Develop and train school personnel and parents in the use of weapons and gang hotlines;
- Develop a system for parent, student, and school safety patrols for during school, after school, evenings, and weekends;
- Provide alternative school environments for severely and chronically disruptive students;
- Institute a system of "straggler checks" to make sure that the school buildings are emptied at night and that all windows and doors are locked;
- Require that all teachers and staff wear photo identification badges;
- Require that all visitors check in and sign in at the principal's office and receive an identification badge for the time of their visit;
- Require that all students wear or possess at all times identification tags or photo identification cards that they display when so requested;
- Develop a system for photographing, recording, reporting, and then eradicating graffiti;
- Clean up the entire school campus and institute a program for all school personnel and students to take pride in their school environment;
- Develop, refine, and practice a system for gun-fire drills and drive-by shooting drills;
- Enforce loitering and curfew statutes to counteract the activities of drug dealers and the confrontations between gangs, and to discourage school intruders and vandalism;
- Institute proven approaches for conflict resolution and peer-mediation activities to promote a climate of nonviolence;
- Develop and implement bullying-prevention programs and enforce them consistently;
- Develop a school-wide disciplinary policy that includes a formal, writ-

ten code of student conduct, specific rules, and consequences that can accommodate student differences on a case-by-case basis when necessary. The code should be a collaborative product of input from school personnel, students, and parents, and it should be reviewed and modified as necessary. It should also include a description of school anti-harassment and anti- violence policies, and students' due process rights. The rules should reflect the cultural values and educational goals of the community. The policy should also include a zero tolerance statement for the illegal possession of weapons, alcohol, and drugs. If there are other zero tolerance policies in the code, they need to be enforced with common sense and on a case-by-case basis, as necessary. If extreme consequences, such as suspension or expulsion, are invoked for students' inappropriate behaviors, school personnel should have a plan to provide services and support for those students who are suspended and/or expelled.

- Adopt a school dress code and/or a policy on uniforms. The code or policy should be a collaborative product of input from school personnel, students, and parents. The code should be enforced consistently and equitably, and it should be re-assessed periodically. Dress codes should address appropriate clothing for daily school attendance and other school functions, and it should include policies concerning jewelry, sunglasses, and hats;
- Require that lockers be shared between students or between students and school personnel;
- Remove students' lockers altogether or institute a system for locker searches;
- Install a telephone or fully-functioning two-way intercom system in every classroom so that teachers can report troublesome situations. Code phrases may also need to be implemented so that teachers can access immediate assistance in a crisis situation. A telephone also allows a teacher to ask students who have disrupted class or otherwise acted inappropriately to call their parents and tell them about it;
- Install closed-circuit cameras or camcorders–to monitor school buses, locker areas, hallways, cafeterias, and other areas where students congregate–to prevent problems and to provide clear evidence to back up any necessary disciplinary actions;
- Require that all backpacks and book bags be transparent, or they will be subject to searches;
- Develop parent-education programs to reduce family violence and to establish successful home–school–community partnerships that will prevent or reduce the likelihood of violence in schools;
- Involve parents and other community members in the development

and implementation of school violence prevention and response plans; and

- Require that all school personnel undergo non-violent crisis intervention training.

IDENTIFYING AND RESPONDING TO
EARLY WARNING SIGNS OF SCHOOL VIOLENCE

In the wake of violence, many school personnel and parents often ask themselves "Did the student say or do something that could have cued us in to an impending crisis?" While there are early warning signs of impending violence to oneself and to others, the signs must be viewed within a context and without labeling or stigmatizing individual students because they appear to conform to a specific profile or a set of early warning indicators.

The early warning signs briefly described below may or may not indicate a serious problem; they do not necessarily mean that a child is prone to violence towards self or others. Rather, the warning signs allow school personnel and parents to check out their concerns and address a child's needs by responsibly getting help for the child before the warning signs of potential problems escalate. It is also important to recognize the fact that children typically exhibit multiple warning signs, and school personnel and parents should not overreact to single signs, words, or actions.

The warning signs should be used to get help for a child early. They should not be used as a rationale to exclude, isolate, punish, mislabel, or stereotype a child. Formal disability identification under federal law requires individualized evaluation by qualified professionals. Furthermore, all referrals to outside agencies based on these early warning signs must be kept confidential and must be done with parental consent (except for referrals for suspected child abuse or neglect).

These early warning signs are presented as an aide for identifying and referring children who may need help. They are not equally significant, and they are not presented in any order of seriousness. The research does indicate, however, that most children who become violent toward self and others feel rejected and psychologically victimized. In most cases, if children who exhibit aggressive behavior early in life are not provided support, counseling, or other assistance, they are likely to continue a progressive developmental pattern toward severe aggression or violence. We remind the reader again that it is inappropriate, and potentially harmful, to use these early warning signs as a checklist against which to match individual children. These warning signs must be used responsibly.

The early warning signs are
1. Social withdrawal. Withdrawal often stems from feelings of depression, rejection, persecution, unworthiness, and lack of confidence.
2. Excessive feelings of isolation and/or of being alone and friendless.
3. Excessive feelings of rejection. Children who are troubled often are isolated from their psychologically healthy peers.
4. Being a victim of violence. Some aggressive children who are rejected by non- aggressive peers seek out aggressive friends who, in turn, reinforce their violent tendencies.
5. Feelings of being picked on or persecuted. Children who feel constantly picked on, teased, bullied, singled out for ridicule, and/or are humiliated at home or at school may initially withdraw socially. If such children are not given adequate support in addressing these feelings, they may vent them in inappropriate ways (violence or aggression).
6. Poor academic performance and/or low school interest.
7. An over-representation/expression of violence that is directed at specific individuals consistently over time in writings and drawings. The guidance of a qualified professional, such as a school psychologist or counselor, must be utilized to appropriately identify and determine the meaning of students' writings and drawings.
8. Uncontrolled anger that, if left unattended, might later escalate into more serious behaviors.
9. A history of chronic behavior and disciplinary problems.
10. Serious threats of violence.
11. A past history of violent and aggressive behavior.
12. An intolerance for differences and prejudicial attitudes.
13. Drug and alcohol use.
14. Affiliation with gangs.
15. Inappropriate access to, possession of, and use of firearms or other weapons.

IDENTIFYING AND RESPONDING TO IMMINENT WARNING SIGNS OF SCHOOL VIOLENCE

Unlike the early warning signs of school violence that were just described, *imminent* warning signs of school violence indicate that a student is very close to behaving in a way that is potentially dangerous to self and/or to others. As with the early warning signs, no single imminent warning sign can predict that a dangerous act will occur. The imminent warning signs are usually evident to more than one person (school personnel, other students, and/or parents), and they require an immediate response because safety must always be the first and foremost consideration.

Immediate intervention by school authorities and possibly law enforcement officers is needed when a student (a) has presented a detailed plan to harm others, especially if the student has a history of aggression or has attempted to carry out threats in the past; and/or (b) is carrying a weapon, particularly a firearm, and has threatened to use it. When students present these or other seriously threatening behaviors, parents should be immediately informed. School personnel should also seek assistance from appropriate agencies, such as mental health centers, psychologists, and child and family service practitioners.

The following are some typical imminent warning signs. The signs are not presented in any order of priority and the list is not exhaustive. The typical imminent warning signs of violence are

1. Serious physical fighting with peers or family members.
2. Severe destruction of property.
3. Severe rage for seemingly minor reasons.
4. Detailed threats of lethal violence.
5. Possession and/or use of firearms and other dangerous weapons.
6. Self-injurious behaviors or threats of suicide.
7. Cruelty to others.
8. Cruelty to animals.

DEVELOPING A VIOLENCE PREVENTION AND RESPONSE PLAN

Effective school personnel create a written violence prevention and response plan, and they form a team to ensure that it is implemented. The plan must be consistent with federal, state, and local laws, and to be effective it must have the input and support of parents, the community, and the local school board.

An effective violence prevention and response plan does the following:

1. Describes how all individuals in the school community, all school personnel, students, and parents, will be prepared to identify the behavioral and emotional signs that indicate that a student is troubled.
2. Indicates what all individuals in the school community, all school personnel, students, and parents, need to do with troubled students when and/or if a violent or crisis situation occurs.

3. Details how school and community resources can be used to create a safe school environment and to manage threats and incidents of violence.
4. Describes the early warning signs of potentially violent behavior.
5. Describes the procedures that will be used to identify students who exhibit signs of potentially violent behavior.
6. Describes effective prevention practices that the school community has taken to be responsive to all students, and to enhance the effectiveness of interventions.
7. Describes intervention strategies that school personnel can use to help troubled students. This includes early interventions for students who are at risk for behavioral problems as well as more intensive and individualized interventions and resources for students with severe behavioral problems or mental health needs.
8. Contains specific suggestions for the immediate response to imminent warning signs of school violence.
9. Contains a clearly delineated mechanism for monitoring and assessing violence prevention efforts.
10. Includes a contingency plan to be used in the aftermath of a tragedy.
11. Clearly states the chain of command in a crisis situation.
12. Provides clear bus routes and an adequate fleet of buses for transporting students to reunion areas or other necessary locations.
13. Clearly states and explains all directions in the plan.
14. Includes a plan for calling on and effectively using volunteer support.
15. Identifies procedures for canceling school, for early dismissal, and for using the school as a shelter for lock-downs, evacuations, and relocations.
16. Includes a plan to establish a phone tree that includes all staff, including janitors, cooks, bus drivers, secretaries, and other support staff.
17. Specifies a mechanism for gathering and disseminating factual crisis information to parents and other community members.
18. Specifies notification and announcement procedures, including assigning responsibility for calls to families.
19. Specifies a back-up plan for additional resource help if the school-level team is overwhelmed.
20. Provides for adequate communication channels at all crisis command post locations.
21. Contains clear procedures for releasing students to caregivers and sets up an accountability system for verifying names.
22. Identifies reunion areas where staff, students, parents, and caregivers should meet in the event of an emergency.
23. Contains adequate provisions to address all students' needs, includ-

ing physically challenged students and students with limited English proficiency.

24. Includes suggestions and resources for support and counseling of staff, students, and community members.

25. Has a defined and specific policy for responding to media inquiries. The plan must be fast, reliable, consistent, and managed by one or two individuals.

26. Contains plans to help parents understand children's reactions in the aftermath of a tragedy.

27. Contains provisions for helping teachers, other staff members, and students with their reactions to a crisis situation. These provisions include debriefing and grief counseling for both students and school personnel.

28. Provides for both short-term and long-term mental health counseling following a crisis situation.

29. Provides guidance for how victims and their classmates can interact and access support when they re-enter the school environment following a school crisis.

30. Specifies procedures for the smooth transition of a previously removed student back into the school community, whether the student was in an alternative school, a mental health facility, or a juvenile detention facility.

FORMING A VIOLENCE PREVENTION AND RESPONSE TEAM

A school-based team should oversee the preparation and implementation of the violence prevention and response plan. The team should involve parents, students, teachers, support staff, administrators, school counselors or psychologists or someone from an outside mental health agency, the school nurse, school board members, support staff (secretaries, bus drivers, cafeteria workers, and custodians), the security officer or a community police team member, and community members. The community members may be drawn from the following populations:

1. Parent group leaders, such as PTA officers;
2. Law enforcement personnel;
3. Attorneys, judges, and probation officers;
4. Physicians and nurses;
5. Mental health and child welfare personnel;
6. Family agency and family resource center staff;
7. Business leaders;

8. Youth workers and volunteers;
9. Local officials, such as school board members and representatives from special commissions; and
10. Any other community members whose advice and support can assist in the effective development and implementation of the violence prevention and response plan. These may be members of the clergy and other faith communities, media representatives, college or university faculty, recreational, cultural, and arts organizations' staff, school public relations officers, and crisis intervention specialists.

While school personnel and students will be the "core team," vested with the responsibility of implementing the violence prevention and response plan, it is essential that members of the greater community accept and support the plan. This is especially important so that everyone can express any concerns they have about troubled students. The team's membership should remain fairly consistent and not have too much turnover or turmoil which can render the team ineffective.

The team should initially agree on a vision and a purpose. Team members should select a leader, secure approval, devise a budget, and obtain resources for its purposes. Team members should receive whatever coaching or training is appropriate; they should practice responding to imminent warning signs of violence; and they need to communicate their activities in an ongoing, structured, and detailed manner so that members of the community are supportive and appropriately involved.

WHAT ELSE CAN BE DONE TO MINIMIZE SCHOOL VIOLENCE?

The prevention and response to school violence and crime must be a coordinated effort among school personnel, students, and members of the larger school community, because the creation of a safe and caring school environment is everyone's responsibility. However, there are some additional suggestions of activities that individual students, parents, and school personnel can undertake to help create safe schools.

Student activities. There is much that students can do to help create safe schools. Students at all grade levels should talk to their parents, teachers, school counselors or psychologists, school administrators, scout leaders, and/or religious leaders to find out how they can get involved and do their part to make their schools safe for themselves and others.

The suggestions presented below are not all-inclusive. The suggestions vary in their effectiveness with the age of the student and the specifics of his or her particular school and home situation. Nonetheless, these are commonly accepted desirable activities for students to engage in so that they can be integral to the communal effort of making schools safe for everyone.

With the support and encouragement of parents and school personnel, students should

- Seek help from parents or school personnel or another trusted adult, such as a school counselor or psychologist, a social worker, a teacher, the school nurse, or a physician, if they are being bullied or harassed, or if they are experiencing intense feelings of anger, fear, anxiety, depression, helplessness, isolation, or they have thoughts of suicide.
- Listen to friends or acquaintances who share troubling thoughts or feelings and then encourage them to get help from a trusted adult or professional. If there are serious concerns about the safety of others, students should share their concerns with parents or a trusted adult or professional so that they can be helped.
- Know their school's code of conduct and model appropriate behavior.
- Be a role model and take personal responsibility by reacting to anger without violence or other aggressive behaviors.
- Refrain from teasing, bullying, and intimidating others.
- Create, join, and support student organizations that combat violence and encourage conflict resolution and non-aggressive resolution of issues.
- Participate in violence prevention programs such as peer mediation and conflict resolution, and practice the newly learned skills at home and in the neighborhood and community.
- Avoid being part of the crowd when a fight breaks out.
- Volunteer to be a mentor for younger students.
- Volunteer to tutor other students.
- Get involved in planning, implementing, and evaluating a school's violence prevention and response plan.
- Work with your teachers and administrators to create a safe process for reporting threats, intimidation, weapon possession, drug trafficking, gang activity, graffiti, and vandalism.
- Use the process or ask for help in using the process.
- Work with community groups to organize youth activities that help students to think of ways to prevent school and community crime and violence.
- Share with others ideas about how to deal with violence, intimidation, and bullying.
- Develop and participate in activities that promote students' understanding of differences and that respect the rights of all parties.

Parent activities. This section presents a limited number of activities parents can engage in to ensure that the schools their children attend are safe and that their children remain unharmed. There are many excellent resources for teachers and parents on what parents can and should do to help their children to remain safe and become successful students at school, and this section will not attempt to review all of the available material but rather presents some activities that are believed to be absolutely necessary. Parents should

- Visit their child's school and become involved. By doing so they send a message to school personnel that they care, are willing to make things better, and are not just complaining.
- Inquire about whether the school has a violence prevention and response plan and team. Parents should advocate for a plan and a team if they are not already in place or if either are in need of improvement.
- Inquire about whether their child's school curriculum includes anger management, character education, peer mediation, and conflict resolution components. If it does not, they should join forces with other parents, community leaders, and school personnel to advocate for them.
- Discuss with their children their day at school.
- Talk with their children about bullying, harassment, ridicule, and teasing and look for signs that might indicate their child is being bullied: trouble sleeping, crying for no apparent reason, unexplained injuries, torn clothing or missing possessions, loss of appetite, a sudden aversion to school, and sullen, withdrawn, clingy, or angry behaviors.
- Take action if there appears to be bullying, harassment, ridicule, or severe teasing problems by talking with the child and meeting with the school authorities to come up with a satisfactory plan of action.
- Ask their children, school personnel, and other parents about where their children spend time before and after school and with whom.
- Monitor children's entertainment, including the Internet, television, videos, and music, and talk with the child about the appropriateness or inappropriateness of these.
- Set parameters and consequences for children's behaviors.
- Model behaviors that demonstrate to children how to resolve conflicts in a non-violent and non-aggressive manner. This includes refraining from the use of physical punishment as a form of discipline as well as not being emotionally or physically abusive of others.
- Become informed about the character-building skills and disciplinary rules that are taught and expected at school. Model and reinforce the skills and the child's compliance with the rules.

- Attend open-school nights and parent–teacher conferences.
- Sign up for school-improvement teams and participate in team building activities that impact the safety and caring atmosphere of a child's school.
- Be accessible to their children to discuss any concerns they have. Parents should communicate calmly and with care and compassion for the growing pains and the school stressors that their children may be encountering.
- Secure weapons, drugs, and alcohol so that children cannot access or use them.
- Talk with children about gangs.
- Encourage and reward children for doing well in school and for behaving appropriately.
- Encourage children to engage in meaningful extra-curricular activities such as sports, band, and the creative arts.
- Model the behaviors that are expected of children.

Other suggested activities for school personnel. In addition to what has been suggested in this chapter and throughout this text, the following suggestions are made for school personnel to use as necessary. The suggestions, like others throughout this book, will have to be modified with respect to the specifics of a particular disciplinary situation.

ALTERNATIVE SCHOOLS. If an alternative school or room location is used for severely troublesome students, clearly specified procedures have to be instituted relative to who supervises students placed there, what students are to do when they are there, and how students will make a smooth transition when they return from the alternative placement to the regular school community. Alternative schools should be more than just isolation wards or a "dumping ground" for severely misbehaving students.

VISIBILITY. School administrators, in particular, must be highly visible to both teachers and students. In many cases, their sheer presence is enough to deter the commission of crimes, harassment, bullying, fighting, and violence.

DETENTION. Detention requires that an inappropriately behaving student spend additional time at school. The detention can take place before school, after school, or on Saturday mornings. The effective use of detention requires that students complete the same academic work that would have been required of them had they remained in their regular classroom. Detention should not be a free time for inappropriately behaving students, and it needs to be closely supervised by school personnel who have the capabilities of managing the behaviors of the students placed there. Parents will need to be involved in those districts where students are bussed to school so that transportation arrangements can be made.

IN-SCHOOL SUSPENSION (ISS). In-school suspension removes a severely misbehaving student from the regular classroom, much like detention. With in-school suspension, the student is placed in a well-supervised, controlled, and well-monitored setting. ISS typically lasts from one to three days, and the student spends the entire day there, including lunch time, with only breaks to use the restroom. In ISS, the students are expected to complete academic tasks just as if they were in their regular classes with additional suspension time levied for continued lack of cooperation. It is a preferred strategy to out-of-school suspension and expulsion.

OUT-OF-SCHOOL SUSPENSION AND EXPULSION. In out-of-school suspension and expulsion, the severely misbehaving student is removed from school altogether. Short-term out- of-school suspensions typically last from one to ten days. Long-term suspensions typically last for any period in excess of ten days during a school year. Limited expulsion is the denial of school attendance through the end of the current school year. Unlimited expulsion is the denial of the right to attend school for a specific period of time beyond the beginning of the next school year or a permanent denial of the right to attend that school.

Both types of out-of-school suspensions and expulsions are controversial measures that some believe should never be used because they oust the student to the streets and the community where they can get into additional trouble. Furthermore, some question whether the misbehaving student views out-of-school suspension and expulsion as punishments, or whether the "freedom from having to attend school" does not in fact function as reinforcement to the very student who most needs to be in school and in a supervised setting. Both types of out-of-school suspensions and expulsions should be used sparingly since they essentially undermine the basic function of schools; namely, to educate students.

It is imperative that school personnel become thoroughly familiar with their district policies and school codes because the grounds for suspension and expulsion vary widely among school districts. There are also differences among state laws concerning what behaviors qualify students for suspension and expulsion, and there are differences in the provisions and procedures that have to be followed if these measures are used with special populations. For example, before a disruptive student with a disability can be expelled, it must be determined by a competent professional whether the handicap is the cause of the student's propensity to disrupt. Thus, there are limits on school personnel's powers to remove a student with a disability from school.

There are also procedural safeguards that vary among districts and states relative to the arbitrary deprivation of a student's right to attend school. The basic principle relative to procedural due process is that some fair procedure is required before a governmental agency, such as a school district, can take a person's "life, liberty, or property," and the right to attend school is considered a property right. Fair procedure requires that students and there parents are presented an opportunity to present their objections about the proposed imposition of suspension or expulsion to a fair, neutral, and impartial decision maker.

Thus, it is common to find the following minimum guidelines that typically govern school administrators' use of suspension and expulsion, although they vary widely among school districts and across different states:

- Before suspension or expulsion can occur, the student must be notified in writing of the charges against the student, and the student has a right to contest the charges.
- Except in emergency situations, the misbehaving student has a right to a hearing before an impartial official, before the suspension or the expulsion.
- Both the student and the student's parents must be advised of their right to attend the hearing, and some school districts allow the student to be represented by an attorney at any hearing.
- In some school districts, the board of education authorizes a committee that is typically composed of certified school personnel: the school counselor or psychologist, a special educator, a social worker, and teachers, to hear student discipline cases and decide to suspend or expel the student.
- "Unofficial" in-school suspension. With "unofficial" in-school suspension, teachers exchange misbehaving or uncooperative students. The students are sent to a class of students of a different age group, not their peers, so it becomes obvious to the other students why the "new" student was sent there. While some object that this practice borders on humiliation, it can serve to motivate the misbehaving student to cooperate so that the student can return to his or her regular class. Unlike the other forms of suspension and expulsion, there is no official record kept, and no paperwork is required.

SUMMARY OF KEY CONCEPTS IN CHAPTER 15

1. Violence and crime in schools is a societal problem, and prevention is a societal responsibility.
2. School personnel should strive to make schools responsive to all students.
3. Schools that are responsive to all students focus on academic achievement, promote good citizenship and character, and foster positive relationships between and among students and all school personnel.

4. This chapter presented numerous suggestions for making the school campus a safe and caring place. Those suggestions should be implemented as per the specifics of a particular school situation.
5. All school personnel should know the early warning signs of school violence.
6. The early warning signs of school violence should be used to get help early for troubled students and not to stigmatize or label students.
7. The imminent warning signs of school violence indicate that a student is very close to behaving in a way that is dangerous to the student or to others in the school environment.
8. All school authorities should be thoroughly familiar with both the early warning and the imminent warning signs of school violence.
9. Effective school personnel create a written violence prevention and response plan, and they form an inter-disciplinary team to ensure that it is properly implemented.
10. A violence prevention and response plan must be consistent with federal, state, and local laws, and to be effective it must have the input and support of parents, the community, and the local school board.
11. Students and parents each have unique responsibilities for helping to make schools safe for everyone.
12. School administrators must be visible to prevent the occurrence of crimes and violence in schools.
13. Alternative schools or alternative placement for severely misbehaving students must be carefully planned for and not merely a "dumping ground" for those students most in need of help.
14. Detention, various forms of suspension, and expulsion strategies must be used with care when implemented with severely misbehaving students.
15. Laws and due process considerations must be taken into account when using the various forms of suspension and expulsion.

REFERENCES

United States Department of Education. (2000). *Safeguarding our children: An action guide.*
United States Department of Education. (1998). *Early warning timely response: A guide to safe schools.*

SUGGESTED ACTIVITIES/ASSIGNMENTS

1. Report on recent violence in local school districts during the last or current school year.
2. Investigate various Internet sites on the prevention of school violence.
3. Invite a panel of teachers and school personnel to discuss the violence they encounter in school.
4. Interview students in various grade levels to get their ideas about how to combat violence in school.
5. Poll parents about what policies they would like to see the local school authorities implement to make their child's school safe.
6. Write a short paper on how younger and older children can successfully deal with the bullying and harassing behaviors of other students.
7. Visit two local schools in two different areas of a community and report on the violence prevention measures that are being used.
8. Collect various school handbooks and compare the disciplinary policies.
9. Discuss your recollections of being bullied or harassed at school.
10. Investigate the extent of gang activity in the local schools. Invite law enforcement personnel to discuss the measures they are using to combat gangs and the occurrence of violence and crime in schools.

REFERENCES

Albert, L. (1989). *A teacher's guide to cooperative discipline.* Circle Pines, MN: American Guidance Service.

Albert, L. (1995). Conferencing with difficult students. *The Cooperative Discipline Connection, 3*(1), 6–7. Circle Pines, MN: American Guidance Service.

Albert, L. (1995). Discipline tips from the expert: Rule is a 4-letter word. *Teaching Kids Responsibility, 1*(1), 2.

Allen, R. B. (1988). *Classroom common sense discipline.* Tyler, TX: Common Sense Publications.

American Psychiatric Association. (1994). *Diagnostic and statistical manual of mental disorders (DSM-IV)* (5th ed.). Washington, D.C.: Author.

Axelrod, S. (1983). *Behavior modification for the classroom teacher.* New York: McGraw-Hill.

Baker, J. N., Shapiro, D., Wingert, P., & Joseph, N. (1987, June 22). Paddling: Still a sore point. *Newsweek,* 61.

Bandura, A. (1986). *Social foundations of thought and action.* Englewood Cliffs, NJ: Prentice Hall.

Bercovitz, J. (1984). *Social conflicts and third parties.* Boulder, CO: Westview Press, Inc.

Bromley, K. D. (1998). *Language art: Exploring connections.* Needham Heights, MA: Allyn & Bacon.

Brophy, J. (1987). Synthesis of research on strategies for motivating students to learn. *Educational Leadership, 45,* 40–48.

Brophy, J. E., & Putnam, J. G. (1978). *Classroom management in the elementary grades.* East Lansing, MI: Michigan State University Institute for Research on Teaching Research, Series No. 32.

Butterfield, G. E. (1991, Spring). Landmark decisions: A balance of rights. *School Safety,* 16–17.

Canter, L., & Canter, M. (1992). *Lee Canter's assertive discipline: Elementary workbook.* Santa Monica, CA: Lee Canter & Associates.

Canter, L., & Canter, M. (1991). *Parents on your side.* Santa Monica, CA: Lee Canter & Associates.

Canter, L., & Canter, M. (1976). *Assertive discipline–A take-charge approach for today's educator.* Los Angeles, CA: Lee Canter & Associates.

Carson, J. C., & Bostick, R. N. (1988). *Math instruction using media and modality strengths.* Springfield, IL: Charles C Thomas.

Carson, J. C., & Carson, P. (1984). *Any teacher can! Practical strategies for effective classroom management.* Springfield, IL: Charles C Thomas.

Carson, P., & Carson, J. (1982). *Don't say you can't when you mean you won't.* Englewood Cliffs, NJ: Prentice Hall.

Cella, C. (1995). You don't have to spank. *The Last Resort, 23*(4), 5.

Charles, C. M., & Senter, G. W. (1995). *Elementary classroom management.* White Plains, NY: Longman.

Chernow, & Chernow. (1981). *Classroom discipline and control.* Parker.

Combs, A. (1979). *Myths in education.* Boston: Allyn and Bacon.

Committee to End Violence Against the Next Generation. (1994, Winter). *The Last Resort, 2,* 3.

Curwin, R. (1992). *Rediscovering hope: Our greatest teaching strategy.* Bloomington, IN: National Education Service.

Curwin, R., & Mendler, A. (1988). *Discipline with dignity.* Reston, VA: Association for Supervision and Curriculum Development.

Curwin, R., & Mendler, A. (1980). *The discipline book: A complete guide to school and classroom management.* Reston, VA: Association for Supervision and Curriculum Development.

Dreikurs, R. (1968). *A parents' guide to child discipline.* New York: Hawthorn Books.

Elrod, W. T., & Terrell, S. M. (1991). Schools without corporal punishment: There are alternatives. *Contemporary Education, 62*(3), 188–193

Emmer, E. T., & Hickman, J. (1991). Teacher efficacy in classroom management and discipline. *Educational and Psychological Measurement, 51*(3), 755–765.

Evans, E. E., & Richardson, R. C. (1995, Winter). Corporal punishment–What teachers should know. *Teaching Exceptional Children,* 33–36.

Evertson, C. M., & Emmer, E. T. (1982). Effective management at the beginning of the year in junior high classes. *Journal of Educational Psychology, 74*(4), 485–498.

Evertson, C. M., Emmer, E. T., Clements, B. S., Sanford, J. P., & Worsham, M. E. (1984). *Classroom management for elementary teachers.* Englewood Cliffs, NJ: Prentice Hall.

Ferre, D. (1992). *Parental involvement in school decision making.* Unpublished Masters Thesis: University of Saskatchewan.

Folberg, J., & Taylor, A. (1984). *Mediation: A comprehensive guide to resolving conflicts without litigation.* San Francisco: Josey-Bass, Inc.

Fredericks, A. D., & Rasinski, T. V. (1990). Working with parents: Involving the uninvolved–how to. *The Reading Teacher, 43*(6), 424–425.

Gardner, H. (1983). *Frames of Mind: The theory of multiple intelligences.* New York: Basic Books.

Gentile, J. R. (1990). *Educational Psychology.* Dubuque, IA: Kendall Hunt.

Gibson, S., & Dembo, M. (1984). Teacher efficacy: A construct validation. *Journal of Educational Psychology, 76*(4), 569–582.

Ginott, C. G. (1972). *Teacher and child: A book for parents and teachers.* New York: Avon Books.

Glass, J. (1993, August). Are you still wearing your childhood label? *Redbook*, 50–56.

Glasser, W. (1968). *Schools without failure*. New York: Harper and Row.

Glasser, W. (1990). *The quality school: Managing students without coercion*. New York: Harper & Row.

Goodlad, J. (1984). *A place called school: Prospects for the future*. New York: McGraw Hill.

Gootman, M. (1988, October). The teacher hit me, Mommy! *Redbook, 131*, 176–180.

Hamachek, D. (1990). *Psychology in teaching, learning, and growth*. Boston, MA: Allyn & Bacon.

Harlan, J. C. (1996). *Behavior management strategies for teachers*. Springfield, IL: Charles C Thomas.

Harlan, G. (1996). Special assistance–The school counselor. In J. C. Harlan, *Behavior management strategies for teachers* (pp. 257–260). Springfield, IL: Charles C Thomas.

Heinrich, L. B. (1985, October). Parent teacher conferences: Include the student, please. *Learning*, 87.

Hereford, N. J. (1993, September). Kids helping kids. *Instructor: Middle Years*, 31–35.

Hester, H. (1989). Start at home to improve home-school relations. *NASSP Bulletin, 73*(543), 23–27.

Hindman, S. E. (1986, August). The law, the courts, and the education of behaviorally disordered students. *Behavioral Disorders*, 280–289.

Hobbs, T., & Westling, D. L. (1998). Promoting successful inclusion. *Teaching Exceptional Children, 34*, 10–14.

Homme, L. (1973). *How to use contingency contracting in the classroom*. Champaign, IL: Research Press.

Hoover, R. L., & Kindsvatter, R. (1997). *Democratic discipline: Foundation and practice*. Upper Saddle River, NJ: Merrill/Prentice Hall.

Jones, V. F., & Jones, L. S. (1995). *Comprehensive classroom management–Creating positive learning environments for all students*. Boston: Allyn & Bacon.

Kagan, S. (1994). The cooperative learning connection. *The Cooperative Discipline Connection, 2*(2), 1–8.

Katz, N. H., & Lawyer, J. W. (1985). *Communication and conflict resolution skills*. Dubuque, IA: Kendall/Hunt Publishing Company.

Kauffman, J. M., & Wong, K. L. H. (1991). Effective teachers of students with behavioral disorders: Are generic teaching skills enough? *Behavioral Disorders, 16*, 225–237.

Kindsvatter, R. (1988). The dilemmas of discipline. In P. Wolfe (Ed.), *Catch them being good–Reinforcement in the classroom* (pp. 32–36). Alexandria, VA: Association for Supervision and Curriculum Development.

Kounin, J. S. (1970). *Discipline and group management in classrooms*. New York: Holt, Rinehart & Winston.

Liontos, L. B. (1992). *At-risk families and schools: Becoming partners*. Eugene, OR: ERIC Clearinghouse on Educational Management.

Luckasson, R., Schalock, R., Snell, M., & Spitalnik, D. (1996). The 1992 AAMR definition and preschool children: Response from the committee on terminology and classification. *Mental Retardation, 34,* 247–253.

Marsh, M. W., & Shavelson, R. J. (1985). Self-concept: It's multifaceted, hierarchical structure. *Educational Psychologist, 20,* 107–123.

Marshall, H. H. (1989). The development of self-concept. *Young Children, 44*(5), 44–51.

Maslow, A. (1954). *Motivation and personality.* New York: Harper.

Maurer, A. (1974). Corporal punishment. *American Psychologist, 29*(8), 614–626.

Mauer, A. (1990). Corporal punishment. *End Violence Against the Next Generation,* 1–2.

McFadden, M. (1987, Fall/Autumn). Corporal punishment: Legalized child abuse. *Education Canada,* 5–6.

McGiboney, G. W. (1993, Spring). Developing a comprehensive school discipline program. *School Safety,* 15–17.

Mercer, C. D. (1997). *Students with learning disabilities* (5th ed.). New York: Merrill.

Mid-continent Regional Education Laboratory. (1983). Discipline. In P. Wolfe (Ed.), *Catch them being good–Reinforcement in the classroom* (pp. 37–46). Alexandria, VA: Association for Supervision and Curriculum Development.

Midkiff, R. N., & Thomasson, R. D. (1993). *A practical approach to using learning styles in math instruction.* Springfield, IL: Charles C Thomas.

Miller, P. (1994). *The relative effectiveness of peer mediation: Children helping each other to solve conflicts.* Unpublished Dissertation, University of Mississippi.

Montgomery, W. (2000). Creating culturally responsive, inclusive classrooms. *Teaching Exceptional Children, 33,* 4–9.

National Coalition to Abolish Corporal Punishment in Schools, 750 Brooksedge, #107, Westerville, OH 43082, pp. 1–2 (includes comments by Fathman, R.).

National PTA. (1993). *The heart of the PTA: Parent and family involvement.* Chicago: Author.

Novelli, J. (1993, July/August). Better better. *Instructor,* 74–77.

Orentlicher, D. (1992, June 17). Corporal punishment in the schools. *JAMA–The Journal of the American Medical Association, 267,* 3205–3208.

Owens, M. R. (1991, March 21). Outlaw corporal punishment. *Congressional Record,* 12–13.

Page, D. R. (1994). *A study of the differences in efficacy ratings of elementary classroom assistant teachers who did and did not receive training in classroom management strategies.* Unpublished doctoral dissertation, The University of Mississippi.

Raywid, M. A. (1976, February). The democratic classroom: Mistake or misnomer. *Theory Into Practice, 27.*

Rich, J. M. (1989). The use of corporal punishment. *The Clearing House for the Contemporary Educator in Middle and Secondary Schools, 63*(4), 149–152.

Rich, J. M. (1991). Should students be punished? *Contemporary Education, 62*(3), 180–184.

Richardson, J. (1993). Teachers in poll seek greater push for parent involvement. *Education Week,* p. 10.

Richardson, R. C., & Evans, E. D. (1993, Winter). Empowering teachers to halt corporal punishment. *Kappa Delta Pi Record,* 39–40.

Richardson, V. (1984). Time and space. In *Learning to Teach* (pp. 73–197). New York: McGraw Hill.

Rogers, C. (1969). *Freedom to learn.* Columbus, OH: Merrill.

Rosenthal, R. (1973). The Pygmalion effect lives. *Psychology Today, 7,* 56–63.

Rowe, M. (1978). Wait, wait, wait. *School Science and Math, 78,* 207–216.

Schnailberg, L. (1994, October 19). E.D. report documents "full inclusion" trend. *Education Week,* p. 8.

Schrof, J. M. (1993, October 25). Tarnished trophies. *U.S. News and World Report,* 52–59.

Schurr, S. L. (1992). Fine tuning your parent power: Increasing student achievement. *Schools in the middle, 2*(2), 3–9.

Smith, T. E. C., Polloway, E. A., Patton, J. R., & Dowdy, C. A. (1998). *Teaching students with special needs in inclusive settings,* (2nd ed.). Boston: Allyn and Bacon.

Squires, S. (1995, March 24). Despite advice, spanking still common. *The Commercial Appeal,* C4.

Stark, E. (1985, April). Taking a beating. *Psychology Today,* 16.

Stomfay-Stitz, A. M. (1994). Conflict resolution and peer mediation–Pathways to safer schools. *Childhood Education, 70*(5), 279–282.

Stulberg, J. B. (1987). *Taking charge/managing conflict.* Lexington, MA: D. C. Heath and Company.

The last resort. (1994, Winter). Newsletter of the Committee to End Violence Against the Next Generation, Vol. No. 2, Berkeley, CA.

Tobin, K. (1987). The role of wait time in higher cognitive level learning. *Review of Educational Research, 57,* 69–95.

Turnbull, A. P., & Turnbull, H. R. (1990). *Families, professionals, and exceptionality: A special partnership* (2nd ed.). Columbus, OH: Merrill/Macmillan.

U.S. Department of Education. (1999). *Annual report to Congress on the implementation of the Individuals with Disabilities Education Act.* Washington, D.C.: Author.

United States Department of Education. (2000). *Safeguarding our children: An action guide.*

United States Department of Education. (1998). *Early warning timely response: A guide to safe schools.*

Walton, R. E. (1987). *Managing conflict.* Reading, MA: Addison-Wesley Publishing Company.

West, N. (1994, April 17). Should a child be spanked? *Parade Magazine,* 12–14.

Wolfe, P. (1988). Expectations and procedures for the secondary classroom. *Classroom management–A proactive approach to creating an effective learning environment.* Alexandria, VA: ASCD.

Wong, H. (1998). *The first days of school.* Mountain View, CA: Harry K. Wong Publications.

Woolfolk, A. E. (1995). *Educational psychology.* Boston: Allyn & Bacon.

INDEX